HEALING CRYSTALS

KAREN RYAN

ALPHA

A member of Penguin Random House LLC

Publisher: Mike Sanders
Senior Acquisitions Editor: Janette Lynn
Book Producer: Lee Ann Chearneyi/Amaranth@LuminAreStudio.com
Copy Editor: Monica Stone
Cover Designer: Jessica Lee
Book Designer/Layout: Ayanna Lacey
Indexer: Celia McCoy
Proofreader: Laura Caddell

Published by Penguin Random House LLC
002-313874-JUN2019.

International Standard Book Number: 978-0-7440-6114-7
Library of Congress Catalog Card Number: 20189600707
24 23 22   5 4 3 2

Interpretation of the printing code: The rightmost number of the first series of numbers is the year of the book's printing; the rightmost number of the second series of numbers is the number of the book's printing. For example, a printing code of 19-1 shows that the first printing occurred in 2019.

Printed in the United States of America

Note: This publication contains the opinions and ideas of its authors. It is intended to provide helpful and informative material on the subject matter covered. It is sold with the understanding that the authors and publisher are not engaged in rendering professional services in the book. If the reader requires personal assistance or advice, a competent professional should be consulted. The authors and publisher specifically disclaim any responsibility for any liability, loss, or risk, personal or otherwise, which is incurred as a consequence, directly or indirectly, of the use and application of any of the contents of this book.

Most Alpha books are available at special quantity discounts for bulk purchases for sales promotions, premiums, fund-raising, or educational use. Special books, or book excerpts, can also be created to fit specific needs. For details, write: Special Markets, Alpha Books, 1450 Broadway, Suite 801, New York, NY 10018.

Trademarks: All terms mentioned in this book that are known to be or are suspected of being trademarks or service marks have been appropriately capitalized. Alpha Books and Penguin Random House LLC cannot attest to the accuracy of this information. Use of a term in this book should not be regarded as affecting the validity of any trademark or service mark.

Reprinted and updated from *The Complete Idiot's Guide to Crystals*

For the curious
www.dk.com

Contents

Part 1: Getting Started with Crystals...1

Chapter 1: Crystals 101 3

    What's in a Word? 4

    The Well of Wellness 5

    Growing Popularity 5

    New Crystals for a New Generation...6

    Spiritually Speaking 8

Chapter 2: The Science of Crystals 9

    Gifts from the Earth 10

        Minerals..10

        Rocks 10

        Crystals 11

        Gems 13

    Scientific Properties of Crystals 13

        Freaky Frequency 15

        Properties of Healing Crystals 15

    Crystals Converted to Other Uses 18

        Cosmetics...18

        Computer Technology..18

    Ethical Crystal Mining...19

Chapter 3: *Metaphysical Mysteries*..21

  Crystal Energy: Myth, Mystery, or More?..22

    Open Up and Learn Something New 22

    There for the Taking 23

  Platonic Solids..23

  Crystal Resonance: Good Vibes 25

  Sacred Healing...26

  You Have the Power to Flip the Switch!...27

  Minding Your Mind with Mindfulness...28

  The Meditative Mind..29

    A Beginning Meditation Exercise 29

    Group Meditation..31

    Into the Alpha State 31

  The Power of Intent..33

Chapter 4: *The Beginner's Guide to Buying Crystals*...35

  So Many Choices!..36

    Hold Me Tight 36

    Be Decisive!..37

  Shopping for Crystals...38

  Crystal Collecting..38

  Gemstone Investing 39

  Initial Introductions 40

  Get the Inside Information 41

Harnessing Power with Familiar Forms 41

    Crystal Pyramids 42

    Obelisks 43

    Crystal Balls 44

    Geodes and Clusters 45

Changes in Thought and Presence 45

Let Intuition Be Your Guide 45

Keep a Crystal Journal 46

Chapter 5: Shifting Energy with Crystals 47

Experiencing Subtle Energy 48

    Eastern Traditions 48

    Restoring Balance to the Subtle Body 48

Chi and Meridians 49

    Yin and Yang Energies 51

    Balancing Yin and Yang 51

Get Grounded 52

    Grounded for Life! 52

    Clearing Blockages 53

The Chakra System 53

    Color Therapy and Chakras 54

    First Chakra: The Root or Base Chakra 54

    Second Chakra: The Sacral, Spleen, or Sexual Chakra 55

    Third Chakra: The Solar Plexus Chakra 55

    Fourth Chakra: The Heart 56

    Fifth Chakra: The Throat Chakra 56

Sixth Chakra: The Third Eye *57*

Seventh Chakra: The Crown Chakra *57*

More Chakras: The Star Chakra and the Earth Chakra *57*

The Chakra Tune-Up Kit *58*

What's Your Aura? 59

What Does Healing Feel Like? 59

Part 2: Crystal Healing Techniques...61

Chapter 6: Crystal Healing Basics 63

Crystal Healers 64

What Is Crystal Healing? 65

How Does It Work? 65

Why Does It Work? 66

Self-Therapy 68

Crystal Healing Starter Kit 69

Post-Cleanse Crystal Integration 70

Reiki and Crystals 70

Combining Crystals and Symbols 71

Ayurvedic Crystal Healing 72

Chapter 7: Crystal Sensitivity Training 75

Awakening Your Intention 76

Nothing to Fear, Everything to Gain 76

Developing Sensitivity to Crystals 77

Crystal Clarity of the Mind..78

    Physical Relaxation...*80*

    Mental and Emotional Relaxation *81*

    Chakra Activation...*82*

    Spiritual Stimulation...*83*

    Visualization Techniques..*83*

Chapter 8: Preparing Your Crystals for Healing......................**85**

    External Cleaning..86

    Internal Cleansing...86

        Salt Bath *86*

        Different Salts..*87*

        Smudging and Bell-Ringing Cleanses.........................*88*

        Fire...*88*

        Recharging Your Batteries...................................*89*

        Sunlight..*89*

        Earth Energy..*90*

        Moonlight Charging *90*

    Wake-Up Call: Activating Your Crystal 91

    Programming for Intent...91

    A Breath of Positive Air 91

    Learn to Attune..92

    Protection Techniques..93

    More Essential Crystals 94

        Kyanite *94*

        Selenite..*94*

        Fluorite..*94*

Calcite 95

Hematite 95

Lapis Lazuli 96

Tourmaline 96

Treat Your Crystals with Care 97

Chapter 9: **More Crystal Power** **99**

Your Personal Agenda 100

Three-Step Program 101

Step 1: Cleansing 101

Step 2: Harmonizing and Integrating 102

Step 3: Stabilizing 102

Maximizing Crystal Healing 103

How Many to Wear 103

The Five Master Healers 104

Clear Quartz: Universal Healer 104

Amethyst: Master Transformer 112

Rose Quartz: The Love Stone 112

Turquoise: Personal Protector 113

Smoky Quartz: Spiritual Warrior 113

Selecting a Constitutional Crystal 114

Using a Pendulum 115

Interpreting the Pendulum's Response 115

Chapter 10: Crystal Clearing Techniques 117

    Vortexes of Energy 118

    Clearing Chakra Congestion 118

        Clearing Chakras 119

        Crystal Therapy System 119

        Intense Release of Energy 121

    Aligning and Balancing Your Chakra in Seconds 121

    Aura Clearing with a Partner 122

    Wand Wonderment 125

    Using a Crystal Wand 125

Part 3: Healing Crystals for Body, Mind, and Spirit...129

Chapter 11: Crystals for Physical Healing 131

    How to Use Crystals for Physical Healing 132

        Healing Takes Balance 132

        Source of Illness 133

        Crystal Selections 133

    Pain Relief 134

        Crystals for Healing and Chronic Pain 135

        Headache Relief 136

        Breathe a Sigh of Relief 137

    Increasing Fertility 138

    Timeline of Healing 139

    Crystals for Physical Healing 139

Chapter 12: Crystals for Emotional Well-Being.................................. 143

How to Use Crystals for Emotional Clearing.............................. 144

    Clearing Anger 144

    True Forgiveness 145

The 12 Love Stones 147

Opening Up to Joy.. 149

Lucky You! 150

Crystals for Emotional Healing... 151

Relationships 153

Chapter 13: Crystals for Spiritual Healing..................................... 157

Deepening Your Spirituality 158

Connecting with Crystal Spirits.. 159

Asking an Angel for Advice 159

    Spiritual Healing... 161

    Crystals for Distance Healing... 162

    Healing Is in the Air 163

Crystals for Spiritual Expansion 163

Pineal Activation 166

The Flow of Fluoride 167

Chapter 14: Crystals for the Whole Family..................................... 169

Even Tough Guys Need Healing.. 170

Crystals for Women's Health 172

Health and Harmony for Teens 175

Crystals for Children.. 176

Healing Animals with Crystals 178

    Healing Pets *179*

    Crystals for Animals *180*

Chapter 15: Multipurpose Crystals **183**

Daily Crystal Use 184

    Crystals for Learning *184*

    Crystals on the Brain *184*

    Crystals for Computers, Cars, and Coffee *184*

Adorn Yourself with Crystals 185

    Wear Them *185*

    Conductive Crystal Energy *185*

    Rings on Her Fingers, Rings on Her Toes *186*

    Bracelets *188*

    Pendants and Earrings *188*

    Pouches of Power *189*

Increasing Prosperity and Luck 189

Feng Shui 190

    What's a Bagua? *190*

    Too Much, Too Little *192*

Crystal Bagua Chart 193

    Changing the Energy *194*

    The Art of Bagua Maintenance *194*

Dream Enhancement 195

Crystals for Dream Enhancement 195

Part 4: Crystals for Holistic Healing...197

Chapter 16: **Crystal Layouts** 199

Patterns of Power 200

Crystal Geometry 200

A Crystal Crown 201

A Ring of Crystals 204

Star of David 206

The Obliging Oval 207

Activation of the Layout 208

Prepare for Crystal Grid Work 209

Chapter 17: **Become a Healer!** 211

Clearing the Space 212

Singing Crystals 212

Ting Cha Ringtones 212

Salt Water Bowl 213

Aromatherapy 214

Assembling Your Crystals 214

"Old Pal" 214

Tools of the Trade 215

Crystal Analysis and Selection 216

Analysis Worksheet for Healing Session 218

Putting Your Lessons to Use 219

Closing the Session 221

Chapter 18: **Transformational Tools** 223

Crystal Grids.. 224

    How to Create a Crystal Grid 224

    Flower of Life Grid 228

Crystal Bagua.. 230

Mindfulness Healing 231

    Labyrinth, a Circle of Healing 231

    A-mazing! 232

    Crystal Healing with Labyrinths 234

    Finger Walking 235

Crystal Skulls 235

    Crystal Skulls for Healing 236

    Selecting a Crystal Skull 236

    Skull Components 237

    Cleansing and Recharging the Skull 238

    Welcoming, Activating, and Naming Your Skull 238

    Maintaining and Working with Your Skull 239

Types of Skull Crystals.. 239

Communicate with Your Crystal Skull 240

Crystal Skull Meditation 240

Crystal Singing Bowls 241

Chapter 19: Crystal Energy Crafts 243

Healing with Gem Water...244

   Mixing Up a Batch of Gem Water 244

   Moon Juice 245

   Other Uses for Crystal Water 246

The Healing Power of Gem Essences...246

Crystal Power Packs...249

Other Crystal Crafts 251

   Money Tree...251

   Crystal Kits and Gifts...252

Part 5: Wellness and Personal Growth...255

Chapter 20: Crystals for Wellness 257

Salt Crystals 258

Kosher and Pickling Salt...258

Himalayan Salt Crystals...259

Healing and Detoxing with Epsom Salts...261

Crystals Can Enhance Your Beauty Routine 262

   Cosmetics Infused with Crystals...262

   Wrinkle Rollers 264

Diffusers 264

Chakra Oils...265

Serene Selenite 266

Shungite 268

Trendy Crystals by Design 269

New Products with Tourmaline 269

Chapter 21: Your Personal Path to Growth and Healing................ 271

Commitment to Working with Crystals 272

Crystal Comments... 272

Imagine the Possibilities! 273

Working with Crystals Every Day 274

Gaining Confidence as a Healer 274

Getting More Training in Crystal Healing 275

Signs of Progress 276

Compassion for All 276

Appendixes

Appendix A: Crystals A to Z 279

Appendix B: Further Reading.. 295

Index.. 301

Introduction

There is growing excitement about crystal healing and its use in mainstream mindfulness and wellness programs. For seekers of spiritual transformation, healing, and growth, crystals provide improved clarity to the mind, alleviate various physical conditions, and can lighten your spirit. Crystal healing is being incorporated into many yoga and meditation retreats and holistic treatments. Massage therapy also includes crystal healing, not just hot rocks! Even celebrities are sharing how they use crystals to reduce stage fright and other issues. Healing—physical, emotional, and spiritual—through crystal energy is powerful and learning more about crystals and their uses is what this book is all about.

Nowadays, crystals are widely available and information about their use is easy to find and shared on social media. Crystals have become so popular, even the fashion industry has added their beauty into fabrics and designs for jewelry. They have become part of the new décor and their intense colors influence mood selection for room design. Their wonderful physical structures are also found in architecture for a new interpretation of spatial design. This is an awesome time to learn more about crystals and to use their natural healing characteristics.

Crystals have also become treasured for their investment value. Rich or poor, anyone can appreciate them and be inspired by these rare beauties. Crystals have been part of sacred art and regal ornaments since antiquity. Crystals are used in scientific instrumentation and medicines. They've been integrated into cosmetics and crafts. Appendix B, at the end of the book, will be helpful if you're interested in acquiring even more knowledge about crystals.

Throughout this book, you will learn about crystal energy used for healing. Crystal healing therapy focuses on using the energy centers of your subtle body called chakras with the energy of selected gemstones. The interaction between the crystals and your subtle energies creates a healing response. To focus that energy, crystal healers rely on their clients having an open mind, a willingness to meditate, and a belief that a healing can occur. The experience of crystal healing can be quite powerful, indeed.

There is a lot of information covered in this book: how to select crystals for purchase, how to get in touch with their energy, and how to use them for meditation and healing. You can also learn some basic crystal layouts for healing the body, mind, and spirit. Explore sacred geometry and the use of crystal grids or networks to amplify and send positive thoughts. As part of your wellness journey with crystals, take them with you on a walk through a labyrinth. Whether you are a skeptical seeker or are already a believer, you will find crystal healing is nothing short of amazing.

How to Use This Book

This book is divided into five parts:

Part 1, Getting Started With Crystals, includes learning about crystals, how crystals were formed on Earth, and their scientific and metaphysical properties. The sacred science behind the mystery and power of crystals is covered, in addition to how to bridge between the physical and the mysterious. Learn some tips on how to select crystals and how to handle them if you're sensitive to them and if they are sensitive to you!

Part 2, Crystal Healing Techniques, prepares you for crystal healing: how to choose and prepare your crystals—and yourself—for healing. You'll learn about energy centers, where they're located on the body, and how to clear and balance chakras, and how to cleanse an aura.

Part 3, Healing Crystals for Body, Mind, and Spirit, discusses which crystals to select for healing on the physical, emotional, and spiritual levels. As well as choosing crystals for the whole family including pets. Explore the multipurpose uses of crystals including energy jewelry, feng shui for harmonizing your home, and dream enhancement.

Part 4, Crystals for Holistic Healing, goes deeper into crystal healing. This part spells out how to do a crystal healing session for yourself and someone else, layouts for abundance and healing, crystal grids that focus and amplify positive thought, how to use a Himalayan salt lamp, and how to take a crystal journey doing a labyrinth walk.

Part 5, Wellness and Personal Growth, leaves you with more information about mindfulness and about new crystal products for health. In addition to suggestions on how to become a crystal healer, I've provided some words from others who have benefitted directly from healing crystals.

Acknowledgements

Thank you to Jessica Faust of Bookends for her encouragement in writing an updated view on crystal healing. Thank you to Janette Lynn for her editorial efforts in pulling the book together and to Monica Stone for the review process. To Dr. Magdalena Konopka, my chiropractor, many thanks for your ability to unknot all the tight spots in my shoulder from many hours at my laptop. To Little Tara, my sweet Lhasa Apso, who gently snored through my long hours of typing, I give my thanks for your companionship. I also want to give thanks and sincere appreciation to Ross Andaloro, my transformational therapist, who guided me towards healing with crystals many years ago and has kept me grounded through all of life's changes, challenges, and transformations. To all those who are searching for the healing power of crystals, thank you for looking for some guidance in this book for your own transformational journey. May you pass along the knowledge about healing crystals to many others!

Trademarks

All terms mentioned in this book that are known to be or are suspected of being trademarks or service marks have been appropriately capitalized. Alpha Books and Penguin Random House LLC cannot attest to the accuracy of this information. Use of a term in this book should not be regarded as affecting the validity of any trademark or service mark.

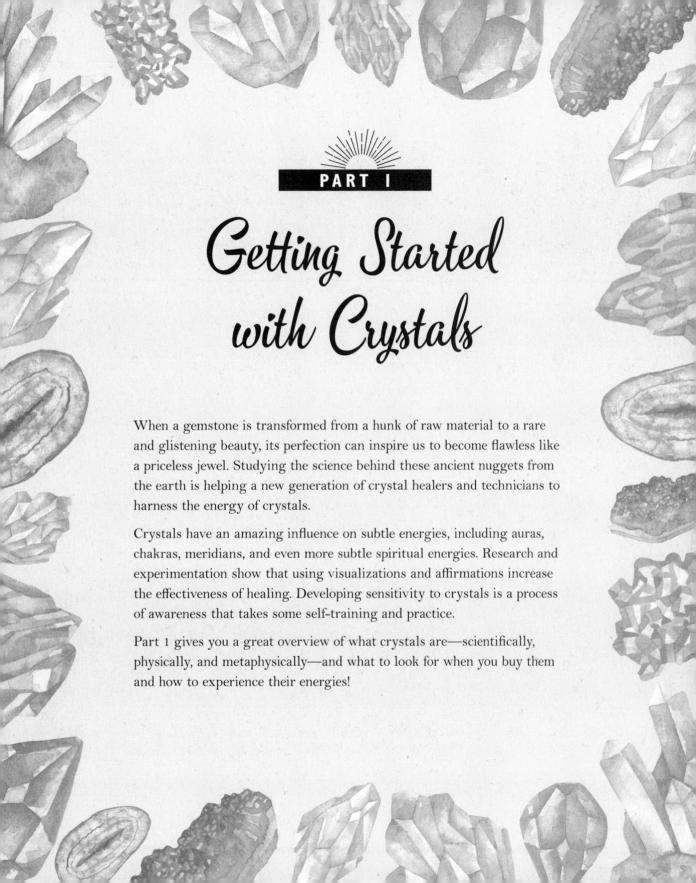

PART I

Getting Started with Crystals

When a gemstone is transformed from a hunk of raw material to a rare and glistening beauty, its perfection can inspire us to become flawless like a priceless jewel. Studying the science behind these ancient nuggets from the earth is helping a new generation of crystal healers and technicians to harness the energy of crystals.

Crystals have an amazing influence on subtle energies, including auras, chakras, meridians, and even more subtle spiritual energies. Research and experimentation show that using visualizations and affirmations increase the effectiveness of healing. Developing sensitivity to crystals is a process of awareness that takes some self-training and practice.

Part 1 gives you a great overview of what crystals are—scientifically, physically, and metaphysically—and what to look for when you buy them and how to experience their energies!

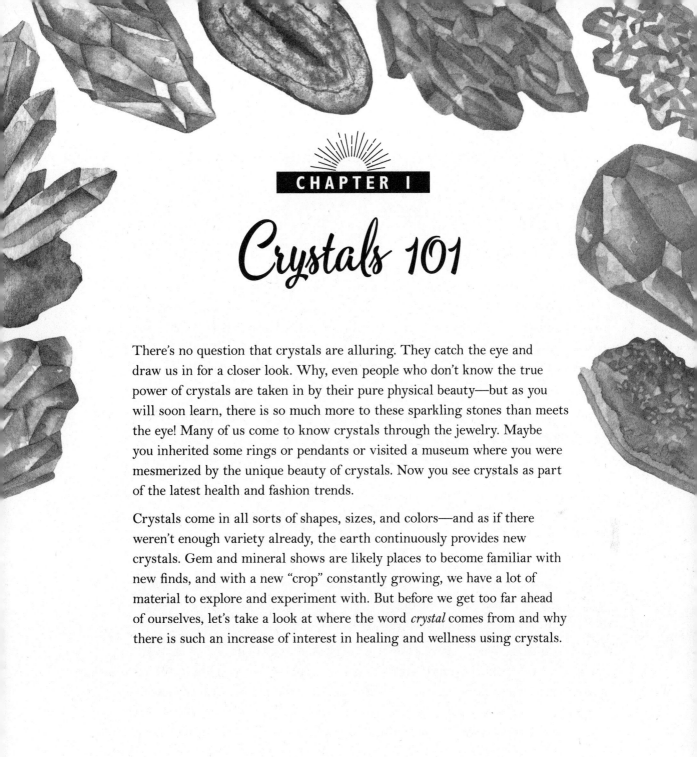

CHAPTER I

Crystals 101

There's no question that crystals are alluring. They catch the eye and draw us in for a closer look. Why, even people who don't know the true power of crystals are taken in by their pure physical beauty—but as you will soon learn, there is so much more to these sparkling stones than meets the eye! Many of us come to know crystals through the jewelry. Maybe you inherited some rings or pendants or visited a museum where you were mesmerized by the unique beauty of crystals. Now you see crystals as part of the latest health and fashion trends.

Crystals come in all sorts of shapes, sizes, and colors—and as if there weren't enough variety already, the earth continuously provides new crystals. Gem and mineral shows are likely places to become familiar with new finds, and with a new "crop" constantly growing, we have a lot of material to explore and experiment with. But before we get too far ahead of ourselves, let's take a look at where the word *crystal* comes from and why there is such an increase of interest in healing and wellness using crystals.

Learn How to ...

♦ Identify which areas of your life could use some crystal support.

♦ Recognize the wellness trends, including crystal healing, and about new crystals.

What's in a Word?

The word *crystal* comes from the Greek word *krustallos* meaning "ice," no doubt because a clear quartz crystal is similar to an ice cube—it's colorless, transparent, and feels cold to the touch. Quartz crystal is a solid mineral comprised of one molecule of silicon and two molecules of oxygen. Crystals come in different shapes due to differences in molecular bonding. Crystals also have electrical properties, and some have magnetic properties, or both.

Crystals are some of the most visually inspiring materials on Earth. Think about it. Literature often refers to the understanding of an idea, a voice, or a concept as being "crystal clear." A lake can be crystal clear, meaning that you can see down to the bottom. A glass of water is also crystal clear, meaning that it's colorless, you can see through it, and there aren't nasty little bits floating around in it. How about the lyrics from Stevie Nicks's soulful song "Crystal": "Then I knew in the crystalline knowledge of you; Drove me through the mountains; Through the crystal-like and clear water fountain…." Ideas are "crystallized" when thoughts are transformed from uncertainty into clarity.

When we use this phrase, we imagine the twinkle and sparkle of tiny little gemstones, providing a light in the darkness or an entirely new way of seeing things. As you read through this book, you'll learn that's really what crystal power is all about!

Healing is a term used to describe a process of change, essentially. When we heal, we're changing or alleviating a condition. We're moving from illness to wellness. We're repairing something that is broken, torn, or not working. Healing can occur at many levels, not just a physical one. When change occurs at more subtle levels, we can call this healing process transformational. We move from what was, to what is. When using crystals for healing, the transformation may be so profound you're no longer the person that you once were. This transformation illustrates the power of crystals.

As you learn about healing in this book, you'll also grow personally by exploring crystals for physical healing and moving into spiritual levels that really expand your consciousness. Your healing allies are crystals that will hold you gently through this transformational process.

The Well of Wellness

When thinking of wellness, do you get the feeling that it means everything is good? Is everything under control and running optimally for you? According to the U.S. Department of Health and Human Services, there are eight dimensions of wellness. Why not run through its list and find out if your "wellness well" is dry or needs some added attention. Later, you'll select crystals to help improve these areas:

- Physical
- Emotional
- Intellectual
- Social
- Occupational
- Financial
- Environmental
- Spiritual

Are you sleeping well; are you happily engaged in meaningful work; are you feeling healthy; and are you secure financially? Do you have time to enjoy your friends, hobbies, and interests? If not, then what would you need to do to achieve well-being and a balanced life? Start by acknowledging where your life needs some extra "currency." By *currency*, I don't mean money, think of energetic currents. The power of crystals can move you beyond your current place and toward a state of balanced well-being.

Why not add luxury wellness as a symbol of your growing economic and social status to the list? Luxury wellness includes organic foods, health retreats and tourism, and healthy pursuits such as stress- and weight-management programs, yoga and meditation classes, and special health diets. Sometimes these are offered at workplaces through employee-assistance programs that increase well-being, motivation, and happiness.

Don't forget crystals! The interest in crystals has grown in response to people's desire to improve themselves at many levels.

Growing Popularity

More specialty stores and mineral galleries are opening all the time. However, it may be easier for you to purchase crystals online; there are even crystal-of-the-month subscriptions. YouTube is a treasure trove of videos by crystal healers. You can learn so much from them! Their outreach invites new customers, but it also provides an easily consumable education that was once the jurisdiction of covens, meditation centers, new-age communities, and secret societies.

The sacred has become part of an urban lifestyle. Executives can now book celebrity crystal purveyors to select crystals for their offices to ensure continued success. Designers incorporate crystals into home and office décor, following principles of Feng Shui and crystal healing energetics. Crystals are classy! Everyone is interested in self-improvement. Even fashionistas have embraced crystal collecting, using jewels both to show off and to talk about their healing energies.

Attendance at gem and mineral shows has swelled. Google noted a 40 percent increase in searches for crystals over the past few years. Crystals are on-trend for home décor with aromatherapy misters, gem-infused water bottles, and gem swizzle sticks that make wine taste better. The Lululemon Lab has a crystal guru who holds crystal classes. Crystals have even been placed underneath the floors in office buildings to balance the electronics and magnetic polarities.

Crystals provide such a wonderful attunement. Why not feel their gentle energy? At a time when there seems to be so much rage and quarrelling over trivial things, can we simply lighten up? Aren't we all looking for peace? However, where do you start to look for it?

First, you must become aware of what needs to change. Can crystals really help here? Yes, they can. Many crystals help clear the mind of unwanted thoughts. Sometimes, it seems there isn't enough room in our brains to handle everything. It's time for a clear out. Chapter 16 provides direction on how to set up a crystals grid that can help settle your mind and emotions and keep them from straying. It's time to focus on your goals and to engage the support of crystals on your path to wellness.

New Crystals for a New Generation

Once available only to rock hounds, crystals have made their way into jewelry pieces, medical and scientific instruments, and even pharmaceuticals and cosmetics. Every generation seems to have new crystals that are mined and brought to the surface to enjoy. Over the past few years, the increased demand for colored gemstones has been outpacing the demand for diamonds. This has led to the discovery of new sources of crystals.

The U.S. Gold Rush helped open up much of the West Coast in the nineteenth century. In the 1970s, a new find of jade in British Columbia, Canada, was the first of its kind outside of China. Other new sources of crystals have been discovered in mineral-rich Morocco such as amethyst. The mine-to-market company Geostone introduced their new found Moroccan amethyst on Jewelry TV. They use special gem cutting to produce a gemstone beauty with showy red flashes from red hematite inclusions. There are also very recent and exciting emerald and sapphire finds in Ethiopia. New Czech locations were discovered for moldavite—a green glassy meteorite crystal. While some gemstone mines have been closed due to being overworked, such as those for opals or tourmalines, new mines are opening up. See Chapter 4 for more thoughts on these new crystals.

You may find some crystals which have been available on the market for some time have been renamed. It's easier to remember the names of crystals when they're given nonscientific names. You can find a list of new crystals on Judy Hall's website (see Appendix B). One such crystal is called *Rooster Tail quartz*, and it provides energy rebalancing. This crystal would be great to use in a layout for rebalancing your chakra energies during a crystal healing session.

How do we know about the healing properties of new crystals? Generally speaking, people who are good at channeling the healing aspects of a crystal can more or less agree on its healing properties. For instance, I was given a new white quartz crystal discovered by a dealer, David Kobliha, and as soon as I held it in my hand, the words *temple quartz* came clearly into my mind. The energy packed into this crystal was immense. Unknown to me at the time, this crystal had already been given to an internationally well-known channeler who'd named this new quartz the *Stone of Sanctuary*. Both of us intuitively sensed that this new crystal provided a sense of calmness, protection, spirituality, and connection with the divine. Perhaps this crystal was revealing its nature to us. To me, it was the reassuring energy of a sacred temple. To the channeler, it was a sanctuary.

You can do this, too, with some attunement to a crystal. At the end of each chapter, you will find "Carved in Stone," a section that contains a short message about a crystal I've mentioned in the book. Furthermore, in Chapter 18 I provide some tips for you on channeling crystals, including crystal skulls.

These new crystals are like getting a new smartphone with lots of new features to explore. You'll definitely enjoy the experience of exploring and working with numerous crystals.

Spiritually Speaking

Crystalline energy is being understood in new ways and under a new mindset of spiritualized science. When crystals are used in healing, is it science or spirituality or both? There's a fine line between what we know as healing through medicine and science and what we term *spiritual healing*.

Now more than ever, we need the power of crystals to help us move past the boundaries and limitations of day-to-day living. As more and more people learn about and become involved with crystals, especially through science and technology, more interest is generated in these gemstones. The idea of wellness is flourishing, and holistic health fields have blossomed.

Healing practices and meditation are becoming more widely supported and accepted by the Western medical community. Crystals can aid these processes, so there's a real connection between accepted scientific research and the more metaphysical aspects of healing. I'm looking forward to seeing where science and medicine take crystal power! Stay tuned to Part 3 to learn about the many different aspects of crystals and crystal-energy healing. I'll delve deeper into the science of crystals in Chapter 2.

CARVED IN STONE . . . .

Diamond: I provide an abundance of light. I am an integrator of mind, body, and spirit, strengthening the subtle energy network in and around your body. I connect you to who you really are.

CHAPTER 2

The Science of Crystals

Learning the differences between minerals, rocks, crystals, and gems is part and parcel of the discussion we'll be having in this book because, although all these things come from the earth, they are not interchangeable—especially when it comes to their energetic properties. Understanding crystalline structures and their properties will prepare you for the greater discovery of crystal healing.

In this chapter, you'll see how crystals relate to and, in many cases, enhance the world around us. For example, you will learn how the science of crystals is applied in computer technology. The same principles and characteristics of crystals that are used in technological applications are the same as those used in crystal healing. This might just lead you to ask the question: Is there nothing that crystal power can't do?

Learn How to ...

♦ Tell the difference between a mineral, rock, crystal, and gem.

♦ Create a spark from rubbing two crystals together.

♦ Define the scientific properties of healing crystals.

Gifts from the Earth

We use several words to describe that rock-hard stuff that comes from the earth—that which forms mountains, glitters in rings, and regulates the timing of our watches and the electrical pulses in our computers. We know these substances as minerals, rocks, crystals, and gems. Are they all the same, related to each other, or separate entities? Let's get down to the details of what makes each group unique.

Minerals

When you were growing up, you were probably told to take your vitamins, but did you also learn to take your minerals? Did you know that minerals are crystals, too?

A mineral must be solid and must have a crystalline structure, which is a repeating pattern of atoms extending in three spatial directions. The process of forming a crystalline structure or a crystal is called *crystallization*.

Minerals are formed from various geologic processes, such as volcanic activity. They have a recognizable elemental structure or chemical composition. The study of the structure, chemistry, and properties of minerals is called *mineralogy*. Some examples of minerals are magnetite, barite, gypsum, and halite.

There are several important minerals that your body needs to function well, including copper, which is a trace mineral used in the formation of hemoglobin and keeps bones and nerves healthy. Your veggies absorb this nutrient from the earth!

Rocks

We seem to name anything that's hard, found on the ground, and looks like a stone a *rock*. That's often the case, as rocks are formed on the surface through a process called the *rock cycle*. A rock is an aggregate of minerals and does not necessarily have a specific chemical compound.

Rock has the ability to transform and crystallize into another form, which is how crystals are made. This ability to transform is a characteristic of the ongoing processes on our planet. Earth really does have the ability to renew its own resources—and does so on a regular basis by moving through the transformative rock cycle.

There are three rock classifications:

- **Igneous rock** Created from a molten state when magma reaches the Earth's surface and hardens. Examples are granite, obsidian, and basalt.

- **Sedimentary rock** Compressed particles that form layers on the surface of the Earth. Examples are limestone and shale, which sometimes creates fossils.

- **Metamorphic rock** Formed when existing rock undergoes dynamic changes from heat, pressure, or chemical activity. Marble is a metamorphic rock formed from limestone, recrystallizing the original calcite under heat and pressure. Other examples include quartz, kyanite, and garnet.

Quartz is crystal that can be formed from any of the three classifications of rock but is principally silica, the most common mineral on Earth. An important note about silica: all the beaches and lake and ocean bottoms where there's sand—that's all mostly silica! Minute silica particles are floating freely in the air throughout the world, and your body also makes use of silica when forming hair and nails and strengthening cells. Your body is already partly crystallized!

Crystals

A crystal is a structure composed of an orderly spatial arrangement of atoms. A geometric arrangement or network of points in which a crystal grows is called a *lattice*. The crystal *lattice* provides a definition of symmetry and geometric shape for each type of crystal based on a three-dimensional axis. This lattice structure also holds the energy within the crystal that is used for healing. In his book, *The Seven Secrets of Crystal Talismans*, Henry M. Mason details each of these crystal lattice systems for their power to attract, protect, and transform us.

The following seven Bravais lattice systems (named after Auguste Bravais) form the basic structure of all crystals:

- **Isometric:** The basic structure of an isometric crystal is a cube. Halite, pyrite, and diamonds are examples of crystals with an isometric crystal lattice structure. This lattice structure is useful to support and to improve ourselves from within but also in our outer lives, such as our goals and ambitions. It helps us to keep order, to form collaborations with others, and to focus on beneficial growth.

- **Tetragonal:** Shaped like a rectangle, an example of a crystal with a tetragonal crystal structure is apophyllite, rutile, or vesuvianite. This lattice attracts someone or something to you.

- **Orthorhombic:** In the form of a rectangular prism with a rectangular base, the orthorhombic lattice helps dispel mental and spiritual issues and eases life's complications, putting things right again. Examples are celestite and topaz.

- **Hexagonal:** A six-sided lattice structure, it is found in crystals like aquamarine, ruby, sapphire, tourmaline, or emerald. This lattice provides direction, purpose, new discoveries, and supports learning and seeking tranquility. Hexagonal crystals align to the power of the mind.

- **Trigonal:** Belonging to the crystal family that includes hexagonal, the two are often combined. Clear quartz is an example of a trigonal lattice, made of six sides with interlaced unit cells. See *hexagonal* for lattice properties.

- **Monoclinic:** A rectangular prism with a parallelogram as its base, the monoclinic lattice is like a guard that protects our material possessions, as well as our spirits, and keeps us from having doubts. Examples are moonstone and other opaque crystals, such as malachite and jade.

◆ **Triclinic:** The least symmetric and with unequal vectors, the triclinic lattice helps to protect us from harmful external forces, such as wars, diseases, and other undesirable elements that we want to keep out of our lives. Turquoise, rhodonite, and kyanite are examples of crystals with a triclinic lattice.

As you can see in the following illustration, there is also an amorphous lattice, in which the crystal holds no particular shape or distinguishable form. An opal is an example of an amorphous lattice.

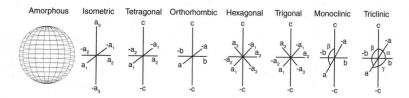

Crystal lattices chart. The internal structure of crystals to a specific pattern of atoms around an axis point is called a lattice, and it can be used to identify a crystal.

Note that for every lattice axis, there's a positive (+) and a negative (-) pole. That's because there are positive and negative ions holding the structure together. Remember, these lattices are three dimensional and give the crystal its crystalline structure as well as its ability to hold energy. For the science folks, did you know that a quartz crystal can be left- or right-handed? Their internal symmetry structure, called a *helix*, can turn either clockwise (right-handed) or counter-clockwise (left-handed).

As humans, we have natural curiosity and want to know how things are put together. We can't really see the DNA that composes our human bodies or, for that matter, the crystalline formation of a crystal. Some of us don't need this deeper knowledge to use a crystal's power, but some of us simply have to know what makes a crystal a crystal and what makes it tick! That's known as *crystallography*, or the study of crystals, including their internal structures and formation.

Gems

A gemstone is a cut and polished mineral, crystal, or other valuable material, such as amber or pearl. (Note: throughout this book when I talk about gemstones, I am referring to the crystal variety.)

At one time, there were two categories of gemstones: precious gemstones like diamonds, rubies, emeralds, sapphires, and topaz, and semiprecious gemstones like amethyst and tiger eye. Some confusion surrounds these terms because the jewelry industry follows fashion trends, and often a gemstone moves from semiprecious status to precious or vice versa. Really, no difference exists between them in the jewelry trade—there are no half-precious gemstones. However, when selecting a gemstone, clarity, color, and style are very important. A transparent gemstone, such as aquamarine, should be flawless with no particles or cloudiness. The color should appear strong, intense, and vibrant. An opaque crystal, such as turquoise, should have a consistently even color.

Scientific Properties of Crystals

There are a number of properties that all crystals have in common to varying degrees due to their unique compositions. The most important property is the crystal's ability to produce a piezoelectric effect or the ability to generate energy in response to pressure.

When resting, the crystal lattice just sits inside the crystal maintaining its structure. The crystal's positive and negative poles are evenly distributed, and any energy stored within is kept in a state of balance or equilibrium. That energy just radiates on its own, within its own circuitry. If you are sensitive to subtle energy, this radiance is what you feel when you are close to a crystal but are not touching it. Once a crystal is disturbed by pressure, the piezoelectric effect separates the energy from the lattice, generating an electrical charge. This release of crystal energy is what is used in crystal healing. Sometimes the release is very fast, like an electrical spark. Other times, the energy is slow to release. Like a battery, it depends on the polarity of what the crystal is in contact with and how much energy is stored inside.

If you apply electricity to a quartz crystal, it will bend, sending out an energy wave. It will vibrate at a precise frequency, much like a tuning fork. Each crystal vibrates at a specific frequency when an electrical current is passed through it. The oscillation of energy is very precise. A clear quartz crystal vibrates at 60 hertz (60 times per second) and can be used for different applications, such as in a watch for keeping time.

When you hold a crystal in your hand and squeeze, the electrical shock isn't very strong. In fact, most people feel nothing. However, when pressure is applied with a mechanical device, 1 cubic centimeter of quartz can produce a whopping 12,000 volts! By comparison, a C-size battery is only 1.5 volts. The release of energy from a quartz crystal has enough spark in the energy charge to ignite gas. As a result, some appliances like gas stoves and barbecues use piezoelectric crystal igniters.

You can see this energy release for yourself by rubbing two quartz crystals together in a darkened room. Enough light energy will be released to see a flare, but little heat energy will be produced. A spark from flint, on the other hand, produces heat when struck. It's commonly used in small lighters and other appliances with combustible fuel.

Piezoelectricity was first discovered in 1880 by Jacques and Pierre Curie, and it led to the use of quartz resonators in sonars during World War I. The Curies discovered a reverse effect to crystals releasing their energy. A transducer sends an electrical signal to a crystal. This pulse causes the crystal to become slightly deformed; the resulting reflected energy wave can be used for determining the distance from one object to another. This characteristic is used in the design of many devices including medical applications.

Freaky Frequency

Here's something you might not know about crystals: their resonance can produce sound. Within the field of biomechanics, sonomicrometry is used for studies of the human heart and with other muscles to measure changes in their lengths. Here's how sonomicrometry works: an electric signal is sent to a crystal planted in muscle tissue. The signal is then transformed into sound. This sound—in the form of an energy wave—passes through a special material that focuses the signal and is received by another crystal. The second crystal converts the sound into electricity, which is detected by a receiver. The distance between the two crystals can be calculated based on the speed at which the sound moves between the crystals. Pretty cool, huh?

I've only met a few people who have heard crystal tones subliminally, and I have heard these tones inside my head occasionally. It's a bit like having earphones on. If you haven't heard crystals sing yet, don't worry, most people haven't. The ring of crystal bowls is the closest you may come to hearing the natural tones of a crystal.

Here's something else that might really get you thinking: each crystal has a specific resonance or vibration and, when suitably charged, it can also emit a color vibration! Some people can even see a colored glow or aura around crystals.

Properties of Healing Crystals

By now you know that a crystal can interact with your own bioelectrical energy fields and that a crystal in itself does nothing without a relationship to another energy source. Now let's take another step toward understanding the properties of crystals used for healing.

The scientific properties of crystals are always there. The bridge to using these properties for healing is a combination of developing the consciousness to direct crystal energy for healing; the intent and compassion to heal; and the use of your breath as a carrier when charging, clearing, and programming crystals. (You'll learn about all these processes in upcoming chapters.)

The following table offers more specifics about the properties of crystals and provides some additional information on techniques to use the properties listed.

10 Properties of Crystals Used for Healing

	Scientific Property	Definition
1	Piezoelectric charge and discharge	The ability of a crystal to convert pressure into an electrical charge. Using the breath to charge the crystal, energy loops from the crystal back to you until a maximum charge is reached. Then the energy can be discharged according to the programming in the crystal and as directed by the intent (thoughts) of the crystal holder.

	Scientific Property	Definition
2	Resonant oscillator/ frequency regulator	The ability to maintain a sound or a wave of energy at a precise frequency. The crystal can maintain a specific frequency or tone at a regular, consistent, and precise vibration. When placed close to an erratic energy signal, the crystal regulates the vibrational frequency.
3	Programmable memory	The ability to store and retrieve information and to repeat a set of instructions. Using the breath, the intent or program is pulsed into the matrix of the crystal.
4	Polarity	The ability to hold positive, negative, and neutral electrical frequencies. When a person is in contact with the crystal, these polar frequencies are activated.
5	Electrical battery	The ability to store a positive or negative charge in the crystal's precise internal structure. The crystal can discharge the electrical impulse according to the thought patterns of the crystal holder either coherently, with preprogrammed intent, or incoherently, without focus.
6	Amplify	The ability to take a pattern of energy and increase its charge into a more intense and coherent energy. Crystals can amplify programming, as well as the energy from other energy sources, including other crystals.
7	Broadcast	The ability to send out energy patterns or information to be received by others, including other crystals. The effect is similar to a radionic transmission and is useful in distant healing.

(continues)

10 Properties of Crystals Used for Healing (continued)

	Scientific Property	Definition
8	Penetrate	The ability to transmit crystalline energy through any substance. When crystals are placed on the body, energy passes through layers of clothing, skin, and bone. This ability applies in distance healing, where energy can be sent and received at a considerable distance.
9	Duplicate energy	The crystal can discharge an energy pattern that can be inherited as an exact duplicate by another similar energy source, such as water or another type of crystal.
10	Conductor	The ability to receive energy through itself with or without altering the energy pattern or program. Used in radios and healing, the crystal is a carrier of energy. Its original matrix and mission is not altered.

Three additional properties which all crystals share are that they can …

◆ regrow after one is removed from its matrix or if it's chipped.

◆ be cleansed of retained energy, such as using salt water to discharge negative ions.

◆ be recharged using energy from other crystals, ultraviolet light, and other subtle energy sources compatible with their individual natural matrix. A crystal resonates a neutral energy flow but needs to be touched to release piezoelectricity. The subtle energy of the crystal is what is used in crystal healing.

Crystals Converted to Other Uses

It's kind of nice to know that crystals are all around us. Some very smart scientists have discovered how to use crystals in some very surprising and yet incredibly practical and familiar ways. So if you think you're brand-new to the crystal world, you probably aren't. Chances are, you've been using them without even knowing it!

Cosmetics

One of the earliest uses of minerals and crystals was in cosmetics. In ancient Egypt, a recipe for eye paint included kohl, a refined soot often containing lead, powered lapis lazuli, honey, and ochre. To obtain green pigment for eye paint, malachite, copper ore, and silvery galena were used. (Galena is lead sulfide and poses as much a health risk today as it did then.) Water was mixed with the powders and extracted from tube-shaped containers using a moistened stick to apply the paste to the eyelids.

Recently, there's been a resurgence of naturally sourced cosmetics using minerals such as titanium dioxide, zinc oxide, and mica. However, the lead found in kohl and some other cosmetics from Middle Eastern and South Asian countries has led to a prevalence of anemia in the population. The cosmetic market in North America is somewhat more strictly regulated under the U.S. Food and Drug Administration (USFDA), but there are still campaigns to alert consumers to potentially hazardous substances in imported cosmetics. Remember to read cosmetic labels and select brands you can trust.

The amazing growth of natural mineral cosmetics has brought increased awareness of the benefits of crystals to consumers. Even my Avon skin-care product has an amethyst infusion in it. (See Chapter 20 for some ideas on using crystals to enhance your own beauty routine.)

Computer Technology

The semiconductor industry uses a variety of silicon to create a material that has an electrical resistance. The lattice of a crystal can be easily modified by adding impurities while the crystal is being formulated in a lab environment for different uses.

If you apply electricity to quartz, it vibrates at a precise frequency, much like a tuning fork. The optimum shape to sustain the vibration was found to be a quartz bar. Thin sheets of quartz are used in delicate instruments requiring an accurate frequency, such as radio transmitters, radio receivers, and computers. In fact, you can use crystals to balance out the energy of appliances by placing one nearby. You'll learn more about this in Chapter 15.

Ethical Crystal Mining

A word needs to be included here about the ethical mining of crystals as it's an important topic. Conscientious miners are moving toward sustainable mining, contributing to social responsibility, planting trees to offset the carbon blueprint, and reclaiming chemicals and water used in processing. Does it make a difference if a crystal comes gently from the earth? Yes, it does. Ethically, your crystal will be pure, and purity helps your healing process. It's a good thing.

CARVED IN STONE . . . .

Adding crystals to your environment is a great way to connect with nature. Did you know that connecting with nature leads to higher rates of productivity, intelligence, and creativity? The more high tech we become, the more contact we need with nature. If you haven't already, have a look around you and notice the crystals that are already in your life. Keep some crystals nearby when you need to take a break and touch nature. Enjoy handling them at least once a day to center and balance your life.

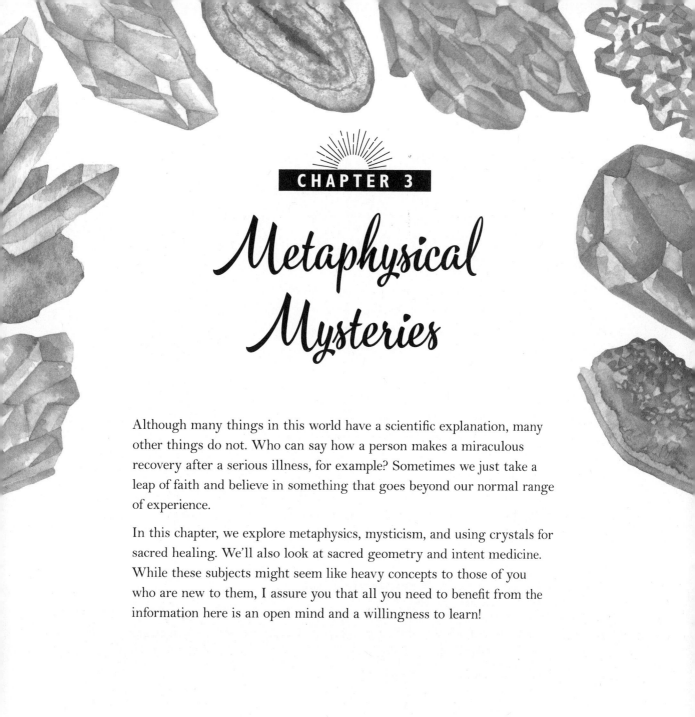

CHAPTER 3

Metaphysical Mysteries

Although many things in this world have a scientific explanation, many other things do not. Who can say how a person makes a miraculous recovery after a serious illness, for example? Sometimes we just take a leap of faith and believe in something that goes beyond our normal range of experience.

In this chapter, we explore metaphysics, mysticism, and using crystals for sacred healing. We'll also look at sacred geometry and intent medicine. While these subjects might seem like heavy concepts to those of you who are new to them, I assure you that all you need to benefit from the information here is an open mind and a willingness to learn!

Learn How to ...

♦ Charge water with loving, healing energy.

♦ Start your journey toward mindfulness using a crystal.

♦ Use crystals for a deeper meditation practice.

Crystal Energy: Myth, Mystery, or More?

Scientists and doctors often want predictable results that can be repeated with consistency before they will declare a theory or healing process as valid. Therefore, science and Western medicine have traditionally pushed alternative modes of healing to the side. However, many things exist that science can't regulate or explain, such as the belief that the spiritual is present in all things.

Fortunately, the spiritualization of science and medicine is emerging, and scientists are beginning to accept the wholeness of the ecological system and the concept of *Gaia*, that the organisms of the biosphere (Earth) regulate the planet to the benefit of the whole. For example, rocks, soil, plants, and the atmosphere all work in harmony. In this shift in thinking, the thin line between knowledge and *metaphysics* is challenged by a new order of *mysticism*. Metaphysics is a philosophical inquiry into the nature of reality and the relationships between things. Mysticism is the awareness of an absolute reality or spiritual truth through direct experience or communion with an ultimate source such as God.

Open Up and Learn Something New

As we grow up, we are told that empirical evidence is the only truth. And yet, as we grow older, many of us find that not everything can be analyzed, charted, or even explained. Often, we don't know what to do with these experiences because they don't match what we've learned to accept as "truth" in the past.

When we encounter experiences that are outside of our expectations, without science to offer us explanations, we become terrified! Breaking through inhibitions and moving beyond artificial boundaries are tasks that take time and a little faith, but it's possible and desirable to do so if you want to change your health or your outlook on life. The result is a wholeness of being that provides a sense of peace and harmony where healing can occur and where a state of wellness can happen.

Keep this in mind as you continue through this book. Nothing extraordinary can take place without the belief that it is possible. And nothing new can take place in a mind that is closed to opportunities.

There for the Taking

It is said that your first crystal should be given to you as a gift from a friend. When your first crystal comes into your life, it's a very special moment. The crystal should be given freely and without attachment as it comes as a gift from the earth. The crystal binds you and your friend with love. Keep your first crystal as a symbol of your connection to universal love.

Without a belief in the wholeness of all things, our perceptions can be narrow minded and our experiences carefully selected to repeat what is known rather than to seek out and explore the unknown. This might be a safe way of living life, but it's also pretty dull—you can miss some extraordinary things that are right in front of you!

Healing energy is always present, but many of us lack the knowledge and the tools needed to access it. We simply need to reawaken the knowledge about giving and receiving healing and then it's ours for the asking. Your first crystal is the gateway to awaken this knowledge.

Platonic Solids

The Greek philosopher Plato believed that everything we need to know about Earth and life on it is accessible to us in five basic shapes. *Everything* is composed of these basic shapes—our physical bodies, DNA, plants, cells, minerals, the cosmos—you name it. These five basic shapes are called the *Platonic solids*, and they compose the structure of every solid material known to us. These solids have the following three-dimensional lattices in solid formation and represent each of the five elements:

- ◆ 3-sided tetrahedron: 4 faces (fire)
- ◆ 4-sided cube: 6 faces (earth)

- ◆ 8-sided octahedron: 8 faces (air)
- ◆ 12-sided dodecahedron: 12 faces (ether)
- ◆ 20-sided icosahedron: 20 faces (water)

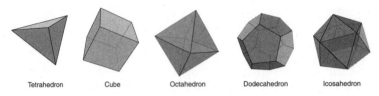

Tetrahedron Cube Octahedron Dodecahedron Icosahedron

The five Platonic solids.

Do these molecular structures have anything to do with the vibrational frequency of a crystal? Yes, very much so! The architectural and mathematical perfection of these natural crystal structures is like a cosmic receptacle for divine energy. They represent complete symmetry. Plato said that it was the dodecahedron (ether) that was used by the divine source to shape the whole universe; and the other four basic elements give us all forms of physical existence as we know it, including chemistry, physics, biology, geography, psychological perceptions, and more. What's more, you can find a set of clear quartz or rose quartz Platonic solids with which to work. In Chapter 5, I present a manifestation exercise that uses a Platonic crystal.

When we use crystals for healing, the structure of that crystal is important. It was formed from the basic elements. The crystal matrix is like a blueprint of the source energy that the divine source forms into matter. On a larger scale, Gaia (Earth) is a cosmic receptacle of divine energy. It is said that the crystals on Earth hold the matrix of divine energy. Each type of crystal provides a specialized link for your lifeforce resonance. Just as a specific train track takes you to your chosen destination, a specific crystal can be used as a tool to repattern your life force.

In the 1970s, experiments at the Scientific Center of Clinical and Experimental Medicine in Novosibirsk, Russia, showed that the DNA in living cells communicates with the surrounding cells by way of energy transmission. Lab results show that energy can move between cells independent of their biochemical and functional organic systems. While that all might seem be a bit much to understand, it simply means that by using crystals you can communicate with and influence cells. If you can send a healthy pattern of energy to stem cells, the cells should respond and repattern themselves to that new energy signature. And those cells would be able to pass that signature along to the surrounding cellular structures.

Crystals, then, are tools that help us to access and to transform the patterns of stem cells, the basic blocks of the crystalline matrix. Because crystals hold the ions of elements from the beginning of time, they can absorb and radiate different frequencies to the fluids in the body that contain electrolytes, minerals that carry an electrical charge. In other words, you can use these crystals to resonate with your own energy and re-create cellular patterns for healing. You could be resonating with the cosmos, with the environment, or with a higher spirit. There's certainly a lot more to explore about crystalline energy.

Crystal Resonance: Good Vibes

The resonance, or vibration, of a crystal is very powerful because it can essentially reprogram the patterns of substances nearby, including—but not limited to—human energy patterns.

Take the work of Japanese researcher Masaru Emoto, as an example. In the late twentieth century, Emoto experimented with the crystallization of water. He found that an intricate matrix was formed by the living consciousness in water crystals when the mind was focused by pleasant thoughts, images, or music. When water was exposed to negative thoughts, the water crystals were incomplete, lacked structure, and generally looked misshapen. If these misshapen water crystals were exposed to ultraviolet light or to certain electromagnetic waves, those changes could be removed.

Why not try changing water into healing water for yourself? Use spring water and two clear drinking glasses for this experiment. In the first glass, place a clear quartz crystal about 1 inch in length at the bottom and then pour 8 ounces (1 cup) of room-temperature spring water over the top of it. If you don't have a clear quartz crystal use rose quartz or amethyst. Hold the first glass about 7-8 inches in front of you and send happy thoughts to the crystal that's in the water. To get you started, think of something that recently pleased you or think of a person you love. Hold that thought in your head and then blow gently over the surface of the glass and water. You could whistle a happy tune. Do this for a few minutes until you feel the crystal and water have been saturated with your love-happy energy. Set the glass aside. The crystal will hold the energy signature in the crystalized water for a bit.

In the second glass, place a smoky quartz crystal about 1 inch in size and pour 8 ounces (1 cup) of room-temperature spring water over the top of it. Hold the glass in front of you and think of all the nasty things you might have encountered or accumulated over the past week. Hold those dark thoughts in your head and then blow over the water's surface. Repeat this until you feel the water is saturated with negative energy. Set the glass aside.

Now, pick up the first glass of crystalized water and take a sip, being careful not to swallow the crystal. This is a time to apply mindfulness training and get in tune with what the water feels like. Does the water feel wetter? Maybe it feels thicker? Does it taste sweet? Does the water look clearer? Do you feel happier?

Okay, now try the second glass. Take a sip and note any sensations. Does anything come to mind? Is the water texture different than the first glass? Do you feel different emotions? Try taking a sip of the first glass again. Now, can you sense a difference?

With pleasant thoughts, you are programming happy cells. There are even happy songs used by cancer patients to improve the quality of cells in the body. Even our thoughts are carried as a resonance in water. Water is very important. On average, your body contains about 60 percent water. The Earth is comprised of about 71 percent water, *and* the most abundant compound in Earth's crust is silicon dioxide, or quartz crystal, at 42 percent. Somehow, through some great creation, crystals are a companion to Earth's resonance. They can resonate their energy through air, water, earth, and even through time and over great distances.

If we can consciously direct the crystal resonance to perform in specific ways, then unhealthy human cells should be able to regenerate from the influence of nearby healthy cells. Crystals can facilitate the focus and direction of consciousness to work with the intent of healing. Visualization helps support this intent.

Sacred Healing

When we take the work of men like Plato and Emoto, and combine it with what we know about crystal resonance on a personal level, we begin to understand how crystals heal the human body, mind, and spirit. It's not just science—it's sacred science! And it's also what we call *sacred healing*, a term used for the processes that are not governed by the conventional application of medicine or medical procedures. It's one of those therapeutic processes that can't be explained by scientists but seems to work well for some people, regardless. It can include all kinds of alternative therapies, such as using crystals for healing.

Maybe you decide to practice mindfulness and, lo and behold, one day you wake up and realize you're feeling better. You've arrived at some level of acceptance, or maybe you've detached a little from your problems. In any event, something has changed inside of you—you've begun to relax your mental efforts and need for a specific outcome. When you realize that you have control over how you see your problems, you see how sacred healing works.

You Have the Power to Flip the Switch!

There seems to be an invisible switch for turning on sacred healing. Some people will turn it on themselves; others need to be led to it. But this switch can be flipped only when the person is ready. Some people describe this as a change of attitude: there's a sense of renewed energy and wanting to find a way to heal. There's a feeling of being reconnected to life and wanting to get out there and do things again.

Spiritual healing is finding a place in many hospitals and clinical settings these days. Doctors know they can provide only so much physical and psychological treatments for their patients. When all the medical avenues have been exhausted, a physician sometimes refers a patient to spiritual services to help a patient find inner healing, spirituality, and prayer in the most difficult times. As one doctor said, spiritual services can help a patient make room for healing to occur. Theologists say it can also make room for a miracle to happen.

Sacred healing comes through many channels, such as meditation, prayer, or visualization exercises, and anyone—and I mean *anyone*—can access these tools. They're already within you! Crystals can play an important role in healing by assisting in these exercises and by providing a connection to the crystalline complex, where healing can happen, and yes, where miracles are possible, too.

Minding Your Mind with Mindfulness

Okay, so now you might be asking, how do you control anger and other unwanted emotions?

That's where mindfulness comes in. Mindfulness is awareness, staying in the present moment, and it includes the practice of meditation. Day-to-day mindfulness keeps us conscious of what we are doing and thinking and of what we bring into the world. By remaining aware, paying attention, and being present, your mind won't wander into negative territory. It will help you become a better human being. In such a hectic world, we sometimes gravitate to mind-*less*-ness. Mind-*full*-ness is the antidote to meaning-less-ness.

Where do crystals fit into mindfulness? Think back to the meaning of the word *crystal* discussed in Chapter 1. The word means "clear." When you carry a crystal or meditate with a crystal, your mind has a chance to resonate with the crystal's clarity. You'll have greater awareness, sharper perception and focus, and attention to stay in the moment.

Try being mindful: keep returning your thoughts to the present moment. People use a lot of supports for mindfulness that can include listening to music, visualizations, incense burning, gongs and bells, and chanting. You can see how this is all sounding so busy! The mind is more capable and flexible to handle life's stresses when we give it the tools it needs for peace.

Now that you have practiced mindfulness, are you ready to go from HOW to WOW? It's so special and so simple!

Now try this crystal mindfulness exercise: sit down, hold a clear quartz or amethyst crystal in whichever hand is most comfortable, be quiet, and don't follow your thoughts—just stay in the moment. The crystal will regulate your physical system, help calm your thoughts, and provide focus for your mind. Stay present, keep your eyes open, relax your mind, and become more aware without your thoughts dashing all over the place. Practice this for a few minutes at first. You may find yourself more relaxed, revitalized, and ready to go forward with your day or night. Mindfulness can be practiced at any moment when you need to reset your energy and to clear your mind. Meditative practice is one of the best tools you can give your mind.

The Meditative Mind

Meditation is an important and integral part of sacred healing, but the very idea of meditation is still quite new to Westerners who've not yet experienced a true form of it. Often, they've been told by ecclesiasts to think of meditation as a time for spiritual reflection or deep introspection. You meditate *upon* something, they say. Well, that's not true meditation because contemplation is still "thinking." There are usually words going on inside your head and some expected outcome from all that thinking. Meditation is about *not* thinking at all. Period. Meditation is an intentional act of being aware of the nature of the mind. It's the discipline of the mind.

A clear mind is a place where true healing energies can take hold and grow. We'll talk more about meditation in the following section and in Part 3, but for now, know that when you use a crystal (such as amethyst, clear quartz, rose quartz, sodalite, selenite, or smoky quartz) during meditation, the results are clearer due to the crystal resonance keeping your energies strong and aligned. For the best results, hold a crystal in your left hand to receive its mind-stabilizing energy.

A Beginning Meditation Exercise

Guided meditation is different from traditional meditation because it uses visualization and other methods to enhance healing. Now that you know what meditation is—and what it isn't—and how it can help flip that sacred healing switch, let's try a simple exercise to introduce you to the process:

1. Sit upright in a chair or cross-legged on the ground. Let your hands fall naturally into your lap or rest them on your thighs. If you have time, go through an inventory of body parts to check for tension. Beginning at the bottom and working up, check your feet, legs, hips, stomach, lower back, upper chest, shoulders, arms, hands, fingers, neck, mouth, jaw, temples, eyes, and, finally, your scalp. Relax everything. With every breath, draw in feelings of relaxation and expel any tension you feel in your body parts.

2. Focus on your breathing for a minute, become aware of your chest moving in and out with each breath. Bring your focus to your nostrils and feel the air slipping into them. Close your eyes, if it helps you focus.

3. Follow your breath as you inhale. Try not to force any awareness. Let your focus be gentle and natural.

4. As you exhale, follow your breath out and feel the air sweep up the esophagus and out the nostrils. Do you have any awareness of the breath from your lungs? Does it feel warm or cold?

You might become more aware during the meditation that your mind is full of "noise" or distractions. Maybe you have some mental yellow sticky notes floating around in there. Perhaps you hear a part of yourself trying to reject your meditation experience. This is all to be expected and is the first stage of many that you go through to achieve an empty mind.

An empty mind is a good thing and an essential thing for healing. In time, the mind relaxes during meditation and becomes like clear water—crystal clear.

Set some time aside every day to practice meditation. Start with 10 minutes, once a day, at the same time and place, if you can. Your body and mind will grow used to sitting quietly. When you feel ready, try two sittings a day for 10 minutes each. The first sitting is to tame your mind. The second sitting will really count, as you will have emptied most of your mind traps during the first sitting. Increase your sitting time each day until you are able to sit quietly for 20 minutes at least once a day, preferably in the morning when there are fewer distractions. And do not be discouraged. It takes practice.

Studies in neuroscience using brain-imaging technology have shown that when the left frontal cortex is activated through meditation, stress and pain are reduced. The medical community is particularly interested in the results of these experiments as a means to decrease healing time and to promote a healthier lifestyle. This is an example of spiritualized medicine that I mentioned earlier.

Group Meditation

When you meditate with others, the harmony created by a group seems to promote better meditation. When you are with people who are all doing the same thing, everyone is putting out the same vibration and the meditative experience is much more powerful for everyone. You may experience a deep sense of peace and a broader awareness.

An experienced meditation leader will usually initiate the group session and may give some guidance on how to conduct yourself during the session so you don't disturb others. You may be asked to sit in a certain way, chant special words, or focus on something to relax your mind. A group session may seem long for a beginner, but it will help your meditation with its shared energy. Check first with the organizers so you know what to expect.

Meditation groups are often found with martial arts organizations, as part of yoga training, or within other spiritual and religious groups.

Into the Alpha State

If you want to know if there is a scientific explanation for why meditation works to heal the mind and body—why, yes, there is!

There are four types of brainwaves that can be measured using an electroencephalograph (EEG):

◆ **Alpha waves:** present when in an awake, relaxed, and effortlessly alert state

◆ **Delta waves:** present only during the deepest phase of sleep

◆ **Theta waves:** present during light sleep and deep meditative absorption

◆ **Beta waves:** present during times of stress or when it's difficult to focus and concentrate

We seem to spend a lot of time in beta states, from the time we wake up, to the time we rest for the night. We rarely slow down long enough to induce an alpha state, let alone a theta state. It's not uncommon for people to feel as though they can't relax—they're just not used to the feeling! Meditation is known to activate the left frontal cortex of the brain and to induce an alpha state of consciousness.

When we don't spend enough time in the alpha state, stress breaks down various mental and bodily functions. Over time, health declines and mental stability is compromised. When we stay in the alpha state for a longer time period, we become more resourceful and more creative. We have less anxiety and more ability to apply concentration to problems. Our immune system strengthens. Even our sports performance is enhanced!

Prayer and meditation are ways to connect to the alpha state when we become peaceful yet attentive. When in an alpha state, you experience calmness and clarity of thought, yet your mind is still and is not chattering on a mile a minute. You can experience the theta state when you rouse yourself from sleeping and just lie there with the awareness that you are awake, yet calm and alert. For some, this is the time when there can be a deeper connection within oneself to the transcendent self or to the divine. It's a time to explore!

Altered states of consciousness from meditation have been found to be highly beneficial to health and well-being. Some of the reported benefits are lower blood pressure, a happier disposition, and fewer stress-related disorders. Research has also shown that when people meditate while physically sitting or lying inside a pyramid structure, alpha brainwave activity increases. These deeper states of consciousness can also be achieved by using the crystals mentioned earlier (amethyst, clear quartz, rose quartz, sodalite, or smoky quartz) to enhance the alpha and theta states.

You don't have to have a physical pyramid to gain the benefits of relaxation. As long as your imagination is ready and willing to do some work, you can simply visualize yourself sitting inside a four-sided pyramid structure. Feel your mind starting to slow down and relax. See how long you can stay aware of the pyramid around you. See if you notice your breathing slowing down or becoming more regular. After a few minutes, allow the image of the pyramid to dissolve like a fading rainbow and slowly bring your awareness back to the room.

By the way, did you know that the 51° angle of the Great Pyramid of Giza is the same as the angle on the face of a quartz crystal? Marcel Vogel, a noted IBM research scientist and leader of crystal healing, cut and angled the tips of lab grown crystals to exactly 51° to focus the "universal life force." In Chapter 4, you'll read more about using a crystal pyramid to help healing and manifestation.

The Power of Intent

A new way of looking at healing exists, called intent medicine or intent healing, which is the application of mental intent to cause a healing response. Intent medicine uses the power of conscious mental intention and can include prayer, meditation, or other like practices. When the power of conscious mental intention is focused on healing, it's been shown to change the pattern of energy.

William A. Tiller, a distinguished scientist featured in the movie *What the Bleep Do We Know?*, leads investigations in the related field of *psychoenergetics* and has shown that thought and visualization together can affect the human energy system. Psychoenergetics is a relatively new field of science that investigates the meeting of consciousness, energy, and matter, and the nature of reality. Teller's experiments have shown that the energy released by healers using thought, intention, and healing hands were capable of releasing electrons and affecting change at a cellular level. Healing doesn't happen in isolation, it's dependent on other factors.

This is one reason why healing circles that gather several people to focus healing on select people maximize their healing intent, even from a distance. We seem to spend a lot of time looking for healing. How many of us really spend the time to look at what we want to happen? We need some new skills for healing, not just new medicines. If we put together the amazing properties of crystals with the power of intent and imagery, we can focus our minds on healing in a very powerful way. Intent medicine is more than a placebo, it's a reality!

In Chapter 4, you'll learn some tips about buying crystals and if there's any investment value in owning a collection. You will also learn more about your crystal and try an exercise to begin connecting with it. You may be surprised what you find!

CARVED IN STONE . . . .

Amethyst: I am the light you seek within yourself. I provide a deeper experience allowing you to sense spiritual reality and to increase your perceptions. I am a safe place for self-development, healing, and spiritual play.

CHAPTER 4

The Beginner's Guide to Buying Crystals

By now, you're probably pretty excited about the potential of crystals and want to get started using them. This chapter is geared toward the beginner, guiding you to the best places to find crystals—and what to do when you get there and find that there are hundreds to choose from!

Of course, after you decide which crystal to buy, your work is really just beginning. Bonding with your crystal is just the first step in the amazing journey you are embarking on with your crystal. Crystals seem to have the ability to find their owners. They come to you for a reason.

Learn How to ...

♦ Select a personal crystal for healing and health.

♦ Connect with your personal crystal and enter the crystal matrix.

♦ Use a pyramid to reduce pain.

♦ Use a crystal ball to receive messages.

So Many Choices!

If there were a type of crystal for every illness, the list of crystals and their meanings would be endless. (Actually, the list could be endless, as far as anyone knows because not all crystals have been discovered yet!) Fortunately for those of us who love and admire these gemstones, there are plenty of crystals from which to choose. But how do we narrow them down to manageable choices? A few tips that might help you pick and choose are discussed in this section.

Hold Me Tight

When you are purchasing a crystal for the first time, selecting a suitable one that you will do great work with is critical to your experience. Keep these points in mind:

♦ Before you head out to buy a crystal, ask for spiritual guidance to direct you to the crystal you need and at a price you can afford.

♦ Set a budget for yourself. In most gem and mineral shops, tumbled stones are inexpensive—usually around a dollar for a small piece. Tumbled stones are smoothed to a glossy finish using a rotary tumbler. It takes several days of continuous tumbling to transform a jagged rock into a highly polished stone.

♦ A rule of thumb is that the better the quality, the more expensive the crystal. Because crystals are like eye candy, it's easy to want many, and you can easily overspend your budget. So concentrate when purchasing, and choose only what really speaks to you!

♦ It's best if you can make your crystal selection when you're not in a negative mood. If you're upset or feeling resentment, your purchased crystal will absorb your bad mood.

♦ If you're buying a specialized crystal, be prepared to pay more for higher quality and larger size. Look for any imperfections, such as irregular coloring, which might indicate that the stone has been dyed. Look for specific markings that are desirable in certain crystal types, such as dark concentric rings in malachite or light wavy lines in blue lace agate or rhodochrosite.

♦ Ask the staff for help in selecting a crystal. They are usually knowledgeable, and they might even preselect some crystals for you to look at.

Once you've narrowed down your choices, you can determine whether you and a particular crystal are a good fit. Crystals will sometimes discharge the energy stored inside them when held. Some people feel this harmless discharge of piezoelectric energy as a small mild electrical wave and might be more surprised than shocked! For most people, holding a crystal causes them to feel calm and relaxed. Sometimes, physical pain lessens, such as a headache that goes away. Sometimes people feel less sad or more energized.

Hold the crystal in your dominant hand at about arm's length. If it has a point or tip, point it toward yourself. Slowly bring the crystal in line with the middle of your chest drawing it slowly closer to your body. You're trying to feel the crystal's power and whether it's connecting and interacting with your energy fields. You might feel a pulling or tingling sensation at your chest, indicating the energy of this crystal is in tune with you.

If you're looking for a crystal to expand your psychic intuition, look for a smaller crystal and hold it to your forehead (your third eye) to sense its energy.

Be Decisive!

Here's a good rule of thumb for any indecisive shoppers out there: if you see a crystal and aren't sure whether you want it, don't leave the store without making a definite decision one way or another. Because each crystal has a unique energy on the planet, there is only one like it. The signature of the crystal you touched will still be with you when you go home. You might even have dreams about that crystal. If you make a connection like that, then that crystal should be with you. And if you go back to buy it and it's gone, you'll be out of luck and missing out on some potentially great healing sessions!

Sometimes crystals feel sticky on the surface. This is usually from many people handling the crystal and leaving negative energies behind. If a crystal feels sticky, it's best to leave it there at the store. Its energy will be depleted, and the crystal will need to be both cleansed and recharged before it can be used.

Be sure your purchases are wrapped up well for the trip home. You don't want to get home and find that the tip on your crystal is chipped. Chipped tips don't hold or direct energy well enough for healing purposes.

Shopping for Crystals

The internet is a great source for finding and learning about crystals, but the downside is that you don't get to hold them or connect with them and see what they feel like until after you've purchased them. For these reasons, I'm a big fan of supporting local businesses when you're making a purchase. You must know exactly what you're getting.

If you are traveling, find out where the crystal shops are and drop in for a visit. You might see something different or unusual to bring back with you. Check out rock hound clubs or gem and mineral shows. Many hobbyists and prospectors bring raw rock and mineral finds from the field to sell or trade at shows. If you find something really special, you can ask a jeweler to make your specimen into a pendant or ring.

I added a special sapphire from the Arctic Circle into the design of a pendant that incorporated a luminescent opal and a matching blue pearl. What a great way to show off a rare gemstone! Why not try your hand at designing your own jewelry?

Here's some advice about wearing crystal jewelry: exercise some restraint. Wearing more crystals could interfere with your energy wiring. Remember, seven crystals at one time is considered the maximum for most healing purposes. I had a neighbor who wore over 40 different crystals all at once in different rings, bracelets, and pendants. She was covered in them and said the more crystals, the merrier. She was shorting out her energy. Just standing near her actually unbalanced my own energy.

Crystal Collecting

I've heard some pretty amazing stories of people who collect masses of crystals. Some people believe that their crystals are precious jewels that will increase in value. Most common crystals, however, don't appreciate as much as you might think. The earth provides a bounty of crystals, but few are rare. Some specialty crystals will sell for tens of thousands of dollars and are handled through known dealers. However, it's difficult to resell a crystal without some documentation, including its original source, lab testing, a gemologist's certificate of authenticity, or an invoice. Is there any value to a casual collector in reselling a crystal? If you think you have a valuable crystal, check it out with a certified appraiser—then you'll know for sure.

There are crystal hunters like Daniel Trinchillo of Mardani Fine Minerals, New York, and others with fine mineral galleries who deal with serious collectors. Remarkable museum quality specimens will go to corporations or private collections, and depending on their rarity, some may be handled as investments. At Sorenity Rocks in Malibu, California, Lenise Soren integrates her boutique of massively large rare crystals with a venue that showcases many forms of art and holds wellness events that offer a unique experience. When large crystals are mined from the earth, everyone benefits whether they are in museums or private collections. Their healing vibration spreads out into the community.

The responsibility of having crystals is huge. Their unique healing signature has come to you in trust. Treat them with the same respect as you would any healing medicine. Keep personal crystals out of the eyes and hands of others. I keep two sets of crystals: One for educational purposes that can be handled, dented, dinged, and chipped without remorse. The other set is a private collection of museum-quality specimens and personal pieces used for healing. None are so valuable that they can't be replaced.

Gemstone Investing

Gemstones have inherent value. However, it requires shrewd investing to have a collection worth anything. It's not stamp collecting. There are numerous crystals in the earth. Miners are facing rising prices to get them out of the land and into gem markets. Gemstones only return value when they are unique, from a limited source, or are really big or flawless.

When buying, your own outlay of cash must be large, in the thousands of dollars, and when selling, it may take a long time and multiple agents to find a buyer. Commissions to agents may also be high. You may not gain much profit since a buyer will be looking for the lowest price. There are other sellers out there, too, as it's a competitive market. Save yourself the trouble of overinvesting in a commodity that's difficult to move into the market and will be slow to resell. Yes, there's currently a décor trend in exotic crystals, but will it last?

Originally, moldavite, which was created from the Nördlinger Reis meteor impact in Southern Germany, was very expensive since it was quite rare. Locations for moldavite were limited to a small area in the Czech Republic. Then new locations of moldavite were found in Germany and Austria. As new sources for this green tektite from the cosmos brought more moldavite to the market, the price went down. They're just now becoming rare again, as supplies are once again reducing.

Similarly, a massive amount of lab-grown gemstones are now available. You can make as many as you want! However, the market demand is currently high because these lovely bobbles are a fashion trend. The new age is the "now age."

If you're a cautious person, you might want to check out any newly available mineral finds with organizations that track materials coming on the market, such as the Hudson Institute of Mineralogy outreach and education website, Mindat.org. It claims to be the world's largest open database of minerals and their localities, deposits, and mines worldwide. Check out your new find and its value with some of their experts.

Initial Introductions

Once you're home and you've unwrapped your new crystal, you'll need to cleanse and recharge it. (Read Chapter 8 for complete instructions on both processes.)

Now you can spend some quality time with it. Remember even the smallest crystal can be effective in opening your consciousness to a whole new level because it's a portal to awareness expansion. After you've chosen a crystal, it's time to really get inside it (and I mean that literally), and see how the two of you affect each other.

A crystal initiation is a session during which one meditates and enters into the crystal matrix. For your first crystal initiation, select a clear quartz crystal with a natural tip— one that hasn't been polished or one that has been polished to a point. This is an all-purpose crystal, perfect for people who've never been through this ritual.

Again, be sure that your quartz crystal is cleansed and fully charged before you begin. Sit quietly in a room that has natural light, which is best for seeing inside a crystal. Spend a few minutes looking outside the crystal and all over its surfaces. Observe its lines, faces, and sides. Be aware of its dimensions. Feel any surface bumps with your fingertips. As you handle the crystal, be aware of your breathing. Maybe your breath becomes quicker; maybe it slows down and is barely audible.

Get the Inside Information

Now, look inside the crystal. Look through the sides of the crystal. Look through it to the other side and observe any distortions. Tilt the crystal and look through the tip. Look down inside to the bottom, to the floor of the crystal.

After you have truly explored the crystal inside and out, select a spot inside the crystal. While focusing on that spot, breathe in and out until your breath slows and becomes regulated by the crystal. When you are ready, close your eyes and feel yourself floating and entering into the crystal. Explore what you see inside the crystal using your inner eye and your deeper connection. Be prepared to see something special. Maybe there's a rainbow of colors. Maybe you hear music. Maybe you see someone there, like a crystal guide to help you in your healing journey, so stay and have a chat! Listen for a message about the healing mission of the crystal. The power of crystals is limitless, so anything is possible here.

When you're ready to return, take a deep breath in and mentally say the word release to bring your consciousness back into this reality. Open your eyes. If you're feeling a bit lightheaded, walk around in some fresh air to get your head out of the clouds and your feet back on the ground.

A crystal initiation is a sacred way to bond with your personal clear quartz crystal. Now that you and the crystal have been introduced to each other, keep the crystal constantly near you for at least three days so your energies become well integrated. See Chapter 8 for some instructions on how to dedicate your crystal for specific use, purpose, or mission.

Harnessing Power with Familiar Forms

In Chapter 3, we talked about crystals that were formed into other geometric shapes and how their crystalline alignment is more powerful. (For example, a pyramid shape can amplify the power of a crystal.) Now, let's talk about some familiar forms of crystals—so familiar, in fact, that many of us don't think of them as crystals at all! And yet, their power to shift and move energy is every bit as genuine as any other gemstone.

Crystals come in all sorts of shapes and sizes—some of these shapes are especially intended to magnify the effect of the crystal's power and can produce amazing effects in your home or on your outlook. They hold powerful energy and can amplify the intent of your layouts. Learn how to use these shapes as part of your layouts and crystal grids in Part 4.

Crystal Pyramids

If you're drawn to pyramids, you might be looking for structure in your life. The pyramid shapes sense from chaotic mental and psychic energies into a logical, creative life force.

Interesting, right? But how do you put this to use in your life? Well, a pyramid structure used during meditation harnesses and focuses your energy. If you have a small crystal pyramid, you can use it as a guide for visualization by placing it gently on top of your head or by holding it over your head. If you're lying down, simply place the pyramid above your head. You can also hold it in front of you and gaze into it.

A crystal pyramid makes it possible to move into other dimensions where information can be accessed and where you can create manifestations on a material plane. Pyramids are the teachers for students learning to use the dynamics of energy!

There are several healing properties of meditating with a pyramid:

♦ **Physical**—It regulates all bodily systems, speeds healing, reduces aging, and smoothes wrinkles.

♦ **Emotional**—It reduces stress and worry, decreases feelings of alienation, and assists in emotional releasing.

♦ **Mental**—It increases mental clarity and dreaming; improves memory, communications, and logic; develops a deeper sense of one's self; and improves creativity.

♦ **Spiritual**—It improves psychic abilities (clairvoyance), enhances spiritual connections with other beings, assists in astral travel, helps access deeper levels of esoteric knowledge, and strengthens all energy fields.

There are pyramids made of many different types of crystal. Clear quartz, rose quartz, and lapis lazuli are popular, among other semiprecious stones. With a genuine crystal pyramid, you have the properties of both the gemstone and the pyramid energies.

A dynamic link exists between the two energies that defies description, although the word *expansive* comes to mind. The bigger the gemstone, the greater the energy, when it comes to pyramid energy.

A crystal pyramid can be programmed to facilitate meditation, telepathic communication, channeling, astral travel, and healing, among other uses. (See Chapter 8 on programming crystals.) With the pyramid shape and the crystalline structure synchronized by its sacred geometry, a full spectrum of light interaction is possible.

Pyramids are great for manifesting your wishes and are helpful for solving problems. For example, as part of a pyramid workshop, I asked 30 participants to imagine themselves within a pyramid about 5 feet high. Then I asked everyone to focus on something they'd like to come true within 24 hours. The next day, I received a phone call from a Reiki master who had attended the workshop. She'd been distressed for several months after misplacing a $1,000 bond. That morning, she had suddenly found the missing bond and she felt absolutely certain that focusing on the bond during the pyramid workshop had helped resolve the issue.

Pyramids can be very practical in other ways as well. Try these suggestions:

♦ Hold the base of a small crystal pyramid against a sore tooth to help reduce pain.

♦ Place a small crystal pyramid inside a filtered water container to energize the water and reduce toxins.

♦ Place a crystal pyramid over a person's photo to send distant healing to that person.

♦ Meditate with a small crystal pyramid made of labradorite or amethyst taped over your third eye to increase psychic abilities.

Obelisks

Obelisks are very popular in home décor. Original Egyptian obelisks were magnificent pieces of stone, often quarried from several kilometers away and carved with the local history of famed rulers. Obelisks are wider at the base, pulling up energy from the earth. At the top of the tall four-sided, tapered spire, the tip is in the shape of a pyramid.

The symbolism is that the obelisk is life-giving. The healing aspects of an obelisk draws negativity from the environment and shoots the energy up the shaft to be replaced on its journey with positive energy. The four sides of the pyramid-shaped tip are like a lighthouse, beaming the positive energies out from its tip over the community or relaying energy to other obelisks, like antennae.

If you have even one obelisk crystal in the middle of your room or home, energies will be kept in circulation, and it will release pent-up energies that have accumulated. When used for healing purposes, place the base of the obelisk over the area of the body to be healed; the obelisk pulls up energies for transformation. An obelisk works well when balanced with a crystal ball nearby to circulate the energy in a room.

Crystal Balls

Most people associate crystal balls with looking into the future. Crystal ball gazing, also known as scrying, is an ancient form of divination using a reflective surface, such as water or a crystal ball. A seer or clairvoyant will look into a crystal ball for images that tell the reader about future or hidden events.

However, crystal balls are not just for gazing. They can be used for healing and for dream work. You can even perform energy massage therapy by rolling the crystal ball over areas of pain or discomfort.

Crystal balls come in different types of crystal, such as amethyst, rose quartz, sodalite, and obsidian. Many clear quartz crystal balls are not perfectly clear and are cloudy with inclusions (flecks or specks in the crystal) or are opaque. Take the time to hold the crystal ball in your hand and listen to it; feel what its energy is telling you without making a judgement about what it looks like. Make your purchasing decision based on your personal interaction with the crystal.

For scrying (which is just a form of harnessing psychic energy with a crystal ball), you'll need a very clear crystal or glass ball. A perfectly clear quartz is hard to come by, but it is worth the money because it provides a clear surface for the mind to project upon. Large glass balls are quite expensive and have less distortions.

Scrying takes practice. You'll need several sessions of sitting with the ball and just gazing softly into it. There's a relaxation within the physical eye after a while, and a connection will open to the inner third eye. You might start to see images. At first, these will be subjective, like seeing your dreams. For those with natural talent, reliable images will be seen along with impressions about them. The interpretation of these images is up to you and your intuition, which of course is strengthened by the crystal itself.

Geodes and Clusters

Geodes are typically formed when volcanic activity spews out lava and forms balls that cool on the outside. The balls contain various gases that promote the growth of crystals inside, such as amethyst. Some geodes are like caves, as big as a person. When they're broken open, you'll see pristine sparkling crystals inside, like a whole colony of crystals. Sometimes, small pieces of the geode are broken off and sold as clusters.

Clusters are groupings of crystals of the same type or different types. They are used in feng shui for balancing energy in a room, in a garden, or in buildings. Feng shui (pronounced "fung shway") is the ancient art of placement based on the principle of an eight-spoke wheel and each spoke represents a part of one's life and environment. Using "cures" for bad influences, objects and colors are placed in areas of the home or in building elements to restore balance and to achieve harmony. (See Chapter 15 for more information on crystals and feng shui.)

Like an acoustical microphone, geodes are cupped to pick up negative energies. They can be positioned within a room to absorb and transmit energy. Place one on each side of a doorway or facing a door to catch and cleanse negative energies on their way in.

Changes in Thought and Presence

As you begin to work more with your crystals, you'll become more comfortable and start to feel enlightened. What's happening here? Is it real? Is there a name for it? There sure is—it's called *intuition*, and it's popping up to say hello. Get used to it because it's going to stick around for a very long time!

Let Intuition Be Your Guide

What is intuition and how do you know if you have it? Intuition is the knowingness that is already inside you. Sometimes people refer to intuition as a "gut feeling;" it's the ability to know when something is right or a warning that something is wrong. Our own intuition is something we trust because it comes from within ourselves.

When you hold a crystal, you may get an energy rush as your intuition awakens and guides you through a new learning experience. Intuition is activated from the energy of the crystal, releasing its energy into your subtle energy fields. It's your own energy that the crystal energy is supporting and enhancing.

If you can sense this awareness or feel other sensations while using a crystal, your consciousness is opening to another level of perception. As your intuition opens, you'll have the ability to know how connected you are to the infinite universe and to the possibilities of love, peace, and healing.

Your awareness expands, and you find that you're living life on a whole new level. Your energy is revitalized, and you become more stimulated by living your personal truth. The positive energies amplified by the crystals can be seen in the way you look, the way you act, and the way you interact with other people. Don't be surprised if others are drawn to you. They feel good in your environment and are feeling uplifted and happy around you!

Keep a Crystal Journal

One of the best ways to keep track of your crystals and your experiences with them is to keep a journal. You can write down details, such as where you purchased the crystal, its cost, the country and area from which it was mined, and special characteristics like inclusions or other crystals growing with it. You might also want to write down your first impressions or images that resonate with the crystal.

Later, you may want to review your notes and identify crystals to help fill your collection or to determine a constitutional crystal (see Chapter 9) for long-term personal use and development.

CARVED IN STONE . . . .

For some, using crystals can be a wild life-altering, mind-expanding experience. You can become captivated by these new treasures you've found. You realize there's more to learn about life beyond four walls. You feel alive with energy. You no longer need to feel separated from nature or feel separated from yourself. You feel reconnected to your own intuition and to higher realms. You are living your truth.

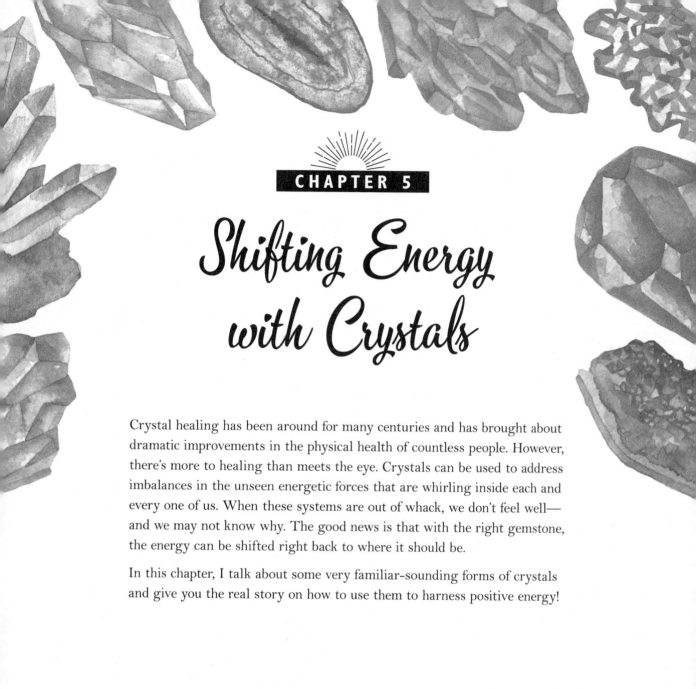

CHAPTER 5

Shifting Energy with Crystals

Crystal healing has been around for many centuries and has brought about dramatic improvements in the physical health of countless people. However, there's more to healing than meets the eye. Crystals can be used to address imbalances in the unseen energetic forces that are whirling inside each and every one of us. When these systems are out of whack, we don't feel well— and we may not know why. The good news is that with the right gemstone, the energy can be shifted right back to where it should be.

In this chapter, I talk about some very familiar-sounding forms of crystals and give you the real story on how to use them to harness positive energy!

Learn How to ...

♦ Balance your yin and yang and rebalance your body's subtle energy.

♦ Get grounded.

Experiencing Subtle Energy

Subtle energy is all around us, even in our bodies. We were born with it, but our knowledge is hidden until we are ready to do something with it.

Subtle energy is made up of the life force that has a connection to a spiritual or divine source. It's so refined, some consider it a vibration. The subtle energy is a complex of interacting energy fields within our physical structure, between ourselves, and even connecting to Earth. We can train to be more conscious and aware of this magnificent energy and can learn more about how crystals are used to connect with this energy as part of the healing process.

Eastern Traditions

In India, where yoga and Ayurveda (the traditional medicine of India) are widely taught, the word prana means "breath." Prana is light and airy and is considered the vital energy in human organisms which flows along a subtle energy network called nadis.

In Tibetan medicine, the subtle body energies are called tsa, lung, and tigle. Tsa are the channels or pathways; lung is the pranic energies; and tigle are the seeds of subtle energy that are like pollen in the wind, moving with the subtle winds of the body and leaving you feeling happy and content. The mind will experience well-being and happiness when there is balance in these channels. Some Eastern traditions teach that there are only five chakras based on the five basic elements, similar to the Platonic solids—earth, water, fire, air, and space. We will learn about the full seven chakras widely accepted in the West since 1918 based on the translation of a sixteenth century Sanskrit text written by the Bengali yogi, Purnanand.

Restoring Balance to the Subtle Body

Subtle energy is an entire network designed to keep you in balance. When the subtle body is balanced, energies float freely without restriction along the channels and feelings of joy, happiness, love, compassion, and well-being flow freely, too. The mind rides along with tigle seeds in the energy channels, like a horse and its rider.

When the subtle body is disturbed through fear and other negative mental states, the tigle seeds of energy become restricted. Because they can't spread around, they start to recede and cause depression, anxiety, and unhappiness. Since the subtle energy is connected to the physical body, illness and disease could manifest if tigle are left unattended.

By working with the subtle balancing energies of crystals, the tigle are influenced and blockages are cleared, allowing our minds to become relaxed and clearer. We're returned to peace and happiness! Constant exposure to crystals and other forms of healing that balance subtle energies help to maintain the subtle body through which we can experience all kinds of love and joyfulness.

Chi and Meridians

Chi, is a Chinese word for "air." In traditional Chinese medicine, chi, like prana, is the life force that sustains a person's vitality. Meridians are the pathways in the body on which subtle energies move about.

We can all increase our awareness of and become more sensitized to our chi. Strong emotions can generate or reduce the flow of chi. Become more aware of when chi increases, such as with laughter, or decreases, as when sad. You can even get positive chi just talking to another person. You'll know because you'll feel good. Taking classes in Tai Chi, Qi Qong, and other Asian methodologies that focus on the movement of chi through the body can help.

Because chi, as a vital force, is all around us, walking or any kind of motion causes chi to flow freely. Meditation also helps stimulate the flow of chi. When chi flows, health is affected in a positive way.

Chi is generally associated with meridians, pathways on which subtle body energies travel similar to the Tibetan tsa. When meridians are imbalanced, our health is affected and our immunity to disease is compromised. When crystals are placed along an imbalanced meridian line, especially at the beginning and end of a meridian line or over the area of imbalance, a rebalancing of that meridian line occurs.

The body contains 12 meridians. Each meridian is a channel for subtle energy to travel along and corresponds to a specific organ and to a set of physical and psychological functions, as shown in the following illustration. You will also find there are two additional chakras in the image, the star chakra or soul-star chakra above the crown chakra and the earth chakra below the feet. These two centers are part of a larger cosmic chakra system. I will cover these two extra chakras in the Chakra System section later in this chapter.

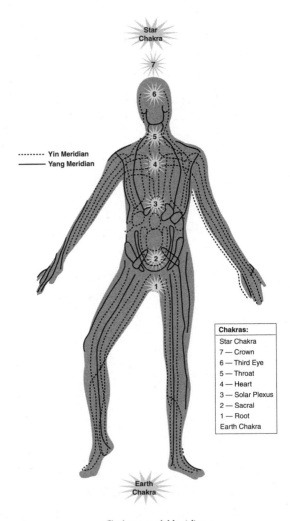

Chakras and Meridians.

Yin and Yang Energies

To understand how chi energy is balanced, you need to understand yin and yang, opposing energies that are contained in all things. Yin and yang represent the balance between positive and negative attributes, and also the balance between feminine (yin) and masculine (yang) energies. Together, they must always be equal in a dynamic equilibrium. Both are part of the whole.

For example, where there is a flood on the planet, there is also a drought somewhere else. If there is too much energy in the subtle body system, there is too little energy in the physical body, which can manifest as illness. When the yin and yang are restored to balance, health and well-being continue. Hopefully, we can do the same for our planet.

Balancing Yin and Yang

When it comes to crystals, some types and forms of crystals will be more yin- or more yang-balancing. Crystals are very powerful for increasing or decreasing energy, and the right crystal must be selected to balance yin and yang energies.

For instance, if you're feeling stressed and a bit hot headed, or feeling upset, this indicates an overabundance of yang energy. To balance this level of yang energy, you have a few choices: find a crystal to calm yourself down by removing or absorbing the excess yang energy; find a powerful yin crystal that will match and balance the high level of yang energy; or select both yin and yang crystals to bring yourself more rapidly to dispel negative emotions and the other to create positive emotions resulting in emotional harmony.

You could select a yang crystal such as the dynamic smoky quartz, best known for absorbing negative energies. You could also select a yin crystal such as moonstone, which is best known for its icy coolness and calming abilities.

Yin crystals include agates, amber, amethyst, aquamarine, calcite, clear quartz, fluorite, jade, moonstone, and rose quartz.

Yang crystals include carnelian, diamond, fire opal, garnet, lapis lazuli, malachite, obsidian, rutilated quartz, smoky quartz, and sapphire.

Hold the smoky quartz in the right male-yang dominated hand and the moonstone in the left-yin dominated hand. This formation works to restore polarity in the body and leaves you feeling relaxed, balanced, and whole.

Get Grounded

Change is difficult for many people because we like familiar ways of doing things. This is not to say we are inflexible. We might grumble a bit if there's no coffee in the morning, but most of us will get on with the day despite the discomfort. Real inflexibility comes when we are asked to change inner parts of ourselves. This is different from changes in the subtle energy body, because these are changes we're consciously bringing upon ourselves. Fortunately, these transitions can be soothed through a process called grounding. Grounding is a method that opens channels in the body and enables unwanted energy to travel into the ground. Grounding helps us keep centered when everything else is changing around us.

Move That Energy Safely

Like a lightning bolt hitting a tree and traveling through the roots into the ground, your surges of energy need a place to go where they aren't going to cause harm to you, to your psyche, or to your loved ones. When you are grounded, unwanted energy passes right through you so that it doesn't harm your physical, emotional, and spiritual bodies. This means that the energies you need for health and healing are readily available, while negative energies are removed altogether.

Grounded for Life!

So how do you do a grounding? It's a fairly simple process that requires focus and a dark colored crystal. Did I mention you can use this method to settle your nerves before an audition or a job interview? Take a deep breath, and follow these steps:

1. Sit down with your feet flat on the floor. Do not cross your legs because it restricts the flow of energy. Feel your weight on the seat of the chair, focused on your tailbone.

2. Place a dark-colored crystal such as garnet or obsidian between your feet. The crystal will provide an anchor for your energy on the Earth plane instead of flying off and getting lost in some other dimension.

3. Visualize energy roots coming from under your feet. See them growing deep into the earth, traveling down until they reach a big boulder, as big as you can imagine, below the surface of the earth. Anchor the roots by winding them several times around the boulder. This is one of the simplest methods of grounding.

4. Draw in a big breath, inhaling the heaviness and stability of that boulder's energy up through the energy roots and toward your feet. You may feel a tugging as your body sinks deeper into the earth. Bring the grounding energies up through your physical body, following the energy pathways, and expanding the energies around you into the subtle body. Breathe in this grounding energy a total of three times. Take your time. You will feel very heavy and really grounded.

Clearing Blockages

When you have repeated stresses such as emotional shock, worry, physical trauma, or feelings of being spiritually shortchanged, the ability to pass unwanted energy through energy pathways becomes weaker. Sometimes blockages form, like the buildup of plaque in arteries when the pulmonary system is overloaded with cholesterol. Some of these obstacles are due to ignoring or failing to recognize signs of physical or emotional distress, hiding emotions, ignoring needs of the self, or staying in a mind space that is harmful to yourself.

The really harmful thing about these types of blockages is that they are a big cause of major imbalances in the body, something I'll talk more about in the following section.

The Chakra System

The word chakra in Sanskrit means "wheel" and describes the spinning centers of energy at various points in the body. They provide circulation of prana to the nadis and contain vital energies as well as spiritual energies.

There are seven major chakra centers, each associated with the glandular system and the general physical health of the area of the body to which it is closest. The chakras are part of the subtle energy of the body and provide for movement of prana.

Color Therapy and Chakras

Color therapy, which is used to balance the chakras, has been around for a long time. Avicenna, the eleventh-century physician, observed that certain colors were connected to disease or healing. For instance, red was associated with movement of disease through the system, blue was cooling (as in calming a fever), and yellow took heat away (as in dispersing inflammation). In the chakra system, red is seen as vitality, blue is associated with healing, and yellow with intellectual pursuits. There are many systems and interpretations of what colors mean. What we agree on is that each color has a special meaning.

In the chakra system, the higher the vibrational frequency of the color, the more it relates to the higher chakras—the seat of consciousness. When positive and negative ions merge as white light in the highest chakra center, the crown chakra, there is such an illumination of energy that ignorance of the mind is dispelled and enlightenment occurs.

On the following pages, you'll find all the information you need to work with and heal the chakras with various crystals. One important note: you will get a bigger self-healing effect if you follow the Chakra Activation instructions in Chapter 7.

First Chakra: The Root or Base Chakra

The first chakra is located between the legs at the perineum, the space between your anal opening and genitals.

The root chakra provides physical strength, the will to live, sexual and reproductive energy, grounding, and the fight-or-flight response.

Colors: Red, black, brown

Crystals: Garnets, rubies, obsidian, black tourmaline, mahogany obsidian, and brown jasper

Sound: LAM; note C

Second Chakra: The Sacral, Spleen, or Sexual Chakra

The second chakra is easy to find. Simply place your hand with closed fingers flat against your stomach below the navel with your thumb just at the navel. In the center of your torso four finger widths down from the navel and just below the little finger on your hand, press and find a soft spot about 3 to 4 inches wide. That is the location of your second chakra—the sacral chakra.

The sacral chakra provides self-esteem, emotional self-awareness, openness to new ideas, connection to others, assimilation of experiences, and definition and identity of our sexuality.

Colors: Orange, orange-red, orange-yellow

Crystals: Carnelian, orange calcite, jasper, and coral

Sound: BAM; note D

Third Chakra: The Solar Plexus Chakra

The third chakra is the soft spot below the sternum in the center of the upper torso. This is the area where many people sense a "gut feeling." Sometimes this chakra moves around, either a bit higher or lower, depending on your interaction with life—trying to get more out of it or trying to hide from it.

The solar plexus chakra provides personal power, self-confidence, logical thought, decision-making skill, and desire for intellectual pursuits.

Colors: Yellow, golden yellow

Crystals: Citrine, golden topaz, golden or yellow calcite, smoky quartz, apatite, yellow jasper, and amber

Sound: RAM; note E

Fourth Chakra: The Heart

The fourth chakra is in the center of the chest, about halfway between the bottom and top of the sternum. This center is usually found in times of great joy or great sadness because it either feels wide open with love or closed down in pain and grief. This chakra can move around as well.

The heart chakra provides compassion for self and others; love; and balance between mind, body, and spirit. This chakra needs both pink and green colors: pink for divine love and green for healing and nurturing. The heart chakra is the seat of compassion and the source of love and radiant light.

Colors: Pink, golden pink, green

Crystals: Rose quartz, kunzite, rhodonite, rhodochrosite, pink tourmaline, emerald, malachite, dioptase, peridot, and aventurine

Sound: YUM; note F#

Fifth Chakra: The Throat Chakra

The fifth chakra is located in the soft spot at the base of the throat, above the well that forms where your clavicles meet. People who use their voices for speaking and singing have a well-developed fifth chakra. The throat chakra provides creativity, communication, spoken truth, and the will to act.

Turquoise is the color associated with healing the fifth chakra, as it is focused on open expression and communication.

Colors: Turquoise, light blue

Crystals: Turquoise, blue lace agate, celestite, aquamarine, blue tourmaline, natural blue topaz, and sodalite

Sound: HAM; note G#

Sixth Chakra: The Third Eye

The sixth chakra is the hardest to locate; it varies with each person. Generally, it is a disc about the size of a walnut located in the center of the forehead. For some, this chakra is lower—slightly above the top line of the eyebrows. When activated, this center tingles.

The third eye chakra provides the seat of your intuitive seeing and knowing, extrasensory perception (ESP), clairvoyance, and a higher understanding of others.

Colors: Indigo, deep blue

Crystals: Iolite, sodalite, lapis lazuli, blue fluorite, sapphire, and azurite

Sound: AH; note A

Seventh Chakra: The Crown Chakra

The seventh chakra is at the top-center of the head. You might have noticed some tingling in the scalp sometimes for no reason. Maybe it was due to incoming messages from beyond!

The crown chakra provides a path to one's higher power, self-realization, and spiritual growth and peace.

Colors: White, purple

Crystals: Amethyst, sugilite, purple fluorite, and charoite, selenite, apophyllite, clear quartz, and diamond

Sound: OM; note B

More Chakras: The Star Chakra and the Earth Chakra

The star chakra or soul-star chakra connects you to the cosmos "out there" and represents the divine or the soul aspect. The earth chakra keeps you connected to "right here" and ensures your connection to the earth for physical well-being and support.

There are two crystals that help align the central energy channel of the body and connect with the star chakra: blue kyanite and selenite. Lie down and place the crystal about 6 to 8 inches above your head, aligned with the center of your crown chakra. Imagine an energy cord coming up from your central channel through your crown chakra, connecting with the crystal and then to the star chakra above the tip of the crystal.

There are two crystals that help connect with the earth chakra: black kyanite and black tourmaline. Lie down and place the crystal about 6 to 8 inches below and between your feet with the tip pointed up. Feel your connection with the earth, draw up energy from the earth into your earth chakra and then into the crystal, and finally up into the lower opening of the central channel. Let this energy radiate through all your energy centers to replenish them.

The Chakra Tune-Up Kit

One of the most important tasks when starting on crystal healing is to assemble a chakra tune-up kit. Keep these specially selected crystals for each chakra handy for when you need them. You will need them for the Chakra Activation in Chapter 7. If you already have a collection of crystals, get them all out and group them together by chakra color to see if you are missing any colors.

Before you start to fill in your crystal collection, look at what color crystals you have already collected the most of. That is a clear signal that you are trying to heal the chakra associated with that color, and you should probably be wearing a crystal in that color as a pendant to increase your vibration in that particular chakra. Now, look at your crystals again. Which color or colors are you lacking? Let's say you have a lack of yellow crystals. This signals that you are trying to avoid issues related to the solar plexus chakra (whose color is yellow), including self-confidence, logical thoughts, and decision-making.

The following table gives a minimum list of crystals for your chakra kit. Crystals should be at least 1 inch in diameter for chakra work, if you can find them, in either tumbled smooth or in raw form.

Chakra Tune-Up Kit

Chakra	Chakra Crystal
1—Root	Garnet or other red crystal such as red calcite.
2—Sacral	Carnelian or other orange crystals.
3—Solar plexus	Tiger eye, jasper, or any yellow crystal such as honey calcite.
4—Heart	Rose quartz or any pink crystal such as rhodochrosite, and green crystals such as jade, malachite, or dioptase.
5—Throat	Turquoise or other light blue crystal such as blue lace agate or sodalite. White coral may also be included.
6—Third eye	Lapis lazuli or other deep blue crystal such as iolite or blue topaz; or golden topaz, apophyllite, or celestite.
7—Crown	Amethyst or other purple crystal such as purple fluorite, or a clear crystal such as selenite.

What's Your Aura?

What is an aura, anyway? An aura is a reflection of the colors of the chakra system. When chakras spin, color projects around the body into different layers of the auric system. Different colors can indicate which chakra and its associated systems are strongest in your body. Depending on the color of the aura, you might be way out of balance! When a chakra is healed or corrected, the aura will also improve. Unfortunately, most people can't see auras, so they have no idea that they're walking around with energy all blocked up somewhere inside their bodies.

What Does Healing Feel Like?

Now that you've been introduced to how crystals can be used to balance or heal systems in the body, the obvious next question is, "How do I know it's working?"

Sometimes the effect of crystals on the human energy field is very subtle and difficult to describe because there is no real physical feeling such as "hot" or "cold." Each person has different levels of perception, receptivity, and sensitivity.

Crystals can definitely warm up in your hand if you hold them even for a short time period. A transference of body heat and other subtle energies into the crystal occurs. If you hold a crystal for a while, put it down, and return to pick it up even after a minute, you will find the heat is still inside. We find it easy to sense hot and cold, but what about more subtle energy?

When you have a pile of crystals laid on your body for a healing session, you can feel very relaxed and often enter a different state of consciousness. Some people feel a tingling when crystals are placed on them. Some say, it feels like a Reiki session, with energy in and around their body like a long soft pulse. Muscles and wrinkles seem to relax and pain subsides. Emotional issues seem less important or resolved. You might feel more energetic and your head is clearer. Sometimes your friends and family will notice the changes before you do! Having a pile of crystals on you is like having multiple healing prayers.

The healing effects of crystals are often experienced as very refined changes to the four levels of being: physical, emotional, psychological, and spiritual. Each will be discussed in Part 3.

CARVED IN STONE . . . .

Garnet: I give you vital energy to direct passion to your life's purpose. I recharge your inner batteries. I generate the flow of kundalini forces to be directed toward spiritual attainment.

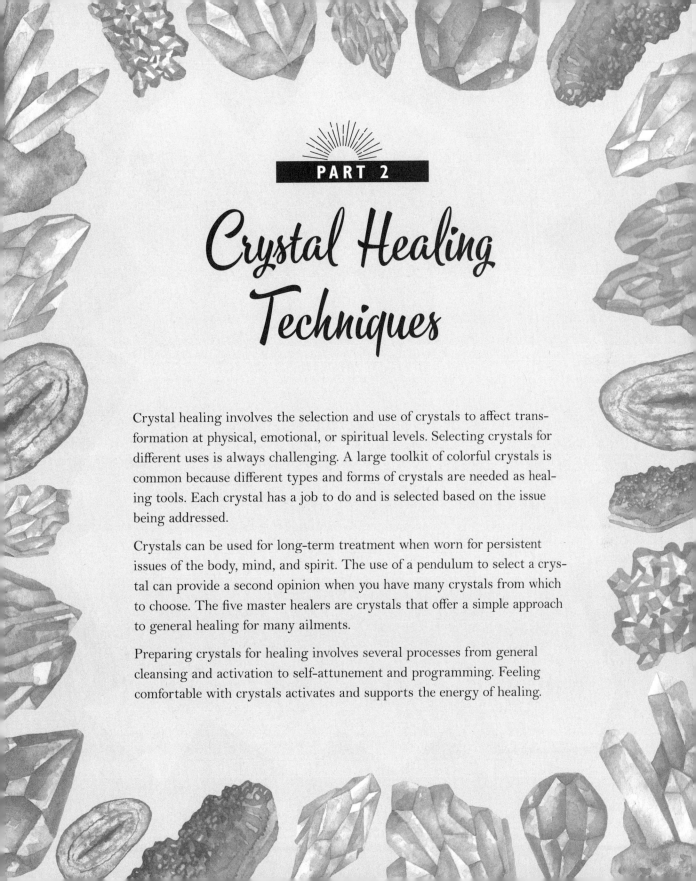

PART 2

Crystal Healing Techniques

Crystal healing involves the selection and use of crystals to affect transformation at physical, emotional, or spiritual levels. Selecting crystals for different uses is always challenging. A large toolkit of colorful crystals is common because different types and forms of crystals are needed as healing tools. Each crystal has a job to do and is selected based on the issue being addressed.

Crystals can be used for long-term treatment when worn for persistent issues of the body, mind, and spirit. The use of a pendulum to select a crystal can provide a second opinion when you have many crystals from which to choose. The five master healers are crystals that offer a simple approach to general healing for many ailments.

Preparing crystals for healing involves several processes from general cleansing and activation to self-attunement and programming. Feeling comfortable with crystals activates and supports the energy of healing.

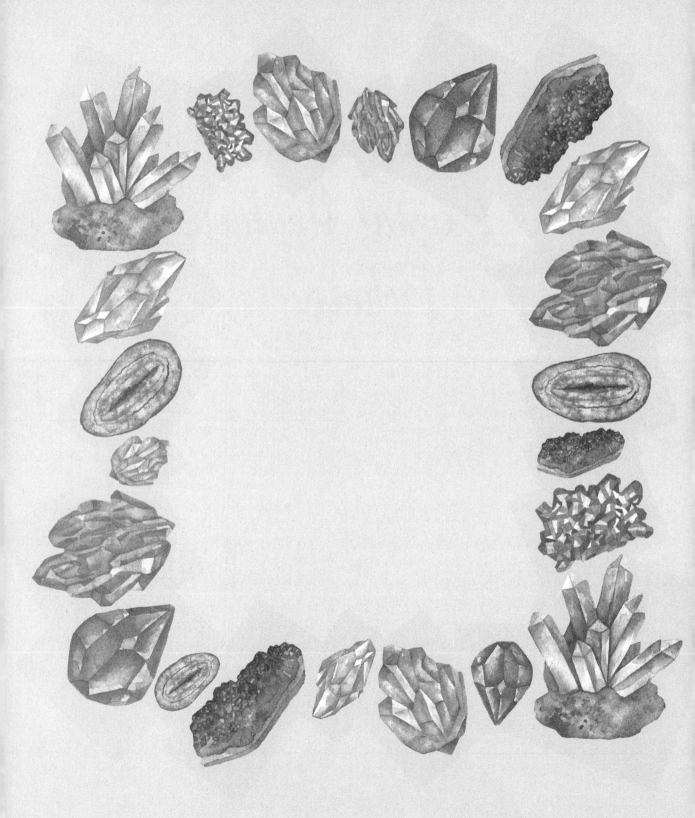

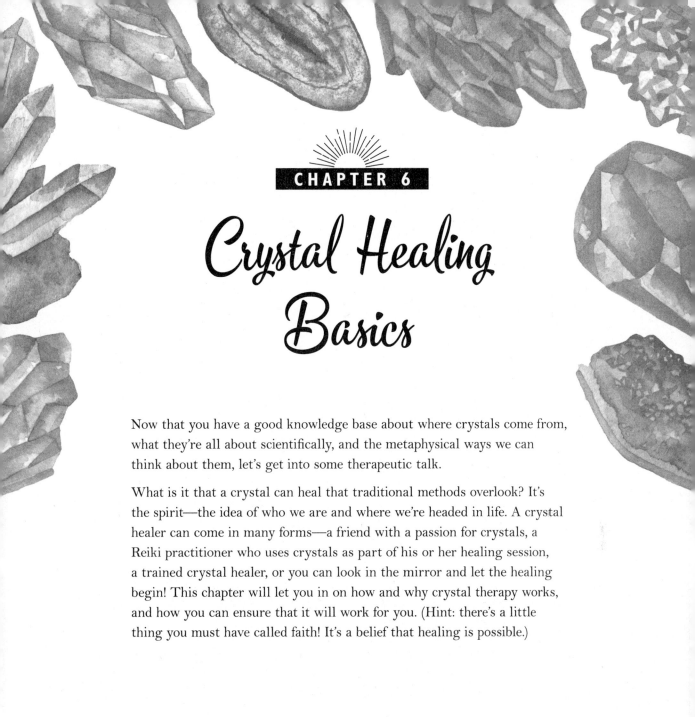

CHAPTER 6

Crystal Healing Basics

Now that you have a good knowledge base about where crystals come from, what they're all about scientifically, and the metaphysical ways we can think about them, let's get into some therapeutic talk.

What is it that a crystal can heal that traditional methods overlook? It's the spirit—the idea of who we are and where we're headed in life. A crystal healer can come in many forms—a friend with a passion for crystals, a Reiki practitioner who uses crystals as part of his or her healing session, a trained crystal healer, or you can look in the mirror and let the healing begin! This chapter will let you in on how and why crystal therapy works, and how you can ensure that it will work for you. (Hint: there's a little thing you must have called faith! It's a belief that healing is possible.)

Learn How to …

♦ Use a crystal starter kit to cleanse and prepare you for self-transformation.

♦ Put a special symbol into the crystal to magnify its image.

♦ Pick an Ayurvedic birthstone by your astrological sign to correct imbalances.

Crystal Healers

Health is a matter of balance between the physical, emotional, and mental states—at least that's what doctors treat if you are ill. Yet, our sense of self and well-being frames how we experience the health of our bodies, our emotional responses, our thoughts, and how we feel spiritually. This is part of living a life of wellness. Sometimes, we need some outside help to initiate our connection between the body, mind, and spirit.

A crystal healer is a person who has the skills or training to facilitate the healing process through the selection and placement of crystals around the client's body. Crystal healers understand the crystalline complex and how to use crystal energy to create a curative transformation at the physical, emotional, and psycho-spiritual levels of being. They may use a variety of techniques and will have a number of different crystal types that are used for different purposes.

Even crystals placed in a room will emit energies or vibrational frequencies that can create a shift in energy dynamics and consciousness. In fact, there are crystal décor specialists who work with the energies of crystals in the environment. There's a growing belief in individual spiritualism making crystals the perfect vehicle for any interpretation. You may find crystals just about anywhere—an office, medical suite, library, and other quiet, reflective, or healing spaces.

Among some Native American groups, quartz crystals are used in healing lodges to provide healing energy throughout the community. Sometimes large crystals are placed back into the land at strategic points to balance spirit energies. The ancient Druids of northern France and England also placed large stones strategically, although their purpose is still a mystery to us. All these cultures have different methods, but they all know one thing: crystals and their healing powers are a natural part of the environment. So, put them in your office or in your bedroom and soak in some crystal healing from your environment!

Within Tibetan Buddhism, crystals represent the highest level of purity and clarity of mind. Why? Well, the crystal teaches us that our minds should be clear and free from afflicting emotions and illness. And like a mother who cannot help but love her child unconditionally, a crystal refracts light unconditionally. If you put a clear crystal ball on a colored cloth, you will see the colored cloth underneath. Put a clear quartz crystal in water and the crystal disappears. Put simply, nothing material seems to stick to it.

Crystal healers know that if we strive to have the same qualities of crystal, we'll hold a higher energy within ourselves and will radiate this light unconditionally throughout our being. Illness will not stick to our bodies, and our minds will be clear. This is ultimately what we hope to find and achieve in crystal healing.

What Is Crystal Healing?

The use of crystals for healing has been around for thousands of years. Ancient civilizations in China and Mesoamerica used jade to prepare the human body and spirit for its journey after death. The Egyptians used copious amounts of gold, lapis lazuli, carnelian, and other precious stones to decorate everyday items included in the tombs of their sacred pharaohs.

The use of crystal healing is relatively new to Western culture, although we do use crystals and minerals in many products, such as fluoride in toothpaste, calcium in stomach tablets, and limestone in cement making. Many other crystals are used in the pharmaceutical industries. Even our computer chips are made from crystal known as silicon dioxide. Other areas of the world use pure forms of gemstones for healing. Indian Ayurvedic medicine uses crushed gemstones, such as sapphires and pearls, and Tibetan medicine uses crushed calcite and turquoise among other crystals in natural remedies. The use of copper worn externally to alleviate body aches and pains is well known through the centuries and in many countries.

We've been using the term crystal healing a lot in this chapter, but what does it really entail? In crystal healing, crystals are selectively applied to the human body or around the body to affect a change in the subtle body energies and promote healing and relaxation. Energy can get stuck in the body. When that happens, it affects every part of the body, mind, and spirit. Crystal healing helps to clear those blockages and get everything back in balance.

How Does It Work?

Before chemistry became a science in Europe, there was alchemy, which was devoted to finding the right composition of raw materials that could be used to manufacture gold that would provide incredible wealth and longevity. However, metaphysicians and philosophers said that the most precious jewel was that of the human spirit. They called this gem the *Philosopher's Stone*—another name for the spirit that lies within us. The quest to find the Philosopher's Stone would lead to enlightenment, bliss, and immortality.

When we have the right composition of materials near us, we can create what we need for personal transformation, ascension, or connection to our higher selves. You've already learned that crystals resonate on particular levels. Their healing properties depend on their resonance.

So, for a broken heart, we want to hold or use a crystal known for its properties of healing the heart chakra. Rose quartz is the perfect choice. For a diseased heart, we use malachite, which is high in copper to help electrical recharging. For psychospiritual healing, we use kunzite, which is high in lithium content to help dysfunctional behavior like alcoholism. For throat complaints such as timid speech or sore throats, you would wear turquoise, known for its ability to open and protect the throat chakra. For back or leg pain, we place hematite, which has magnetic properties, along the spine or leg.

Knowing which crystals to use for which issue is only part of the healing work. There's also the person's individuality to consider. A crystal healer will have a greater understanding of the crystals and their uses and will be able to activate the crystal resonance for healing purposes.

Why Does It Work?

We tend to attribute certain values to crystals, as we do with gold. The rarer an item is, the more interesting it is and the more value we place on it. But there really is a transcendent nature to crystals. Realization of this nature depends on the user having an open mind—something we call a consciousness opening or a spiritual initiation.

There actually is some real energy in the crystals, too, of course. You can even measure their properties scientifically for electromagnetic energy, piezoelectric energy, luminescence, and for known chemical substances. But when you learn how to use these physical attributes on an esoteric level, crystal energy can be used even more effectively.

There's also a line between the physical and the metaphysical. With crystals, your mindset—your intention—is a carrier for energy. This is not pseudoscience, it's the nature of the metaphysical world.

I owned a crystal store for two years before moving into full-time crystal healing. A number of people came into the store looking for healing. On some occasions, people received spontaneous healings. Here's a few stories that will help you understand that crystal healing is magical but not magic:

♦ A young man had swollen hands and asked if there was a crystal to use for his complaint. I suggested halite, which is also known as rock salt. I asked him to put a small piece in his hands. During the next few minutes, his hands started shaking and when he opened them there was a puddle of water in his palms that ran off onto the counter. The swelling in his hands had shrunk, and he claimed he could bend his fingers more easily.

♦ One man came into the store to tell me how a healing crystal he had purchased only a few days previously had helped his family. He said that his son had cut off the tip of his finger. He had quickly wrapped his son's finger with a bandage and the newly purchased clear quartz crystal. He said that it seemed like a good idea to wrap the crystal in his son's bandage. His son felt no pain, and the surgeons were amazed to find the damaged area was in good condition for this type of injury. The doctors were also a little startled to see the crystal drop out of the bandage. They sewed the tip back on, and the son healed more quickly than expected.

♦ An elderly woman came into the shop to ask me if I recognized her. I didn't. She reminded me that the last time I'd seen her was about two months prior and that she'd walked in using two canes. Clearly, she had no canes with her this time. She said she used the copper and garnet that I had suggested for her arthritis and it had worked so well that she no longer needed the use of her canes.

♦ Others have told me that their thyroid medication had been reduced after using crystals, usually amethyst. Amethyst is known to work on the subtle energies related to both the pineal and thyroid glands.

Crystal healing is satisfying for many people because they can participate either actively or in a passive manner—whichever is appropriate to their healing. Remember, there's no room for healing with a closed mind. Sometimes, the crystals do all the work. Other times, the person does all the work. And sometimes, a higher force does all the work.

Self-Therapy

The good news is that you don't need to seek out an energy healer to get the benefits of crystals. Many books, including this one, compile the meaning of each crystal and will guide you on your way to self-therapy. (See Appendix A for a good selection of crystals for your collection.)

Let your intuition guide you to which crystals you need. Experiment with your feelings by selecting a crystal and wearing it throughout the day. Make a note of any changes you feel in a journal and add any specific events that might have been unusual for you and any reactions from other people. (Were they friendlier toward you? Less friendly?) For instance, I've noticed that whenever I wear turquoise earrings, people stand closer to me and I seem to be more engaging. Try wearing turquoise for a job interview. Maybe you will be sending out an irresistible vibe.

Is there a vibration to crystals like an earthquake or a truck rumbling by? No. The vibrations of healing crystals are subtle and very gentle. Many people need to be led to open up another level of consciousness, to actually feel and use the energy of a crystal. Without this knowledge and sensitivity, the crystal is just a rock.

It's easiest to wear crystals in jewelry, hold them in your hand, or just have them near you. Give each crystal about three days wear to settle into your energy matrix and begin to resonate with your own vibes and then try a different crystal. Explore each crystal one at a time and be aware of the specific message each one brings to you. Remember, sometimes the healing is on more subtle levels, so check how you feel physically, emotionally, psychologically, and spiritually.

When you get used to their energetic output, you might want to wear one crystal type to get a special effect over a longer period of time, such as a few weeks. It's okay if you want to wear more than one crystal of the same kind. Their effects will be stronger. Try wearing two different crystals at a time and later add one more for optimum healing. You can actually wear up to seven crystals at one time. Any more than that and you might feel overwhelmed!

Crystal Healing Starter Kit

Buy three crystal point pendants, one each of rose quartz, clear quartz, and amethyst (1½ inches long by a ½ inch wide) and place them on a sturdy necklace that reaches your heart chakra. Instead of crystal points, you can use three tumbled stones at least 1 inch around and ½ inch thick and place them in a drawstring pouch or medicine bag. The pouch or bag should reach your heart chakra at mid-chest. This is your crystal healing starter kit.

21-Day Crystal Healing Cleanse

This crystal cleanse can be initiated any time you feel a need to move forward by opening your heart, opening your mind, and opening to new possibilities.

As you go through this 21-day cleansing period, remember to record your impressions in your crystal journal. If you find the cleansing experience is too intense, limit the wearing duration or wear smaller crystals. Remember to cleanse and recharge your crystals every three weeks for maximum benefits. And yes, you can remove them to shower.

Week 1—Rose Quartz—The Love Crystal
Begin by wearing only the rose quartz at the heart chakra to open the subtle energies of the mind and heart. Give yourself some self-love and support during a period of vulnerability while letting down your barriers to love and opening to a higher level. Feel more relaxed and in balance with your surroundings. Feel the expression of love!

Week 2—Clear Quartz—The Universal Healer
Add clear quartz to your necklace or pouch to generate and direct healing energy using your mind. This crystal can filter negative energy from others and promotes self-healing at all levels (physical, emotional, mental).

Week 3—Amethyst—The Master Transformer
Add the third crystal, amethyst, to your necklace or pouch. This purple crystal is a natural transformer of negative energy into positive energy. Align your subtle energies to a higher vibration for a deeper meditative experience. Integrate all energies (body, mind, and spirit).

Post-Cleanse Crystal Integration

After you've been wearing all three crystals for a week, the energy of the crystals integrates into your physical, emotional, and psychospiritual levels. The crystalline energy of the rose quartz, clear quartz, and amethyst merge into a new harmonic, producing a single crystal oscillation that can be used for a higher spiritual purpose. The result is your mind is clearer and sharper. You may experience less physical pain and less emotional stress. Solving problems might come more easily because you can see more clearly what needs to be done. You react less emotionally to uncertain situations. You may sleep better and dreams are brighter and more memorable. You are also more intuitive, and your psychic powers are much stronger. The longer you wear your crystals, the more benefits you will have and the deeper the healing.

A final word of caution: if you feel light-headed or dizzy, take the crystals off for a while to allow you time to integrate the changes. You may also need to work with fewer crystals over a longer period of time until you build up your stamina for crystal energy. Try a grounding crystal, such as black tourmaline, bloodstone, or lepidolite, to help you get adjusted to your new awareness of subtle energies and the changes in your subtle body.

Learn to trust your feelings about crystals. By developing sensitivity to subtle vibrations, you'll be able to select crystals for yourself and others and make a positive impact.

Reiki and Crystals

Many Westerners are already familiar with the practice of hands-on healing or the "laying on of hands" within a spiritual context. The Bible refers to this ability, and healing through touch has been practiced throughout time. Even the Shaolin monks in China perform a type of powerful energy healing using the hands. Reiki is a hands-on healing technique that increases the body's natural ability to heal physical ailments and release the causes of disease. The word *Reiki* is a Japanese word for the universal life force and our personal life force. The Reiki healing energy is focused and channeled by a Reiki healing therapist. Universal life force energy is gently absorbed into the body to heal at all levels. Reiki evolved out of the experience and dedication of Mikao Usui, a healer who started Reiki healing schools in the 1920s in Japan and was introduced to the West during the 1980s.

Many people receive benefits from Reiki energy therapy—adults, seniors, children, and even pets. Reiki has been used to treat stress, burn-out, hyperactivity, depression, and related psychological imbalances, as well as various diseases including HIV, cancer, and addiction. Reiki can also assist in recovery from sports injuries, car accidents, and so on, wherever gentle healing is beneficial to promote well-being and health.

Reiki is an ideal treatment for seniors and disabled persons who may respond well to healing touch therapies. A person receiving Reiki can expect to feel deeply relaxed and balanced with a general sense of well-being. It can be a profound experience of deep relaxation and inner quiet or it can allow you to shift gears into a deeper sense of self and personal priorities. Reiki is a way of being that assists in creating more peace, harmony, balance, and a state of grace in your life.

The use of crystals in Reiki is not part of the traditional Usui teachings. However, crystals certainly provide a benefit and are used to augment a Reiki healing session. A Reiki practitioner will hold the crystal for a while to place Reiki energy into it before placing the crystal on the client. Advanced crystal Reiki practitioners will put universal energy symbols into the crystal, which is something I'll talk about in the following section. When the crystal is placed on the client's body, the energy pattern is released and transferred. This is a powerful way to use crystals for healing as it blends two healing systems.

Combining Crystals and Symbols

We know from Chapter 2 that one of crystal's properties is that it can hold an energy pattern constant. If we put another energy pattern—such as a symbol of peace ☮—into the crystal, it will also retain that energetic structure. This means the energy of the symbol is available to be energized by the crystal. When the crystal discharges its energy, that energy includes the pattern and force of the symbol and transfers the resonance of both the crystal and the symbol. Some samples of symbols are a white dove representing peace or a red rose representing love. Maybe you can think of some others.

If you would like to experiment using crystals and symbols, here is an exercise to try. First, select a cleansed clear quartz crystal. Ensure that the crystal is fully charged (more on these processes in Chapter 8). Then follow these steps:

1. Place the symbol in front of you and gaze at it for a few minutes while holding the crystal in your right hand. If you close your eyes briefly, you should see an image of the symbol in your mind. If you do not have an actual image of the symbol, think of one and hold that image in your mind for a few minutes. Close your eyes if it helps to visualize the symbol more clearly. Still don't know what symbol to use? Try a happy face ☺ or a symbol of faith.

2. Hold the crystal in front of you a few inches away from your mouth, and view this image in front of the crystal. Hold the image steady in your mind and when ready, draw in a deep breath and blow sharply out over the crystal. This transfers the image into the crystal and is a form of crystal programming. The breath is an energy carrier for the image. The crystal will resonate with the symbol in its structure, just like Emoto's crystalized water.

3. Take the crystal and hold it to your heart chakra or third eye chakra. See if the image of the symbol appears in your mind, or note what you feel from the symbol. As an experiment, give the crystal to a friend to hold it up to their third eye and ask what they see or sense. Maybe they will suddenly have a happy smile on their face!

You may find that holding the crystal energized with the symbol makes you feel tingly—that's okay because it means your energy is being activated by the crystal with the vibration of the symbol. Try sleeping with the crystal under your pillow and record any dreams stimulated by the symbol into your crystal journal. You can also use this technique to put a symbol into a crystal for use in a crystal grid or layout.

Ayurvedic Crystal Healing

Since ancient times in India and other countries, astrology has guided and governed people's lives. When people are born, the planets may be aligned in both auspicious and inauspicious ways. According to Ayurvedic beliefs, we can wear crystals or gemstones when we need some help to balance the energies that are out of balance due to the planetary weaknesses present at the time of our birth. The word *Ayurveda* refers to the Hindu method of healing, which has been practiced for thousands of years. Ayurvedic gemstones are believed to balance any cosmic energies that were out of balance when you were born. These gemstones also increase the strengths with which we were born.

The natural electromagnetic radiation of gemstones helps with the alignment of glands, organs, and chakras. As subtle energy interacts with the body and mind, subtle corrections are made. A person wearing gemstones to balance energy will benefit from a longer life and be more free from the effects of illness and other discomforts than someone who doesn't have access to gemstones selected for his or her health.

If you're interested in this approach, it's best to consult with a trained Ayurvedic gem specialist or Vedic astrologer. The following chart is a rough estimation only. A gemstone is usually selected by birth date and time and other considerations such as location and your parents' birth dates. The gemstone, known as a *jyotish* gemstone which means "divine light," is carefully prepared according to ancient formulations. The gem must be completely natural and not be chemically treated. It must have clarity and sattva, meaning "sweetness" or a sense that one feels desire for the gemstone and can sense the life of the crystal itself.

Ayurvedic Gemstones by Astrological Sign

Astrological Sign	Ruling Planet	Birthstone
Aquarius	Saturn	Blue sapphire
Pisces	Jupiter	Yellow sapphire
Aries	Mars	Coral
Taurus	Venus	Diamond
Gemini	Mercury	Emerald
Cancer	Moon	Pearl
Leo	Sun	Ruby
Virgo	Mercury	Emerald
Libra	Venus	Diamond
Scorpio	Mars	Coral
Sagittarius	Jupiter	Yellow sapphire
Capricorn	Saturn	Blue sapphire

In Ayurveda, gemstones are selected for each person based on planetary alignments at birth and karmic predispositions. Jewelry, such as a pendant or ring, must be worn over the proper body part for healing and balance. Thus, the gemstone will provide subtle energy and vibrations to correct the imbalance within a person's life or body caused by planetary imbalances at the time of birth. Usually the gemstone is worn for the person's entire life.

Numerous people are trained to work with crystals, such as crystal healers, crystal energy therapists, crystal Reiki practitioners, Ayurvedic astrologers, and traditional medical doctors, among others. The knowledge about healing crystals has been around for a long time and is part of the fabric of many different cultures. Maybe the new age did bring back some of the old crystal healing ways and some of the traditions got lost in new-age spirituality. Today, crystals are seen as part of wellness and a compliment to finding some peace of mind and healing in the "now age."

CARVED IN STONE . . . .

Lapis lazuli: I lift your mind and spirit to new levels. I clear the way to acting on your highest ideals and for your highest purpose. I provide the attunement and protection needed as a light healer.

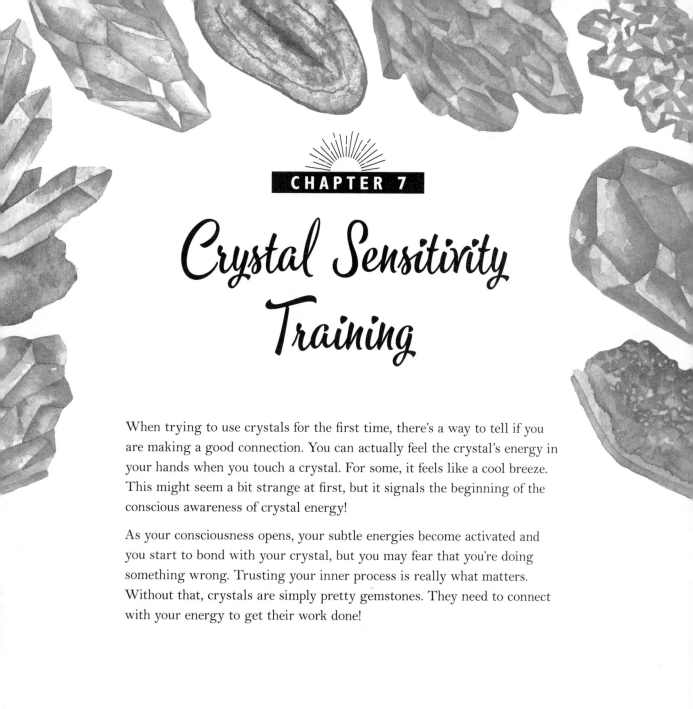

CHAPTER 7

Crystal Sensitivity Training

When trying to use crystals for the first time, there's a way to tell if you are making a good connection. You can actually feel the crystal's energy in your hands when you touch a crystal. For some, it feels like a cool breeze. This might seem a bit strange at first, but it signals the beginning of the conscious awareness of crystal energy!

As your consciousness opens, your subtle energies become activated and you start to bond with your crystal, but you may fear that you're doing something wrong. Trusting your inner process is really what matters. Without that, crystals are simply pretty gemstones. They need to connect with your energy to get their work done!

Learn How to ...

♦ Develop sensitivity to crystals.

♦ Use crystals for mental and physical relaxation.

♦ Use your crystals for chakra activation.

♦ Create special chakra oils.

Awakening Your Intention

You might have opened this book to learn about crystals for personal reasons or because you want to help yourself or someone else in the healing process. Maybe it's to heal from drug or alcohol abuse, sexual or psychological abuse, disease or illness, bodily trauma from an accident, bad luck, unemployment, or family stress—the list of possibilities goes on and on. The problem doesn't really matter. What matters most is whether you're truly ready to heal. Without that intention, healing can be difficult. To heal, we need to get to a place of wholeness in body and spirit, and that can only happen if the person who needs healing is open to experiencing that healing. So, if you're trying to help a friend or loved one, you must wait until that person is ready to heal.

When you start working with crystals, an awakening begins. It helps if you have been practicing mindfulness. Through mindfulness, you become more aware of your surroundings; you may feel energy moving more freely through your body; your mind will be more alert; and your breath will be deeper as you breathe in new life, sending oxygen into your body. You may find your surroundings more pleasant. Your emotions will be more balanced, and it will be easier to express them. Your eyes will be brighter, and you might have a spring in your step. In short, you'll have a feeling of hope—one that you perhaps haven't felt in years!

Nothing to Fear, Everything to Gain

Fear is a huge factor in life. It's what slows us down and holds us back. Some people don't believe in crystal energy, yet others fear it. Keep in mind that crystals have been sitting in the ground for hundreds of thousands of years without causing any problems whatsoever.

Crystals provide a means for connecting to a vast energy network to promote healing and meditation.

Some of you might be thinking, "I don't know what to expect", "What will I experience?", or "I'm afraid of not knowing what's going on." Challenge yourself to take one small step at a time. When you become more familiar with the crystals and their healing energy, you'll feel more confident.

Crystals work on scientific principles and have been successfully used by countless people for centuries! In fact, many people wear crystals in their jewelry. If you are married or engaged, look down at your hand and chances are that you are already wearing a very popular crystal, a diamond in your engagement ring!

If you are looking for a place to put feelings of skepticism, put them into a spot called *wonderment*. You already know this place—it's where you were as a child, enjoying unrestricted access to new information and investigating the world around you. As long as you enter a learning process, wonderment should be there. Whether it's learning about computers for the first time or designing a new injection mold for plastics, let your life be one long learning process.

Developing Sensitivity to Crystals

Bonding with your crystal is a way to align your biochemical energy structure with the crystalline structure in the crystal. Having a crystal close to you for a while to harmonize your energy with the crystal's is an important first step. You'll also open the subtle energy bodies, and your consciousness will become more attuned, which will help you become more sensitive to crystals. You'll want to get started with a crystal right away.

To train yourself to feel the energy of crystals, begin with a cleansed and charged clear quartz crystal, 2 to 3 inches long with a single point at one end. Hold the crystal, point down about ½ inch away from the surface of the palm of your hand. Make small circles running the point above the surface of your palm. You might immediately feel some pressure or tingling at the surface or under the skin. If you don't feel it right away, keep trying. Your consciousness will eventually open up to these sensations. It may be something you have never felt before. They don't teach this in school, so be patient learning something new.

Now, run the point of the crystal up and down your fingers, barely touching the skin's surface. Play around at the tips of the fingers. The crystal will help to activate your internal electrical energy system, clearing meridian lines that carry chi energy and opening up subtle energy channels called nadis.

Your feet are also very sensitive to energy. Run the point of the crystal over your toes and ankles. You can also run your crystal over your arms and legs, lingering over any sore spots. What does it feel like on your face? Run the tip of the crystal around your eyes and frown lines where there's so much tension. Now you can see why crystals are added to cosmetics. That's one way to treat a wrinkle!

If after 4 or 5 minutes, you still aren't getting a feeling of energy, heat, or tingling, put the crystal down. Open and close your hands several times. Rub the palms of your hands together and shake them lightly. Pick up the crystal and try running the crystal over your hands again, keeping the tip ½ inch away from the skin's surface. Experiment by moving the crystal 2 inches away and going back and forth toward your skin surface. You're seeking a subtle energy, like a breeze. You may not even notice it at first. Give yourself time to feel it.

You're finding a new sense, your sixth sense. Your sixth sense is your intuitive strength and your ability to perceive subtle energy. When you do find it, take a bow, because many people live their whole lives without knowing or even using this sense due to its subtlety. This is really a moment of personal discovery and wonderment.

Crystal Clarity of the Mind

In Chapter 3, you learned about the beginnings of mindfulness and meditation. Now, you'll combine these techniques with crystals to amplify the experience and obtain even more benefits. The benefits of meditation have been recognized by the scientific and medical community for years. Some people associate meditation with Eastern religions and steer away from it because they're afraid it conflicts with their own beliefs. Although meditation originated in Asia, it's so commonly used these days that it isn't tied into any particular religion. In fact, you've probably meditated without realizing it. Do you remember watching the clouds float by as a child and the way you could shut off your mind and not think about anything? That was sky meditation. Now as an adult, you can do mindful meditation. And although you can certainly meditate without crystals, using a crystal can help you calm the erratic energy of a busy mind. The crystals that are most frequently used for sitting meditation are clear quartz and amethyst because they help regulate the mind's activity. If you have a very noisy mind that constantly chatters or wanders off, using a dark crystal, such as smoky quartz or obsidian, help to ground and center the mind.

Incense or essential oils are sometimes used to help focus the mind during meditation. Do not use perfume because most of them contain chemicals and alcohol that disturb subtle energies. Some natural scents that are commonly used include sandalwood (for quieting the mind), patchouli (for focusing the mind), jasmine (for calming the mind and emotions), and amber (for alerting all the senses).

Start this basic crystal meditation by holding a clear quartz crystal in your left hand (your receiving hand for energy) with the point facing toward you. Alternatively, you can place the crystal 6 to 8 inches in front of you so it's in your energy field. In this instance, it should point up or toward you. Then follow these steps:

1. Sit either cross-legged on a cushion or in a chair with your feet flat on the floor. Let your hands relax into a natural position, in your lap or on your thighs.

2. Bring awareness to your breath as a way to quiet your mind of thought. Inhale through your nose for a slow count of eight. Pause, then exhale through your nose for a slow count of eight, relaxing your diaphragm completely.

You'll know you're in a state of meditation when your body is relaxed, your mind isn't in thought, and you feel awake and aware, yet totally at ease in your body. If your mind starts to wander off, bring it back gently by focusing on your breath for a while and then relax again into mindfulness. Rest in meditation for as long as you can. Stay present. It's not unusual for beginners to be able to meditate for only a few minutes. Each time you practice, hold your meditative state a bit longer, eventually extending your session to 20 minutes.

To enhance your meditative experience, try the following tips:

♦ Try to find a place where you won't be disturbed. This means no distractions. No kids, no pets, no loud or jarring sounds that will knock you back to reality before you're ready.

♦ Be aware that music can help or hinder the meditation process. If you find that music distracts you, try white noise instead, such as running a fan. The constant sound numbs background noises.

♦ Light a candle. Preferably, use one made from ecologically clean beeswax. It will help purify the air by pumping fully balanced negative ions into the air and either sending dust, toxins, and odors to the floor or eliminating them all together.

♦ Plan a regular time when you will meditate. As your meditation becomes habitual, your mind and body will go into a meditative state more easily. Try not to mediate when you are already sleepy because you risk falling into an actual deep sleep.

If you're having trouble getting yourself into a state of relaxation, try a guided meditation video or app. These tools provide helpful visualizations and mental stimulation that slide you into a state of relaxation and then into a deeper meditative state. However, it's best to not become dependent on them. There are some really great apps for smartphones and devices, such as Muse, that can provide some basic guided meditations and instruction.

Physical Relaxation

We hear it all the time: "Relax! Take it easy!" Why should we slow down the physical body? Won't we have time to rest when we're old and weary?

It's important even for healthy younger folks to take a physical break once in a while. When your body is relaxed, your subtle energies flow more easily, and your mind becomes quiet and still. And when both mind and body are relaxed, a deeper healing (physical and emotional) can happen on many levels.

Here are some guidelines to achieve a deeper state of physical relaxation using a crystal relaxation technique for 10 to 20 minutes:

1. Put on some light and airy instrumental music or turn on a fan to block out any background noise. Lie down, comfortably supporting your neck and shoulders with pillows and cushions. Prop your knees up with a pillow underneath them to support the sacral area and to flatten the stomach.

2. Place a clear quartz crystal at the solar plexus chakra to help alleviate emotional stress. Draw a light blanket over yourself to prevent your body from losing heat during this process. Perform the grounding exercise visualizing yourself anchored to the earth by roots.

3. Bring your focus to your toes and feet. Wiggle them gently to release any tension. Next, focus on your ankles, calves, and knees. If there's any tension there, draw it in with the breath and release it on the exhale. Check in with your thighs, buttocks, lower back, and lower torso (groin). Search out tension in your middle torso, upper chest, and back and shoulders. Be aware of any tension in your fingers, hands, lower arms, and upper arms. Do you feel tension in your neck, jaw, cheeks, mouth, eyebrows, or temples? Finally, feel your hairline, your scalp, and the back of your head where it meets the pillow. Breathe in and out to release any tension found in each area.

4. Allow your back to sink into the mattress or ground. Let your body feel heavy. Feel each joint drop into the floor, fully supported by the earth.

5. Bring your awareness to the crystal sitting in your solar plexus chakra. Now, visualize a bright golden radiant light like the sun. See this golden light spreading throughout your body. First, send the light through your bones. Then send it through every organ. Finally, send the golden light to your skin.

6. If there's a particular area of physical healing your body needs, focus the golden light intently on that area for a while. When you're ready, bring your focus back to the golden light above the crystal at your solar plexus and let your mind relax there.

This relaxation exercise unifies mind and body energy and provides a healing awareness. When you're ready, take the crystal off and get up gently, trying not to disturb your energy. You will feel quite refreshed, and your vital energy will be restored.

Mental and Emotional Relaxation

Once you've settled your physical body, it's time to work on your mental body and your emotional body. Your mental body is all the subtle energy of your thoughts. Remember how a thought can have so much energy, you may feel like you might explode with all those thoughts going around and around in your head. Similarly, your emotional body is comprised of all the emotional energy based on those thoughts, experiences, and perceptions, and whether they're good or not so good. Think about when you feel anger. There's so much energy in anger that you may even feel it at the physical level as excess heat. Crystals are often selected for relaxing, balancing (meaning neither too much nor too little), and integrating both the mental and the emotional body. You're right if you're thinking that healing the chakras will help at all levels—physical, emotional, mental, and spiritual. Before you get to chakra activation and healing, you'll still need to focus on your mind and emotions to provide a place for the crystal healing energies to work.

To promote mental relaxation before working with crystals, perform the breath-in-and-out technique when meditating or whenever you seek to relax your mind of its troubles. For settling your emotions, hold a clear quartz crystal in your right hand (your sending-energy hand) over your solar plexus. Breath in and out to complete an energy circuit that will help ground your energy.

Chakra Activation

You might already know about the energy centers of the body called *chakras* and are ready to begin with a crystal energy exercise that will open up those centers for deeper healing. A chakra is a wheel of energy that responds very well to subtle energies from crystals, light, and sound. Chakras contain a lot of emotional energy. Releasing excess energy in the chakras and balancing these energy centers will also benefit your mental state.

A way to stimulate deeper healing is by using sound and visualization techniques with crystals for chakra activation. When a chakra is active, its structure is in motion, rotating and distributing energy to other parts of the subtle body system. Why would anyone need to exercise their chakras? Well, sometimes a chakra will be sluggish in its rotation or be blocked with excess emotional congestion. The following chakra activation alleviates these symptoms and promotes health in the chakras. You will need your Chakra Tune-Up Kit.

First, find a quiet spot free of distractions, lie down. Get comfortable and grounded. As a reminder, use the visualization technique of seeing roots growing from under your feet down into the earth, anchoring your energy.

Place one of the chakra crystals directly on top of each chakra while visualizing the chakra color. Sing the chakra sound for a few seconds to activate and awaken the chakra energy. Do this one by one for each chakra, starting at the root chakra. Let the crystals rest on top of your body for 3, 7, or 15 minutes to soak in all the energies and rebalance the body.

When you want to get up, remove the crystals or let them fall gently off as you roll to one side. Get up slowly and gently. You have had an energy workout, and getting up too quickly might be a bit of a shock to your system. Drink some cool water and walk around a bit to restart your not-so-subtle energies.

When chakras are open and clear, you might feel more vulnerable about certain issues. It's worth noting what those issues are in your crystal journal because they indicate which chakra might need more work.

Spiritual Stimulation

Are you looking to open up your consciousness to higher realms? Perhaps you wish to engage in dialog with entities from those realms. Okay, what are those realms? The etheric body is one of your aura's outer layers. Most people aren't aware of it. It holds the expression of our highest potential, our divine expression. This is where sacred geometry works to provide the alignment between ourselves and our divine perfection, our perfect symmetry with all that is. It's where the perfect geometry of crystals merges with your mental intent and brings an alignment to the healing process. Let's try a crystal manifestation exercise using visualization.

Visualization Techniques

You just used a visualization technique with the image of a colored ball for your chakra activation. Now let's try something a little more complex to create something you'd like to happen, such as winning a sports competition. This is where you will pattern your intent at the etheric level.

First, select one of the crystal forms from the set of Platonic solids mentioned in Chapter 3. Remember that Platonic solids contain the elements of all things. If you don't have a Platonic solid crystal, use a generator or channeller clear quartz crystal. (See Chapter 9 for types of quartz crystals.) Start with a cube or tetrahedron Platonic solid at first and then move to the more complex shapes. If you don't have one, use a clear quartz crystal. Assume your position for meditation or visualization. You know the drill by now—find a quiet spot with no distractions.

Hold the crystal in front of you and gaze softly at the crystal. Think of something you would like to have happen in the next few days. Alternatively, you can think about an upcoming activity you'd like to successfully navigate.

Now visualize the image of yourself inside the crystal going through each and every motion very clearly, right down to the words spoken and what people are wearing—imagine as many details as you can. See the complete scenario from beginning to end in the most positive way. Move through it slowly, deliberately, and whole-heartedly. The crystal will store the energy of the visualization. Keep the crystal with you and then see what happens.

By now you will be quite attuned to your crystals. You will feel centered and confident using crystals for your chakras. They know your energy and you know theirs. This is just the beginning of a beautiful relationship!

CARVED IN STONE . . . .

When so much seems out of place and you can't get things into any order, isn't it wonderful that you can reach out for something that is beyond the chaos? Crystals connect you to the bigger picture. This unchanging connection to the divine is in all of nature. It is yours to connect to your divine nature.

CHAPTER 8

Preparing Your Crystals for Healing

Before using your crystals for healing or meditation purposes, begin by physically cleaning the crystal of any mud or other debris. Then, using a cleansing technique, remove any negative energies from the crystal.

For maximum healing effects, energize your crystals by charging them with fresh energy. Then "wake up" your crystal, activating it to its role and mission. Finally, program your crystal to direct the energy for a specific outcome or for support during a healing session.

Learn How to ...

- ◆ Cleanse your crystals inside and out.
- ◆ Activate your crystals and program your intentions to it.
- ◆ Protect yourself from negative energies.
- ◆ Care for your crystals.
- ◆ Build your collection with more essential crystals.

External Cleaning

When removing dirt from your crystal, be careful, because the crystal might be softer than the matrix it grows in! A warm water bath in a high-foaming liquid dishwashing detergent and a flexible, soft toothbrush is best for fragile or brittle crystals. Be wary though, some crystals are not meant to have a bath, such as halite, which is salt and is water soluble. For fragile crystals, use a soft dry brush or light pressurized air to remove any dust. Check out the "Smudging and Bell-Ringing Cleanses" section for more on cleaning water-soluble crystals.

For really tough cleaning situations, soaking the crystal in chemical might be necessary. For example, the matrix on clear quartz crystal is usually yellow and somewhat caked hard, and it requires a bath of oxalic acid to dissolve the matrix.

Internal Cleansing

After you have physically cleaned the crystal, the next step is to cleanse the crystal of unwanted vibrations and energies from other people who handled the crystal before it reached you. Crystals tend to take on energy indiscriminately and, like wearing someone else's clothing, you can feel that something's just not quite right.

Salt Bath

A salt water bath is really good for removing negative energies from most crystals; however, some crystals like angelite, barite, and howlite, and some marbles and pearls are sensitive to salt, and their surfaces can be damaged quickly in a salt bath. Some polished crystals may also pit and lose their shine. For those, you can use the smudging technique found at the end of this section.

To cleanse a crystal you wear regularly, give it a salt bath for 7 hours every 2 weeks or so. Get a plastic bowl large enough to hold your crystal or crystals. (Glass is fine, but it's a hard surface and you could chip your crystal easily.) Fill the bowl with enough room-temperature water to cover the crystal.

Add about 1 teaspoon of salt for every 8 ounces of water. The perfect cleansing solution is a 30-percent solution of sea salt and spring water. (If you have genuine sea water, use that!) I usually just throw a handful of salt over the crystals in a small bucket and leave the entire thing in the sun to soak up the UV rays and recharge the crystals.

When you pour off the salt water, do not touch the water because you will be transferring the negative energies back onto yourself. Rinse any salt residue from your crystals with fresh water. Let the crystals dry on newspapers or tea towels. If you leave them in the sun while soaking, you can also charge them!

Different Salts

You might wonder if there is a difference between using sea salt and table salt (rock salt). There is. I find that sea salt leaves the crystals with a different energetic feeling than table salt.

Sea salt has a more refined energy signature with a lot of small rainbow-colored vibrations. Table salt is like a workhorse—it's less subtle, is more coarse, and has clunky yellow and gray-blue vibrations. If you plan to use a crystal at the upper chakras (third eye or crown), cleanse it in sea salt because these centers are very sensitive and prefer a subtler vibration.

To feel the energy signatures from different salts, get a variety of them from health or food stores or pick them up while traveling. I have tried ordinary table salt, Celtic sea salt, Dead Sea salt, Hawaiian red clay sea salt …. Each provides its own type of energy signature and vibration.

It's time for another experiment. Try soaking two quartz crystals separately in two different salt solutions overnight. After a rinse, see whether you can tell the difference energetically by holding one and then the other.

Salt is so very important to cleansing not only your crystals but also for clearing your environment. Chapter 20 includes a section with further information about Himalayan salt crystal lamps and how they help your health and wellness.

Smudging and Bell-Ringing Cleanses

As I've mentioned, some crystals should not be soaked in salt water. These are generally porous or water-soluble crystals such as halite, marble, angelite, and barite. Salt can also pit the shiny exterior of a polished crystal. As an alternative to a salt bath, cleanse these crystals by smudging with sage, sweet grass, Palo Santo wood, or incense such as frank-incense or copal. To smudge something is to use smoke to clear it of negative energy. This is a particularly good method to use if you have a cabinet full of crystals or some that are very large and awkward to bathe.

Spend about 3 to 7 minutes doing a smudge, fanning the smoke over the crystal with a turkey or peacock feather fan. As the smudging smoke rises, it pulls the negative energies away from the crystal. Fan the smoke away from the crystal, preferably near a window, or go outside to smudge and dispel the smoke into the air.

Another alternative cleansing technique uses sound to cleanse crystals. Ring small Tibetan chimes called *ting cha*, larger Tibetan hand bells, gongs, or singing bowls within 4 to 6 inches of your crystals. The crystals get the full force of their pure sound vibration. Anything that's not harmonic (aligned to your highest purpose) will be attuned. Ring the bells or chimes gently for 1 to 3 minutes.

For a room full of crystals, you can smudge everything, or ring the bells until you feel the unwanted energy lift from the room. You'll know when you've done that because the bell will ring clearly and will vibrate for a longer time. Sweet!

Fire

Fire is an ancient method for cleansing. Not too many people know about using fire for cleansing crystals, probably because the crystal heats up and singes your fingers if you're not careful. In India, fire represents Agni, the Vedic fire god, and it is used in sacred purification rites such as during wedding rituals.

This method of cleansing by fire works best if your crystal is fairly long and is easy to hold between your fingers. Using a candle, preferably a beeswax candle, pass the crystal back and forth over the flame a few times. You can say a purification prayer such as the following one or a mantra from any traditional belief system, using the flame of divine consciousness to purify unwanted energy.

> I ask through my connection to the Divine Spirit to cleanse all unwanted negativity, thoughts, suggestions, and influences from this crystal at all levels. Let positive, healing light permeate this crystal and be sealed with triple protection.

Then visualize the triple protection as three layers of color encapsulating the crystal: silver (awakening to the cosmic mind), gold (enlightenment and divine protection), and white light (the transcendent and higher dimensions, angelic connections, and ultimate purity and truth).

Recharging Your Batteries

A crystal grows and is nurtured by yin or feminine energy from its mother, the Earth. To develop, the crystal takes nutrients from the ground like gases, water, and various minerals. When it is harvested from the earth, the crystal is removed from the maternal energies that fed it and now needs yang or masculine energy as its source of energy renewal.

Sunlight

Sunlight recharges crystals with UV light, sometimes called *light radiation*. The UV light from sunlight provides the full spectrum of light and restores the crystal's depleted energies.

The time to recharge depends on the crystal's capacity to absorb light (its individual crystalline energy structure has a lot to do with it) and the stage of energy depletion within the crystal. Typically, I find 4 hours in bright sunlight once a week keeps a small crystal energetic and alert.

Keep your crystals by a window for continual recharging. Some people say that glass refracts the UV rays, but if that were so, then plants raised in glass greenhouses probably wouldn't survive. Exposing your crystals in direct sunlight during the strongest UV rays of the day is best.

Earth Energy

Another way to both cleanse and recharge larger crystals is to use the earth. Wrap your crystals in a natural linen or burlap cloth or stick them directly into the earth at least 3 to 4 inches down or even as deeply as 12 inches below the surface. Cover the crystals with soil and mark the location. Remind yourself in a few days to dig them up. The natural energy currents of the earth will be attracted to the crystals and will realign their energies back to earth-natural.

Moonlight Charging

Let's talk about charging crystals in the moonlight. Notice, I said "charging," not "recharging." When a crystal has spent its energy, it's best to recharge the crystal in the sun, with other high-energy or high-frequency crystals, or on a piece of selenite. Moonlight is good for charging a crystal using the gentle yin energies that birthed the crystal in the earth. Moonlight helps restore the original energy of the crystal. It's energy is calming. Any and all crystals can be charged in moonlight, the reflection of the sun's rays that gives light to darkness. The energy flow of moonlight is fluid, magical, and mystical. Sunlight is yang energy and is very active and dynamic. But there are times when the Mother Moon is needed for gentle healing, especially during deep transformative periods.

This is good news for some crystals that could fade in direct sunlight, such as amethyst, angelite, aquamarine, celestite, fluorite, kunzite, rose quartz, and some smoky quartz.

Put your crystals outside in the night before, the night of, and the night after a full moon. I find the moonlight energy is very soft and gentle, but also that it dissipates within 5 days.

There is an extra strong energy connection during a special moon event or a time of year that coincides with religious celebrations, such as the autumn harvest or Chinese spring moon festivals, eclipses, comets, meteor showers, and other special planetary alignments.

Create a sacred space outside for your crystals. Smudge the area. Place other supporting objects nearby, such as flowers and other crystals to magnify the energy of the moon.

Wake-Up Call: Activating Your Crystal

Sometimes, a crystal can be a "sleeper" and needs a little nudge to be made aware that it's going to be used for healing or meditative purposes. You can activate your crystal through a self-initiation ritual or by simply holding it, rolling it quickly back and forth in your hands, sleeping with it, gazing at it, washing it, and even talking to it. Keep it with you throughout the day to bond to the crystal's energy.

To awaken its consciousness through ritual, offer some sage or sweet grass and indicate your intent for the use of the crystal (e.g., for healing, for world peace). In the Attunement section, you'll see a short dedication prayer that can be used.

Touching a tuning fork to the crystal or using the sound of bells will also initiate its energy by sending a harmonic signal through to the crystal's structure as a wake-up call.

Programming for Intent

Each crystal has its own mission or its own program for healing. Crystal people, or healers, sometimes say that a crystal resonates with a particular chakra, or that it has a mission to clear a past life. We don't want to mess with that preprogrammed energy. But here's the interesting thing: each crystal also comes with its own blank database, a subtle or spiritual energy center that can store new instructions, just like humans have an infinite capacity for instruction and spirituality. The crystal can translate and absorb an energy signature from outside itself and store it within its own crystalline energy structure.

The crystal will then resonate with those instructions, amplifying, broadcasting, and projecting the new set of energy patterns in its work. I mentioned these properties of healing crystals in Chapter 2. Now this is the real esoteric work of a crystal!

A Breath of Positive Air

When we're talking about programming crystals, we're really talking about infusing them with positive, helpful energy. Here are some different programming techniques used with crystals:

◆ Write a thought on a piece of paper, then place a crystal on top of it to absorb the thought energy. The crystal magnifies the written thought pattern and sends the thought in its amplified state to the universe. Use a clear quartz crystal for this or any other crystal that is similar to your request. For instance, for fertility, use garnet; to increase wealth, use citrine.

◆ Program your crystal with your breath by holding it in your hand, breathing in through your nose, thinking in your mind of what you want, and forcefully breathing out (snort!) through your nose into the crystal. The intent is programmed into the energy matrix of the crystal. Do this on each side or face of the crystal. There are six sides to a clear quartz crystal; for a tumbled or round crystal or gemstone, hold it in your hand and snort directly over it three to six times. The reason you pass air through your nose is that the mouth is considered vibrationally inferior—you cough, say bad words, and eat using your mouth, so the vibration is not as pure for passing the subtle energies as through the nose.

◆ Hold the crystal in your right hand a few inches away from your nose. Focus your mind on your intent. Use a circular breath by breathing slowly and naturally through your nose into the crystal, then breathe energy back in from the crystal. Repeat this circular breath for 3 to 5 minutes. This is an effective meditative technique and is quite powerful for directing your mind for positive results and building up programmed energy in the crystal matrix.

You can put as many thoughts, affirmations, or images into your crystal as you like. Whenever you want to clear them out, just hold the word *clear* in your mind and then forcefully breathe (snort) through your nose into the crystal three to six times to clear the crystal of unwanted programming.

Learn to Attune

Now you are ready for the process of attunement to your crystal. Attunement is the process of aligning your energy with that of a particular crystal.

To become more attuned to crystal energy and to open your sensitivity to subtle energy, hold a clear quartz crystal at the center of your heart chakra about 4 inches away from your chest. Run the crystal in clockwise circles very slowly in 3- to 4-inch circles around the center of your heart chakra. Feel the sensation of crystal energy in your heart chakra. Stop and hold the crystal in front of you at your heart chakra and say the following dedication prayer or one of your own choosing.

> I dedicate this crystal to the Universal Purpose. From this moment on, I undertake to utilize its energies to benefit all life. For I am one with the creative mind and, therefore, one with all life forms. In that which I am, I now activate the life energy within this crystal in order that its power will be utilized to serve the Universal Purpose.
>
> (Reprinted with permission from Sharon Ellis, www.facebook.com/sharon.ellis1)

Then, simply place the crystal pointing up against your chest over the heart chakra. Lie quietly with the crystal on your chest for 15 minutes to get a full attunement with the crystal and its mission. Make note in your crystal journal about any images or thoughts you receive during this time.

Protection Techniques

As you work with crystals and open up energy centers, you may feel vulnerable and will want to feel protected from any harm or misdeeds (such as negative energy). This is where special protection techniques can be used.

Recite a protection prayer, preferably three times, to express your higher will. You can make up your own prayer or modify the fire cleansing prayer. Simply ask for spirit guides or angels to stand guard over you. You can envision a golden net with white light over the room, sealing out any unwanted energies. Maybe you'll envision a ring of fire for protection. Use your imagination. Whatever works for you will have more meaning and power behind it.

More Essential Crystals

Now that you know how to get started with your crystals, I want to tell you about some more crystals that many crystal healers would not be without. I'm not saying you have to add them to your kit right now, but somewhere along the way, you'll want to make sure to pick these up for their healing benefits.

Kyanite

Blue kyanite is known to energetically align chakras, both vertically and horizontally. For a full alignment treatment, hold the crystal at each chakra for a count of 7 or 21 seconds, or up to 3 minutes for any particularly stubborn chakras. Your hand might wobble a bit with the energy at first, but it will steady itself as the chakra becomes aligned. Kyanite is one of several crystals that do not need cleansing due to its unique internal structure that constantly provides its own alignment. Kyanite should be in every healer's tool kit!

Selenite

There is no doubt that selenite opens the crown chakra and offers esoteric information telepathically to those who wish to know. You might even be able to access Merlin's knowledge!

This crystal can be used at the highest levels for healing—to align chakras, to cleanse the aura, to remove obstructions such as tumors, to open to higher states of consciousness, and to increase creativity.

Selenite is another crystal that does not need cleansing because its lustrous light and internal structure eliminates energy from being absorbed in the first place. I discuss different forms of selenite in Chapter 20.

Fluorite

Fluorite comes in various colors and has a natural octahedron shape, like two pyramids end-to-end attached at their bases. Green fluorite is used for physical healing. Yellow fluorite is used for mental stimulation and creativity. Also look for rainbow fluorite, which is banded with many colors, for a full spectrum of healing.

When there are stubborn blockages in the chakras, drop a purple or rainbow fluorite into the chakra for several minutes to loosen up those emotional and mental strongholds.

Fluorite is a master of the mind and intellectual matters. Fluorite is for people who work with large amounts of data requiring thoughts to be quickly and accurately processed.

Use fluorite at the crown chakra in a layout to clear energy passages from the third eye to the crown and to provide an increase in intuition and clairvoyance. For crystal grid work, fluorite provides keen mental focus for intent and helps maintain strength to the grid's energy structure.

Calcite

Like fluorite, calcite comes in many colors such as orange, green, yellow, and blue. Calcite isn't a very hard material, so you'll need to be careful not to drop it or bang it up too much.

Calcite is cooling and calming for emotions, dousing the intensity of stress. It's commonly used to fill energy gaps in the chakras. It absorbs energy and has the ability to set things right. It can calm upsets whether they are emotional or physical (if your tummy is upset). The crystal is effective for supporting learning projects and helps retain memory. It is also used for healing bones, soft tissues, and skin.

Used in a crystal grid, it supports and amplifies the crystal energy structure. Calcite works the same way in a layout, it harmonizes the crystals within the layout and offers its healing to the specific chakra by color.

Hematite

The natural magnetic quality of hematite makes it a perfect crystal to use instead of commercial magnets to ease nausea and for pain reduction at specific points on the body. Obtain several flat pieces of highly reflective, polished hematite for your crystal healing tool kit, and tape them onto joints and the spine to reduce pain and increase energy. As blood pumps by the crystal, it picks up needed magnetic energy and increases the circulation in the area of the crystal.

Hematite is also a blood purifier and calms and reduces anger and eliminates toxins stored in the liver. It provides protection, reflecting back unwanted energies, and operates as a shield for stress and stressful situations. In a healing layout or a crystals grid, use hematite for grounding and for helping to manifest your dreams and aspirations.

Lapis Lazuli

This opaque noble blue crystal is known for its high vibrational rate and abilities to enhance communications and psychic perceptions. It's a protector of healers, knowledge seekers, and mystics. It's a perpetual cleanser and protector to the aura and third eye and crown chakras. Lapis is a crystal that enhances channeling abilities and for opening communications with ascended masters. You can also use it in your crystal grid with mental focus to actualize your intent.

This crystal helps to settle people, even children, who have psychic abilities but sometimes seem lost or unable to access or use their abilities. Lapis creates an energetic connection and loving support for their journey of self-discovery and transformation. It provides courage to take on a worldly role when they may be conscious that their origin and quest is from beyond. Consider lapis lazuli as a gift for those who are seeking something to fulfill their void, no matter what it is.

Tourmaline

Tourmalines are one of the most versatile crystals for use in physical, emotional, mental, and spiritual healing. Tourmalines are available in a range of colors of black, green, blue, pink, yellow, aqua, and multicolored and are known under different names. While hematite is magnetic, tourmaline is a potent electrical healer when in contact with the body. Tourmaline is well suited to healing numerous systems, including the nervous system, meridians, and mental complexes, as well as on the DNA and cellular levels. Used in layouts, tourmaline is capable of aligning all layers of the aura. Tourmaline can impart knowledge telepathically about topics that one might not even have been studying.

Tourmaline is best known for bringing in a full, pure light spectrum and focusing color rays, depending on their color. For that matter, tourmaline helps guide a new soul to its parents. It is great for performance sports and for enhancing psychic development.

Tourmalines are not very big in general, and they can be rare and quite expensive. The largest one I ever held was a green tourmaline as long and as thick as my forearm. When I held it in both hands, it felt like a lightning bolt went through my whole body. The healing power of tourmaline can be quite remarkable.

Treat Your Crystals with Care

As you begin to build your collection of crystals, you'll want to have a number of different crystals available for various physical, emotional, and spiritual issues. Keeping your crystals together is actually helpful because they tend to resonate to the highest crystal frequency. When they are all together, they share healing memories, so they learn from one another.

For third eye or crown chakra crystals, a container kept separate from heavier crystals will keep the softer and more refined crystals protected. Finally, if there are any crystals that have not been cleared of negativity, the vibration of the other crystals will clear the crystal.

In the next chapter, you'll learn more about the types of master crystals and the three steps to healing with crystals.

CARVED IN STONE . . . .

Calcite: I provide chakra attunement and adjustments from induced change. I push you forward beyond your self-limitations. I stabilize your emotions. I provide release, expansion, and vitality to your energy field.

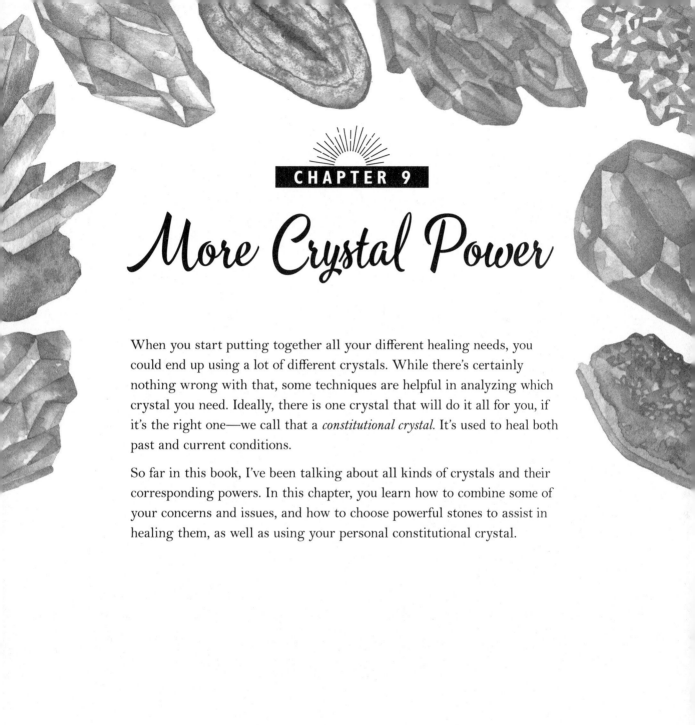

CHAPTER 9

More Crystal Power

When you start putting together all your different healing needs, you could end up using a lot of different crystals. While there's certainly nothing wrong with that, some techniques are helpful in analyzing which crystal you need. Ideally, there is one crystal that will do it all for you, if it's the right one—we call that a *constitutional crystal*. It's used to heal both past and current conditions.

So far in this book, I've been talking about all kinds of crystals and their corresponding powers. In this chapter, you learn how to combine some of your concerns and issues, and how to choose powerful stones to assist in healing them, as well as using your personal constitutional crystal.

Learn How to ...

♦ Use the three-step program to initiate esoteric healing.

♦ Select your constitutional crystal for long-term healing.

♦ Identify the five master healers for clearing emotional, physical, or spiritual issues: clear quartz, amethyst, rose quartz, turquoise, and smoky quartz.

♦ Use a pendulum to select your crystals.

Your Personal Agenda

The first step to understanding your own healing needs is looking at yourself. When choosing crystals for healing, you need to first assess the problem areas in your physical, emotional, and spiritual lives. If you have been collecting crystals for a while, take a look at your personal crystal collection. Your collection will reveal your healing needs and ultimately help you identify your personal healing crystal.

If you have a dominant color choice, that color and the chakra to which it relates is often where your healing attention needs are focused. Being in balance takes some effort. Crystals can create a much bigger story than you can handle, and that energy can get away from you.

So, what are you doing or avoiding doing? Line up all your crystals now and have a look. It will be very revealing.

To identify areas that are ripe for healing and identify the type of constitutional gemstone you will need, jot down your answers to the following questions in your journal:

♦ What is your dominant crystal color or colors?

♦ Which chakra or chakras are tied to your dominant colors? How does this reflect your healing needs?

♦ Would you like to address any long-term physical issues, emotional problems (feelings), or spiritual questions?

◆ What three things are you really good at? Do your crystals support those areas?

◆ What three areas would you like to improve (i.e., which areas are underdeveloped)? Do you have crystals that could help?

Excellent! In the next sections, you'll read about a healing program that takes you through the different stages of healing with crystals. Then, you'll read about the master healers and other powerful crystals. You want to select your constitutional crystal and other crystals to work with your personal strengths and weaknesses. Follow the three-step program to maximize the benefits.

Three-Step Program

After cleansing and dedicating your crystal, it's time to move on to a program that will help you integrate the healing energies of your selected crystals into your subtle body. When you wear a crystal, you are initiating a powerful esoteric healing process that requires time to adjust to your subtle energy vibration. This is accomplished in a simple three-step process.

Step 1: Cleansing

In the first week or so, the crystal is making tremendous adjustments within your energy field, matching the matrix of your energy to a larger outer universal energy field that will be used in your healing. We call this the *cleansing process.*

It is important to keep the crystal on you 24 hours a day for at least the first 21 days for this cleansing process to be initiated and completed. This is also a period of time where the blockages of energy that are causing the imbalance are removed and purified.

Sometimes a healing crisis occurs during these early days. This might occur as a sudden release of energy—an emotional release, a sudden increase of pain, vivid visions, intense dreaming, or other physical or psychological phenomena. Remember, crystals accelerate the change process, so this is normal.

Allow these processes to occur without interruption by continuously wearing the stone or crystal until you complete the next two steps. If you find the process is too intense, remove the crystal and wear it for a shorter period of time to let your energies adjust during the initial 3-week period.

Cleanse your crystal every week and recharge it in the sunlight for at least 4 hours weekly throughout the initial healing process.

Step 2: Harmonizing and Integrating

During the second stage, around the fourth week of wearing the stone or crystal, you might notice that your face looks more relaxed. This is due to a harmonizing connection that's being made within yourself and your subtle bodies. Your mental outlook, thoughts, feelings, and even opinions can change significantly. All aspects of your energy will be activated, and the result will be a very positive feeling. However, you're not quite finished yet!

You might notice physical and emotional changes during either the first or second steps as your physical, mental, emotional, and spiritual bodies come into alignment. Some of these changes are caused by throwing off toxins and negative energies during the cleansing process, which will continue during the entire healing process.

You may not feel much physically. If you have pain, you might find it lessens. If your mind has been dull, you might find it's sharper. If you have been down a bit emotionally, you might find your mood has improved. Mostly you will see your awareness grow, and with that comes spiritual confidence—the acknowledgement that you are transforming into the person you want to be.

Step 3: Stabilizing

The third step can take 3 to 4 months, or possibly even longer for some people, depending on the intensity of your original condition. When you are committed to wearing a crystal for stabilizing purposes, you will wear it for a long time, occasionally changing it for a new one of the same type. With continuous wearing of a stone or crystal, you will achieve stability in the changes you have achieved, whether they are emotional or physical.

"Will I be dependent on this crystal forever?" you might be wondering. No, you won't. So how do you know when it's safe to remove it? You can test your stability by removing your crystal from time to time—maybe just for a few hours or perhaps for days at a time. If you are able to go for a few days without your stone, but then notice you are slipping back into your old ways, consider wearing it for another week or more or only at bedtime before taking it off again. As you develop deeper sensitivity for crystal energy, you might decide to keep the crystal on much longer to complete the healing process.

Maximizing Crystal Healing

A crystal should be worn next to the skin for best results. The size of the crystal might be relative to your budget. Many semiprecious crystals such as rose quartz are inexpensive, costing around $1 to $2. The crystal should be what you can afford and should be no smaller than the fingernail on your ring finger, symbolic of your spiritual heart's minimal need. Your commitment to the crystal is part of the healing process. Let the crystal do the work for you. The length of time it takes to obtain the desired outcome depends on the quality of the crystal (size, color, and energy charge), where and how long you wear it, and the crystal's appropriateness to your healing.

How Many to Wear

If you are new to crystal healing, it is best not to wear more than two or three stones at any one time since many people find the effects too distracting. You can, however, wear up to seven crystals in a leather or silk pouch and wear them at the heart chakra. The heart chakra redistributes the energy all over the body, so you don't need to wear a crystal on a specific chakra. Why seven? With seven chakras, the workload is distributed over the energy system. The heart chakra is generally the regulator of the energies. However, remember there are other systems in your body such as meridians; the nervous, lymphatic, and glandular systems. You don't want to overwhelm these systems all at once. It takes time to integrate the energies. Seven is enough to do the job.

To help you select your constitutional crystal, review the characteristics of the following crystals thoroughly to see if any one of them would be a good personal crystal for you. You can use your pendulum to help divine which crystal would be best. (See the end of this chapter on how to use a pendulum.) Take your pendulum with you on your shopping trip, hold it over the crystals you have selected, and ask which is best for your long-term use as a personal healing crystal.

The Five Master Healers

The five master healers are crystals that work well to repair a lot of troubles that we humans get into. They can be used for many purposes at the physical, emotional, and spiritual levels of healing. One of them may become your constitutional crystal.

These crystals are easy to find and genuinely work as indicated. You don't have to worry about getting the perfect crystal within each master class because they are very forgiving crystals. For clear quartz, however, it's helpful to know about the various configurations so you can use the one that's right for you. Let's start there.

Clear Quartz: Universal Healer

The basic building block of all crystals is clear quartz, or silicon dioxide. When you first receive a clear quartz crystal, you will probably look it over, but unless you know about this crystal's interesting formations, you might miss something!

In general, clear quartz crystal is part of the hexagonal lattice system and has six sides and six faces. Because the sides and faces can have different lengths and widths due to growing conditions, different configurations arise. I've put together the 10 basic configurations of clear quartz in the following sections. Keep your eyes open to look for these crystals to add to your crystal collection. One of them might actually become a personal crystal that you'll keep with you for years ahead.

Generator

A generator is a crystal where all six sides of the crystal join together at the tip to form a uniform apex that generates energy. Finding a good generator is rare because each face must be perfectly formed to meet at the tip with all the other faces. Most polished crystals are ground by machine to accomplish this level of perfection. This type of crystal is the most basic formation, and as such, is a good crystal for a beginner. As a universal healer, generators are useful for stimulating healing through all subtle body levels, although they are best used for...

   ♦ Wearing anywhere on the body to generate healing energy for a specific area, such as a chakra, in an area for physical healing, or to keep your aura purified.

   ♦ Opening the crown chakra while sleeping or during guided meditation.

- Teaching yourself about crystals and their basic energies.
- Filling in any gaps in an energy field and stabilizing disorganized energy in the aura.
- Balancing polarity, the positive and negative electrical charges.
- Setting into a ceremonial wand to generate and to direct energy.

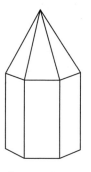

A generator crystal

Double-Terminated

A double-terminated crystal has six faces at each end of the crystal. The ends might be like a generator, with all points coming to a common tip, or they might be different. Energy in this crystal moves bidirectionally—in both directions concurrently. Energy is either drawn or is transmitted, depending on the crystal's programming. Look for a crystal with a good center so that energy can flow freely and uniformly.

Double-terminated crystals are best used for…

- Active wear in the center of the body, for balancing yin-yang energy, and balancing dark and light energy.
- Chakra alignment. Place the crystal vertically at each chakra for 3 minutes for chakra balancing.
- Telepathic communication. If friends each have a double-terminated crystal and carry them for three days to pick up an imprint of their energies and then exchange their double-terminated crystals, they can be in telepathic communication with each other.

A double-terminated crystal

To send a message with a double-terminated crystal, hold it and visualize the message being sent out of one tip of the crystal and being received through the tip of the other crystal. The message will be stored for your friend to pick up later and can be accessed by holding the crystal and inhaling deeply, allowing the message to form in his or her mind.

Channeler

A channeler crystal has a single large face framed by seven sides. This face represents the seeker of wisdom. On the opposite side is a small, three-sided face in the shape of a triangle. The triangle represents the seeker of truth. Hold the crystal in front with the seven-sided face toward you, and tip the crystal back to see the secret pyramid on the other side. This type of crystal should be in everyone's collection to help channel higher energy.

Channelers are best used for...

♦ Seeking answers to gain information. It can be about something specific, such as healing information during meditation or for self-development.

♦ Channeling. The seven-sided face represents wisdom as the seven soul qualities: love, knowledge, freedom, manifestation (the ability to project and create), joy, peace, and unity. The three sides of the triangle represent creativity, truth, and expression through speech.

♦ Opening the third eye. For a small channeler, place the crystal at your third eye chakra. For larger channelers, place your thumb on the seven-sided face and your index finger on the three-sided face. Keep your mind clear, focus on your third eye, breathe, and let images and impressions come to you spontaneously.

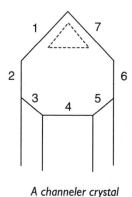

A channeler crystal

Transmitter

A transmitter crystal has a seven-sided face that sits on either side of a three-sided triangle face. These two seven-sided faces should look identical. The edges of the triangle should be uniform and look sharp, clear, and in proportion. The crystal should be clear and feel slightly heavy, illustrating the crystal's ability to hold a greater energy charge.

Transmitters are best used for…

♦ Providing focus during meditation by holding or placing the crystal in front of you.

♦ Receiving and transmitting programmed messages and energy.

♦ Setting into a wand for use in healing the body.

♦ Focusing thoughts and intentions through the three-sided face.

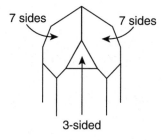

A transmitter crystal

Trans-Channeler

A trans-channeler, also called a *dow crystal,* combines both a single seven-sided channeling face and a three-sided transmitter face to the left and right of the main channeling face. An even more rare configuration is the alternating of three-sided faces and seven-sided faces to form a special 3:7:3:7:3:7 configuration. Trans-channelers are hard to find but very valuable spiritually.

Trans-channelers are best used for...

♦ Achieving higher states of consciousness and intense focus for accessing higher energy levels and spiritual dimensions during meditation.

♦ Providing access to cosmic consciousness and awareness.

♦ Opening the third eye or crown chakra to direct questions and receive answers.

♦ Requesting spirit energy to work with. The triangles provide energy portals for the spirit, and the seven-sided faces provide communication portals.

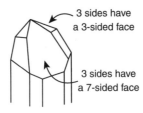

A trans-channeler crystal

Window

This crystal is a real find! A large diamond shape is created from sloping angles of other faces on the front of a crystal. Like real windows, the best window crystals are ones you can see through. Some crystals have more than one window—one to show you the past (in a smaller face to the left of the major window) and one to show the future (in a smaller face to the right of the major window).

Some crystals have more than one major window. These are time windows, showing you snapshots of certain events. A window crystal can also be used for unblocking creativity, like writer's block.

Windows are best used for...

♦ Clearing the mind and accessing other realms. Gaze into the crystal for several minutes before meditation or to relax before going to sleep.

♦ Opening awareness to who you really are. Gaze through the window and ask intently to see yourself in your truest form.

♦ Reading auras. Have the crystal window in front of you, pointing toward your third eye. Draw an imaginary line between the crystal and your third eye to enhance imaging.

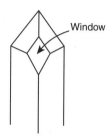

A window crystal

Record Keeper

On the surface of the largest face of the record keeper crystal are small, slightly raised triangular bumps. These small bumps can sometimes also be found on smaller faces. Don't look into the crystal, just look on the surface of the face.

This crystal is sometimes called a *teacher* because the information has much to do with planetary origins, cosmology, and planetary evolution; healing information; and higher states of consciousness. If this is so, do not give this crystal away. It has come to you and is meant for you to keep and to learn from.

Record keepers are best used for...

♦ Accessing information. Rub the ridges on the fleshy part of your thumb over the little bumps. At the same time, breathe in fully and slowly. Information—whatever you are concentrating on—will be deposited for later retrieval through dreams or when needed.

♦ Catching bad dreams during sleep. Bad dreams might just become a thing of the past with a record keeper next to your pillow to catch the bad ones.

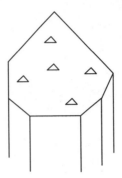

A record-keeper crystal

Self-Healed

Due to shifts in the ground and other interventions, the bottom of a self-healed crystal will often appear to be broken off. When the crystal regrows, small triangular faces cover the bottom. If a crystal has a large self-healed area where it has started to regrow, it has had a long time to heal with many lessons learned along the way. An older crystal would be better to learn from than a younger one, which is still in the process of rehealing. Newly broken crystals have a glassy, fish-eyed look to them at the bottom, and the edges might still be quite sharp.

Self-healed crystals are best used for…

♦ Reminding yourself that you can heal. If the crystal can re-form through its own internal coding, so can you.

♦ Sending messages of self-healing to the body. For emotional issues, project your disharmonious thoughts into the bottom of the crystal and let the crystal organize them. Turn the crystal around after a few minutes of meditation and receive the organized energy.

A self-healed crystal

Rainbow

Rainbows inside crystals are caused by changes in the optical quality of the crystal due to a fracture inside the crystal, probably caused by rough handling such as geodesic shifting, dynamite, or even being dropped during extraction from the earth.

Another way rainbows are created is when a crack or fissure has opened up due to thermal stress. Cooling and heating expands and contracts at a weak point in the crystal's material and a fracture occurs, creating a space between the walls of the fracture. The various colors of the rainbow are caused by the thickness of the gap picking up a certain part of the light spectrum.

Rainbows are best used for...

♦ Inhaling the colors of love and joy into the heart chakra. Breathe out to dispel negativity and sorrow.

♦ Remembering there is love all around. Rainbows are especially great for children to connect to their inner light during times of trauma or depression.

♦ Wearing. At the heart level, the rainbow light will wink and twinkle, and fill in color gaps in the aura and fill up the chakras with light.

Veil

A veil is a thin reflective silvery wall or a white wispy cloud inside the crystal. Veils show you the future—not to see the future exactly as how it will unfold, but as a potential of what will come to be, allowing you to prepare in advance. Sometimes inclusions look like veils. It looks like a transparent curtain. You might even see what appear to be little bubbles.

Veils are best used for...

♦ Showing how trauma is transformed into wisdom and beauty. We can see behind the veil of ourselves to the beauty masked by our shadows.

♦ Teaching us about our own darkness and about transforming our hidden fears, negativity, and anger. With transformation of our own negative states, we hold a greater capacity to help heal others of their own negativity.

Amethyst: Master Transformer

If you were limited to choosing only one crystal, amethyst would be the one to pick. As a major transformational crystal, amethyst is also a purifier of the aura. Its job is to take lower dysfunctional vibrations and clear them by transmuting them to a higher vibrational level. It is very protective of the wearer's energy and acts as a filter for negative energies coming from both the environment and other people. Wearing an amethyst anywhere on the body will provide some degree of healing.

Amethyst heals all things at all levels. Use it for physical problems, for dispelling negative emotions, for changing negative thoughts into higher aspirations, and for accessing higher spiritual planes. If you are using amethyst for meditation, choose a polished single-point generator—the larger, the better. Amethyst will need frequent charging and cleansing because it is subject to burnout. Keep it fully charged as much as possible.

Rose Quartz: The Love Stone

Rose quartz is the heart chakra opener, oozing compassion into all centers of the body. It's a powerful healing crystal and bestows divine gifts. The wearer becomes aligned with a gracious and gentle energy that can smooth over even the toughest emotional wounds.

When used for physical healing, results can be remarkable. For instance, here's a story about a man who had an inflamed scar behind his knee. During his heart surgery 10 years earlier, a vein had been removed from his leg. After only a few minutes of holding a 3-inch rose quartz to the scarred area, the redness completely disappeared. The man declared to me that it was the first time since the operation that he finally felt comfortable!

As a master healer, rose quartz gently releases emotional pain and encourages trust and forgiveness of oneself and of others. When gentleness and calming of any situation is needed, rose quartz can provide the emotional support. It is a great healer for that hole in the heart, for loss and grieving, and for alleviating a sense of despair. For heartbreak, go to rose quartz for healing love and relationship issues. This crystal is indispensable for healing raw emotions expressed from the solar plexus and not yet evolved to the level and understanding of the heart chakra.

Turquoise: Personal Protector

Turquoise is a protector of the physical body. It aligns all subtle bodies and works with the meridians to unblock and promote the flow of chi.

This crystal is best known as a stone of communication, working enthusiastically with the throat chakra. It supports the expression of creativity, not only vocally through speech and singing, but also through activity, such as the arts and crafts, music making, and construction. This is a crystal that supports your career ambitions. While wearing it, you will feel the power of leadership. It protects during travel, changes of location, and for job changes. It is mentally relaxing, reduces anxiety, and brings good fortune.

As a master healer, turquoise dispels negativity by providing a detoxifying influence, knocking out self-sabotage and self-harm to those who are near the stone. It's a stone of many virtues and is highly versatile for use with various diseases and ailments.

Smoky Quartz: Spiritual Warrior

Smoky quartz is known for its intensity for absorbing and dissolving negativity. Some unwanted energies will be neutralized or transmuted but much will be absorbed into the quartz's structure. Larger pieces of smoky quartz tend to amplify negative emotions, so be sure to cleanse your crystal often and wear an appropriate size for your emotional nature. If you need more protection from gossip and bullying, keep a piece near you.

Smoky quartz is highly grounding, yet it carries a lot of light in its structure. This crystal is usually used in the middle and lower chakras because it provides a field of confinement for emotional issues, dissipates outbursts and uncontrolled anger, and handles negativity toward others from you or from others toward you. Help ease a panic attack by running your fingers over the surface or sides of a smoky quartz while clasping it to your solar plexus. Because it's a grounding tool, wearing a programmed piece can help manifest your goals and help direct chaotic or focus flighty thoughts to more practicable applications.

Selecting a Constitutional Crystal

Now that you are more familiar with some of the major healing crystals, finding a crystal that is good for your constitution or your individual makeup is a holistic consideration. I would advise selecting a crystal that's beneficial for your personality at all levels of physical, emotional, and spiritual healing—one that could be worn continuously.

Similar to the use of constitutional homeopathy, select a constitutional crystal that aims to treat your current health concerns, mental and emotional states such as fears and aversions, and your spiritual aspirations such as love and ascension.

Consider the areas where you seem to have the most trouble—again, this might be physical, emotional, or spiritual in nature—or it could be that it's all tied together. Perhaps you have trouble speaking your mind, and that's the issue that bothers you the most. Do you also suffer from frequent sore throats? Feel blocked as a creative writer? A number of crystals could be used individually for these problems, but one in particular would cover most of these symptoms in one compact package. Have you guessed? I covered this one earlier as one of the master healers—it's turquoise.

Crystals are amazing. Let them lead you to health and healing. A constitutional crystal will support you through your self-transformation. You can trust your constitutional crystal because it is an extension of you, and who else knows you better than yourself? Your constitutional crystal is intended for long-term use. Use other crystals to support short-term healing for your body, mind, and emotions. It may take a bit of detective work to find your crystal. Check the eight dimensions of wellness list noted in Chapter 1 and answer the questions at the beginning of this chapter as starting points.

With a constitutional crystal, you would wear the crystal much longer (maybe years) to provide ongoing healing benefits and to alleviate specific conditions. Remember, the crystal will need to be cleansed and recharged regularly to get the most from the stone. It's not unusual to change your crystal every two years or so if you feel you have moved past the stone's capacity.

Using a Pendulum

At any point while working with crystals, you can also use a pendulum to help you select an appropriate gemstone for healing. A pendulum is a crystal or metal, charged with positive intent, and suspended from a chain or string. It is used to answer your questions about the future or to hone your intuition. Wherever there's a choice to be made, the pendulum works on the basis that your subconscious already knows what you need to know. The pendulum will show you the answer by picking up and amplifying the subtle vibrations from your subconscious, causing the pendulum to swing. As mentioned before, set your mind with intent and focus on the question before using the pendulum.

Hold the pendulum between your thumb and index finger with your elbow slightly bent at your side. Use the hand that feels most comfortable for you and relax. It is important to let the natural vibrations of your own body move through your hand to the pendulum. Your questions should be phrased in such a way that they can be answered with a yes or no.

Interpreting the Pendulum's Response

For many people, when the pendulum swings left and right, this can be interpreted as a no. If the pendulum swings up and down (to and fro), this can be interpreted as a yes. If your pendulum swings elliptically, clockwise, counterclockwise, or even stays rigidly still, you must interpret this as best you can.

Here are some tips:

♦ Ask your pendulum something that is true, such as, "Is my name _____?" Note the response. This demonstrates the yes motion.

♦ Now, ask your pendulum something that you know is not true, like, "Is my name Queen Elizabeth?" Note the response. This is the pendulum's no motion.

♦ Finally, ask it a maybe question. Something you don't know the answer to, such as, "Is it going to rain later?" (Provided that you haven't watched the weather forecast). This is your maybe motion. It's important to structure your question properly to make a yes or no answer possible.

Consulting your pendulum is not the same as asking a doctor for informed and reliable information. Seek professional care if you're concerned about a medical issue.

CARVED IN STONE . . . .

Turquoise: I am your protector in all things. I dispel your fears and doubts. I unite your broken and wounded parts into a healed whole. I bring tranquility to your life.

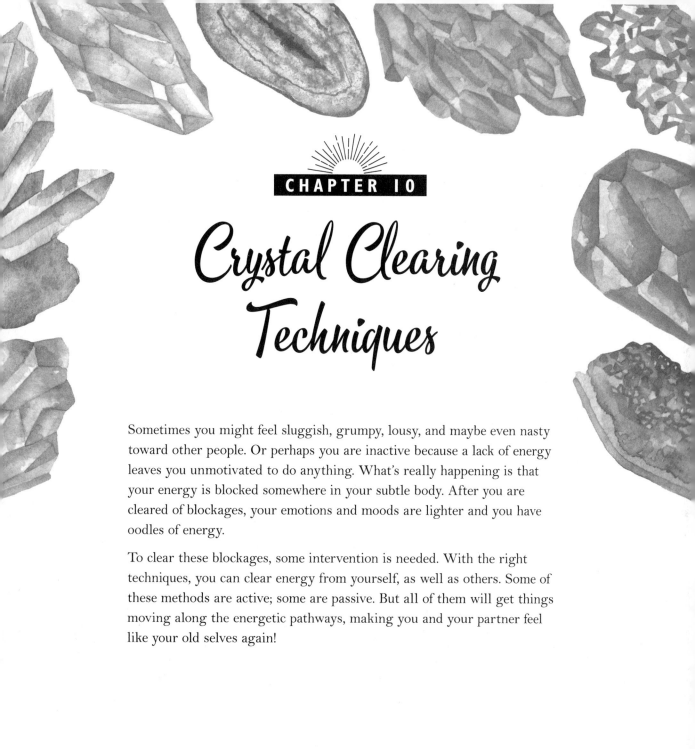

CHAPTER 10

Crystal Clearing Techniques

Sometimes you might feel sluggish, grumpy, lousy, and maybe even nasty toward other people. Or perhaps you are inactive because a lack of energy leaves you unmotivated to do anything. What's really happening is that your energy is blocked somewhere in your subtle body. After you are cleared of blockages, your emotions and moods are lighter and you have oodles of energy.

To clear these blockages, some intervention is needed. With the right techniques, you can clear energy from yourself, as well as others. Some of these methods are active; some are passive. But all of them will get things moving along the energetic pathways, making you and your partner feel like your old selves again!

Learn How to...

♦ Clear congestion in chakras.

♦ Align and balance your chakras.

♦ Cleanse the aura of your partner.

♦ Use a crystal wand.

Vortexes of Energy

In Chapter 5, we talked about chakras, the "wheels" or centers that help distribute energy throughout the body. Before we go any further into cleansing techniques, I want to make sure you have a clear idea of what we're talking about. Think for a moment of a sink full of water. When you unplug the sink, a funnel of water slowly swirls in a clockwise rotation (or in the opposite direction if you are in the Southern Hemisphere), and it zips down the drain, creating an energy vortex. An energy vortex is the rotation of energy that swirls around a center. The speed of this energy is faster at the center than at its outer boundaries.

Chakras are a little bit like that, taking in energy and pulling it into the central channel called the sushumna. The sushumna is the central channel in the chakra system to which all the chakras are joined. It runs parallel to the spine and links the other chakras and subtle energies (the nadis) of the body.

When a crystal is placed near a chakra, it influences the subtle energies of all the chakras. The whirling chakras pull the energy modified by the structure of the crystal into the sushumna and nadis for distribution by following the programming in the crystal and the intent of the healer.

Obviously, the chakras are quite sensitive to crystal energy. Even if you aren't fully aware of changes in your own subtle energy, it's best to start out slowly with the crystal exercises in the next section. As your subtle body becomes more energized and your awareness expands, you will become more and more sensitive to small changes. For this reason, I recommend that you always ground yourself very well before beginning this type of work.

Clearing Chakra Congestion

Like a magnet, a crystal has the ability to pick up and absorb energy of all kinds. When a crystal absorbs negative energy, you can easily cleanse it by smudging it or placing it in a salt water bath. But sometimes our chakras get cluttered and need a good cleaning, too. Up until now, you've done this by either wearing a crystal or placing one on your body or at a chakra. Now, you are going to learn another way to clear unwanted energy quickly from centers of energy.

When using a crystal for healing the chakras, you need to be very gentle and move slowly. Chakras are as delicate as tissue paper. Although they are a bit more elastic than paper, you need to be respectful of their capacity for change. Slow and steady wins the race when it comes to transforming negative energy to positive.

Clearing Chakras

Why do you want to clear your chakras? Like a storage battery, chakras can retain energy and fill up with day-to-day clutter and need to release stored energy. We hold onto negative emotions such as grief or uncertainty and stressful experiences such as trauma. We don't always have time to empty it out. Press in at your solar plexus right now and you may find it's a bit tight and sore! This physical awareness of your solar plexus is from tense emotions held at the physical level. When you massage the area (gently), you are easing the physical condition. Some people work out at the gym and engage in physical activity to ease pent up emotions. See how closely emotions are to the physical body? But how do you release the more subtle emotional level in the chakra and keep it in balance?

The whole system can be optimized for peak performance by routinely cleansing the chakras. The results are positive energy and an improvement in overall health and wellness. Emotions are calmer because they have a place to go and are more efficiently processed. Your mind is eased of troubles and there is improved mental focus. You may even find yourself whistling while you work!

Crystal Therapy System

Let's try an easy exercise using a more advanced crystal healing technique so you can see the effects of clearing a chakra using crystal therapy. Whereas holding a crystal or wearing one is a passive way to work with crystals, this technique is part of the Crystal Therapy System (CTS) that I teach at my crystal healing school, the Crystal Alchemy Academy. The methodology is based on energy medicine and dynamic techniques for opening, clearing, calming, rebuilding, and rebalancing energy using crystals.

We'll use the throat chakra for this clearing exercise because many people seem naturally more sensitive in this area. Later, you can try this with your heart or solar plexus chakra. Please read through the instructions first to ensure you understand and are comfortable with the entire process.

Your intent for this session is to clear any blockages in the throat chakra. Follow these simple steps:

1. You'll need a clear quartz crystal such as a generator or laser crystal about 1- to 2-inches long that is cleansed and fully charged.

2. Program the crystal with this affirmation: "I, [your name], now gently release all that is needed for my highest good."

3. Before you go any further, you'll need to ground yourself very well to help reduce a healing crisis. (Think of roots growing from under your feet.) Relax your body by taking some deep breaths.

4. Spend a few minutes in meditation and focus on your throat chakra. This will help bring your energies to a ready state.

5. Hold your crystal in your right hand and slowly bring it up to your throat chakra, positioning the tip about 4 inches away. Hold the crystal still, pointing the tip into the center of the chakra. Let the chakra and the crystal unite in their energies. You might begin to feel a heaviness, a tingling, a gagging response, or some other sensation as the crystal starts to work in your energy field. (Be patient—there's no right way or exact time frame for this!)

6. As the crystal bonds energetically with the area, the throat chakra will begin to open. Any negative energies that are ready to be released will be attracted to the crystal and be pulled from the chakra. Some of these negative energies will be transmuted into white light by the energy of the crystal. Other energies (such as blockages) will start to break up and stick to the crystal. Gather these energies from the chakra by slowly moving the crystal in a clockwise circle 3 to 4 inches wide.

You are creating an energy vortex with the crystal to pull out unwanted energies. Flick the unwanted energies away several times from the end of the crystal until you feel free of the constriction.

7. Your breathing will probably change into deeper cleansing breaths as you relax further. This is a sign that you have finished clearing. As the clearing happens, you might also experience related energy releases such as yawning. Just think, all that energy was stuck there! Clearing it now helps reduce the possibility for disease or emotional issues later.

8. Next, place a soothing crystal such a turquoise, rose quartz, or jade on your throat chakra for a few minutes to calm down the chakra. What did you experience? Write it down in your journal.

Intense Release of Energy

To reduce the intensity of the session, you can also use a smaller crystal or hold the crystal farther away. Move it 10 to 12 inches away from your chakra, and hold it steady instead of moving it around the chakra. Everyone's sensitivity is different because we are all made of different energies, experiences, and DNA.

Remember, it's just your own unwanted energy that has been stuck trying to release itself. Breathing deeply and quickly can help alleviate any discomfort. Stay with the feeling. It's like exercising a muscle. There are bound to be some cramps along the way, but it's worth it for the result.

Remember to put the crystal aside for cleansing with a salt bath or smudging and for recharging the next day. This type of dynamic crystal energy work runs down the crystal's internal battery, but your own energy should feel lighter because you have cleansed the energy that might have been dragging you down.

Aligning and Balancing Your Chakra in Seconds

Chakras not only need to be cleansed, but they also need to be aligned every so often. As humans, we encounter many bumps, both emotional and physical, along the road of life.

Releasing and realigning energy keeps us moving at a steady clip and prevents major breakdowns.

The chakras are fragile yet substantial enough for almost everything we experience throughout our lives, including falling off bicycles, falling in love, walking down grocery aisles, or walking down the wedding aisle. Chakras respond to everyday stresses by floating around a bit in their positions. They are structured like a flower with petals that open and close to protect subtle energy from damage.

Some shocks are just too much and can cause a misalignment of the subtle body energy. Doctors and physiotherapists work on your physical body, but the subtle body also needs repair.

You can confirm how aligned your chakras feel by using a pendulum to ask if all your chakras are aligned. If you get a no answer, ask one by one which chakra should be realigned. When you are in alignment, you will find yourself standing and sitting tall and your response to everyday stress will be minimal.

The use of kyanite for chakra work is not widely known or practiced by many, yet it is very effective. For this exercise, you'll need a piece of blue kyanite, which has a natural align-ment in its structure and can align energy sideways as well as up and down. It balances like your head on your neck. Kyanite is sometimes called a kyanite wand because the crys-tal is often long, flat, and split like a wooden stick. Kyanite is recommended as part of the healer's crystal toolkit.

The kyanite crystal should be a length no less than 2-inches long and ½-inch wide. Hold the crystal with one end pointing directly into the center of each chakra for a count of 7 or 21 seconds each, depending on whether you need a minor adjustment or a bit more work.

Another nice benefit of kyanite is that you don't need to worry about cleansing or charging it because it's one of the few crystals that is constantly charged and never needs cleansing! When placed close to other crystals, it helps align their energies as well.

Aura Clearing with a Partner

Now how would you like to do some more crystal healing, but this time with a partner? The following exercise is part of the aura balance and clearing techniques taught in my crystal classes. The exercise helps warm up the aura by circulating energy and activating the subtle energies. You'll be using a crystal to sweep the aura of impurities. The aura will be balanced, meaning that the energies will flow smoothly. Your partner in this exercise needs to be willing to participate and remain open minded to experiencing crystal energy work.

As with any crystal work, grounding is important. Before beginning this exercise, both you and your partner should stand facing each other, and each of you should visualize roots under your feet anchoring you deeply into the ground for a minute. Breathe deeply and regularly.

As the healer in this case, select a cleansed and charged quartz crystal point 3- to 5-inches long in either rose quartz, clear quartz, or amethyst. These master healing crystals already know how to work with the human aura and are gentle balancers of energy. You may also use a selenite wand for this exercise.

Before you begin, inform your partner that you can stop at any time—and be sure you do stop if you're asked to. When a person closes up his or her energy, there's no point in continuing anyway. If your partner says nothing but seems uncomfortable, offer to stop. Checking in from time to time is standard practice among healers.

Now follow these steps:

1. Stand facing each other. As the crystal healer, you can call in your own healing spirits or those of your partner for help in this session. Recite a simple prayer request to initiate the session such as "Masters, guardians, teachers, and guides, I ask for your protection and assistance during this healing session. Please provide for conscious awareness and direction for healing [name of the partner]. Let all activity be conducted for the highest good of [name of the partner]."

2. Hold your crystal in your right hand close to your heart chakra for a few moments to receive its energy and to warm up the crystal and connect with your energy at the heart level.

3. Point the crystal at a spot between your partner's feet about 6 to 12 inches below their arches. This is the earth chakra and represents the person's anchoring point to the earth. It's the place to start clearing the aura.

4. While visualizing white light radiating from the tip of the crystal, start slowly moving your right hand to the left and visualize sweeping up under your partner's feet. In a continuous flow, continue to visualize a white light coming from the

crystal. Draw the crystal up, following the right side of your partner's body about 2 to 4 inches away from the side of the body. You are drawing an outline of the person's aura.

5. As you draw the crystal up, you might feel tugging, pushing, or pulling. This is resistance in the energy flow of your partner's aura. The crystal is working very hard to remove impurities, negativity, and imperfections from the aura, so you need to go slowly, not only to feel what's going on, but to also allow your partner to adjust his or her energy as the crystal passes.

6. If you feel the crystal becoming saturated with negative energies, gently withdraw it from the person's aura and gently shake it free of negative energy. You can also breathe in, think the word *release*, and visualize white light streaming out over the crystal and transmuting the negativity into white light. Return to the point in the aura where you left off and then continue the cleansing motion.

7. Continue moving your crystal in a clockwise direction around your partner's aura, slowly tracing up and over the person's head and down the right side. Stop when you feel a sticky area, wiggle the crystal a bit to release the energy, and focus on clearing the patch before moving on. If you find that the hand holding the crystal gets tingly, shake your hand out to remove excess negativity.

You can't go wrong with this exercise because the crystal is doing all the work, and you aren't working on the more sensitive chakras. Your partner might experience tingling and some feelings of pressure as the crystal encounters blockages in the flow of the energy in the aura. He or she might also feel some swaying back and forth with the changing energy flows. These are all typical responses to energy activation and clearing. It can be a very nice experience, and at the end, you'll both feel relaxed from sharing the healing experience.

If you and your partner are going to switch places, be sure to go through the grounding exercise again and have your partner use his or her own cleansed and charged crystal to work on your aura.

If you have been the healer, make sure you cleanse your hands of any negative energies picked up from your partner. Wet your hands in cold water and rub the skin lightly with sea salt to purify the energy and cleanse the hand chakras. Rinse the salt off your hands with more cold water. Cold water is used to help close down sensitivity in the hand chakras after handling crystals. Be sure to cleanse and recharge your crystal before using it for other healings.

Wand Wonderment

In ancient traditions a wand with a crystal is called a scepter and is used as a symbol of authority. Just holding a wand generates a lot of energy. When crystals are placed at the tip of a shaft, the energy generated can be amplified and directed to disperse in a very powerful and focused way. The wand can be moved around to direct the flow of energy. If you have a crystal wand, you can use the Dedication Prayer in Chapter 8, or use the Activation prayer found in the next section.

A wand can be used in place of the crystal for the clearing auras exercise in the previous section. Test the wand on yourself first to ensure its energy is activated. (The test can be as simple as pointing the tip at the opposite hand to activate the hand chakra.) You may feel a tingle or coolness. Perfect!

Using a Crystal Wand

Before you begin, smudge the wand and then hold the wand in your hand to warm it up for several minutes to excite the molecules and generate an energy charge. It's like starting a car on a cold morning. The crystal and metal or wood shaft will unite their energies for a more powerful wand attunement.

Now it's time to activate the wand. While sitting, hold the wand on your knee and lower thigh. Roll the wand back and forth on your knee or between your hands, visualize a white light surrounding you, and recite the following Activation prayer:

- ◆ I now invoke the love and wisdom of my higher self to be present and guide the energies for this wand activation.
- ◆ I now dedicate the healing energy of this wand to benefit all others in the highest service of all mankind.
- ◆ I now encapsulate this wand in the triple healing light—pure white light, green healing light, and the purple transmuting flame to seal and protect this wand from any misuse.

♦ I now call on my masters, teachers, and guides to help me serve in the highest intention for use of this healing wand.

♦ I now activate this crystal wand for the highest good of all who may receive healing from this tool.

The wand is now ready for focusing and moving energy into alignment for healing purposes. You can hold the wand by either one or both hands and point it a few inches above the surface of your body to send healing energy. Try visualizing white light or colored chakra light coming from the wand's crystal tip into your body. Look just past the tip for an aura of energy. You will become more attuned to the crystal's light the more you work with it.

At psychic shows, I often use a crystal wand as part of a crystal healing demonstration. I ask for a volunteer who has no prior experience with crystals to come up to the stage to have their aura cleansed. This is the same aura cleansing exercise done with a partner as explained previously, but using a crystal wand. For demonstrations, I use a really large 30-inch copper wand with a 3-inch-wide amethyst crystal at the tip, which packs a powerful punch to just about any sceptic's aura. Often, someone in the audience will gasp out loud, surprised that they can see white light pouring out from the tip of the crystal wand. The volunteer sometimes sways gently back and forth, feeling the amplified power of the crystal.

If you want more practice using a wand, try these exercises:

♦ To send energy out farther for distance healing, hold the thought of the person in your mind or gaze at a photo of the person. Aim the wand toward the visualization or to their photo and at any special areas that need healing. Hold the wand steady for several minutes. You can either say an affirmation for the person or ask for a healing or a blessing. If you find the wand shaking, it's just energy and should stop shaking when the broadcast is complete.

♦ For joint pain, focus the crystal tip at each joint, first at the base and then tip of the joint. This will stimulate circulation and reduce pain.

♦ To literally pull a headache out of someone's head, focus the wand a few inches from their pain point. Wait until the energy has gathered, about 20-30 seconds, and then gently lift the unwanted energy away. Flick the negative energy off the crystal and see it dissolve into white light. Repeat a few times.

You can also use your crystal wand to align energies for crystal layouts and crystal grids. Your crystal wand is an important tool in your healing toolkit. A wand is strong yang energy. To keep your wand energized, keep it wrapped up in a red silk cloth. Cleanse it in smudge, such as sweet grass, and leave it in sunlight or moonlight to recharge it.

You learned in this chapter to use some basic healing techniques for chakras and the aura. Your connection to your crystals will be stronger when you use them on yourself and others. As you gain more knowledge about crystals and your intuition broadens, try new crystals and try different ways of working with them. Let your intuition guide you. In the next part, there are suggestions for specific crystals used in healing the body, mind, and spirit.

CARVED IN STONE . . . .

Kyanite: I open the dimensional portals. I provide the connectivity between different energy sources and etheric layers. I unify the frequencies for communications and direct energy flows.

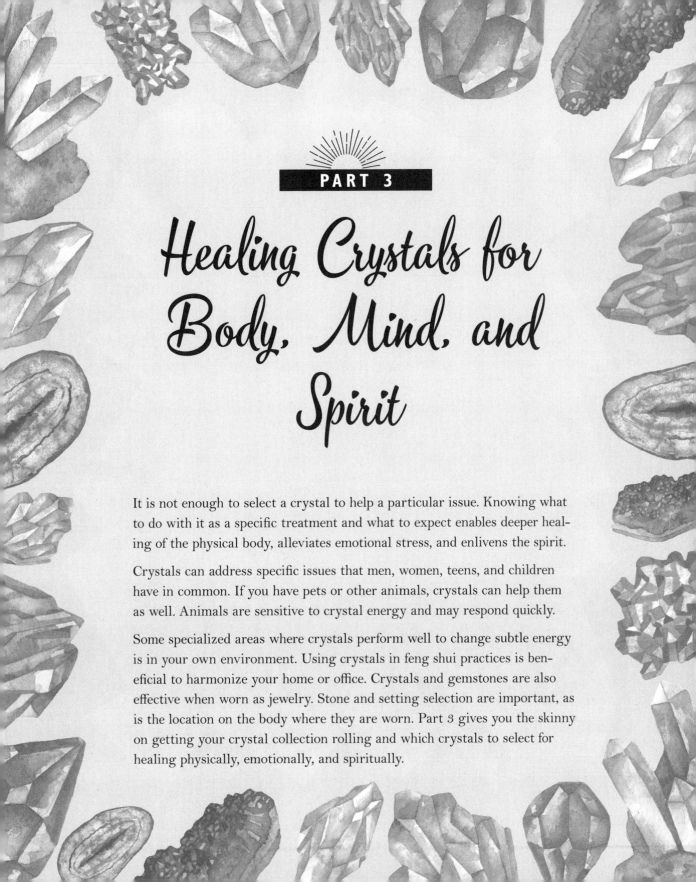

PART 3

Healing Crystals for Body, Mind, and Spirit

It is not enough to select a crystal to help a particular issue. Knowing what to do with it as a specific treatment and what to expect enables deeper healing of the physical body, alleviates emotional stress, and enlivens the spirit.

Crystals can address specific issues that men, women, teens, and children have in common. If you have pets or other animals, crystals can help them as well. Animals are sensitive to crystal energy and may respond quickly.

Some specialized areas where crystals perform well to change subtle energy is in your own environment. Using crystals in feng shui practices is beneficial to harmonize your home or office. Crystals and gemstones are also effective when worn as jewelry. Stone and setting selection are important, as is the location on the body where they are worn. Part 3 gives you the skinny on getting your crystal collection rolling and which crystals to select for healing physically, emotionally, and spiritually.

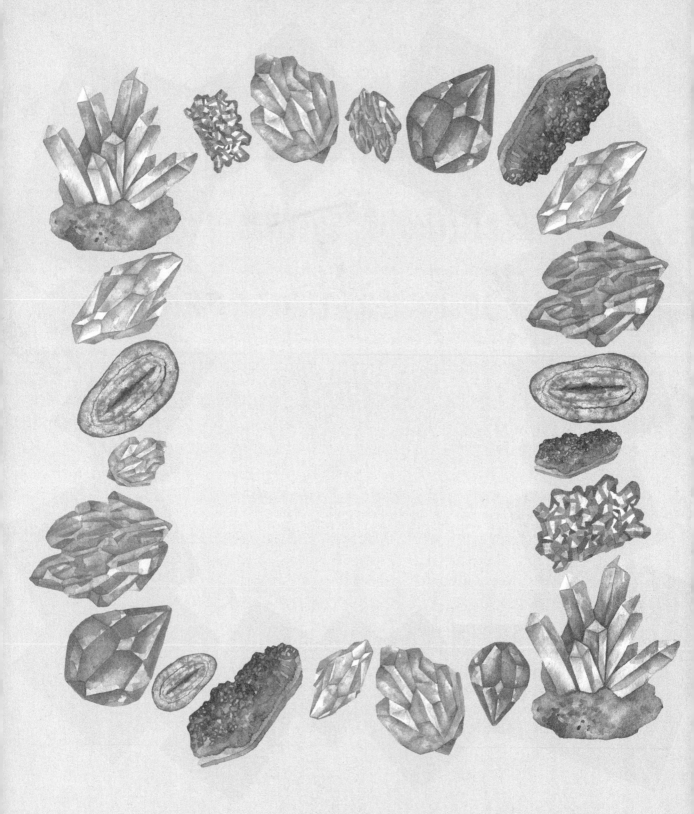

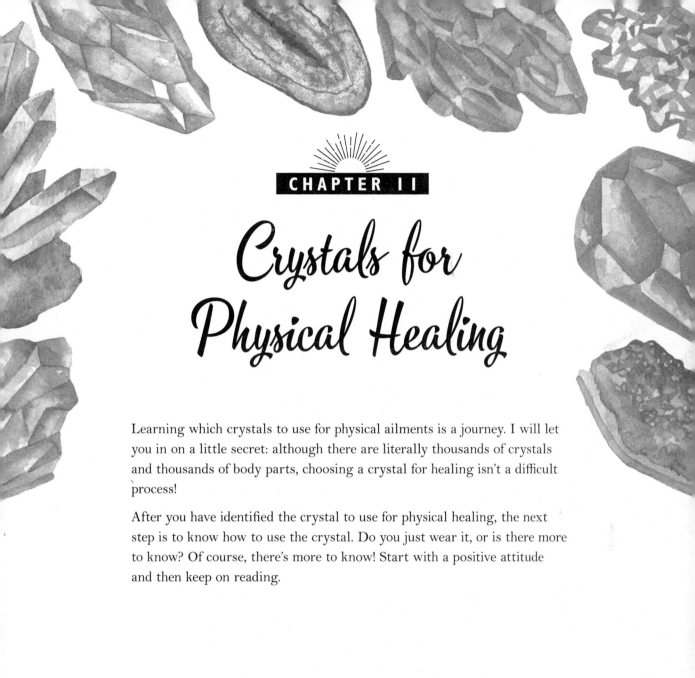

CHAPTER 11

Crystals for Physical Healing

Learning which crystals to use for physical ailments is a journey. I will let you in on a little secret: although there are literally thousands of crystals and thousands of body parts, choosing a crystal for healing isn't a difficult process!

After you have identified the crystal to use for physical healing, the next step is to know how to use the crystal. Do you just wear it, or is there more to know? Of course, there's more to know! Start with a positive attitude and then keep on reading.

Learn How to...

♦ Alleviate headaches and heal a cut.

♦ Reduce pain and speed healing of an afflicted area of the body.

♦ Select crystals for different types of illness.

How to Use Crystals for Physical Healing

Crystals can facilitate the healing process by providing focus, but they do not replace quality medical care. As always, consult a medical professional for your health issues and use common sense. If you need some help learning how to heal, now is a good time to seek a healer or healing facilitator. A healer provides knowledge and guidance and creates an environment for healing to occur, just like a sports coach provides guidance for self-growth.

Healing Takes Balance

When we are disconnected from the source of wholeness, our physical and emotional energy systems can go out of balance with our spiritual side. Returning to wholeness requires a multilevel approach of body, mind, and spirit to restore balance and health. Healing is the ability to direct energy to restore that balance.

Focused intent, breath work, and visualization are all part of the healing "team" that assists crystal healing work. Intuition is very important and helps guide us through that process. Healers use crystals on their third eye to open the center of intuition so they can see and feel what healing intervention a client needs.

If you have some doubt about crystal healing and are the type of person who wants to see something physically happen in front of your eyes before you believe it can actually happen, here's an experiment for you. Try healing a small, superficial paper cut.

Using a clear quartz crystal 1- to 3-inches long, hold the tip of the crystal about ¼-inch above the cut. Follow the line of the cut, moving the crystal very slowly back and forth over it for about 5 minutes, letting the energy from the crystal align with the internal skin structures. Repeat this exercise two or three times during the day. You should find that the cut heals quickly. You might also see a black carbonized line where the cut was, signifying the power of the crystal to accelerate healing of the tissues.

With body, mind, and spirit working in harmony to balance subtle energies, health will be restored. Be sure your mind is aligned, too, as it is an essential component to the healing process. The stronger the connection to the spiritual side, the stronger the energetic connections made for physical healing.

Source of Illness

Every system in the body can break down or run into problems. That's just the nature of being human. Fortunately, there is a crystal for just about everything. It's important to choose the right crystal based on the locale of the illness or problem and the spiritual connection to its manifestation. Having some intuitive sense in knowing which crystals are best for a problem is very helpful, too.

Crystal Selections

The first step in healing is selecting the crystal to use for the physical ailment. Choose from either the list of crystals for healing chronic conditions and pain in the next section or from the list of crystals recommended for various parts of the body at the end of this chapter. If you are unsure which crystal to use, select the crystal according to the color of the chakra which is closest to the trouble. For instance, if you have a sour stomach, the nearest chakra is the solar plexus. You could select from the list of solar plexus chakra crystals such as amber or calcite. Place it over your stomach for 5 to 10 minutes to calm excess acid.

A general rule is that red and orange crystals invigorate, blues sedate, pinks and greens soothe, yellows neutralize, and purples and whites purify. There are many healing systems, but for crystal healing, these colors work well for these conditions. I've also included information on infusing and increasing energy:

- ◆ **To remove excess energy**—Over the affected area, place four pointed clear quartz crystals, each ½-inch wide and 1 to 2 inches in length, with the tips pointing in each compass direction—north, south, east, and west. Place a physical healing crystal such as smoky quartz, purple fluorite, or turquoise into the center of the affected area to cleanse negative energy from it. This crystal layout should remain over the area for

3 minutes to 5 minutes to allow unwanted energies to escape; however, this is just a guideline. If you feel more time is needed, then listen to your intuition and leave them in place as long as necessary. (See Chapter 16 for more layouts.)

♦ **To infuse energy**—Again, place four pointed clear quartz crystals, each ½-inch wide and 1 to 2 inches in length, over the affected area at the north, south, east, and west, but this time point the tips inward toward the affected area. Place a physical healing crystal in the center to boost healing energy to the afflicted area. Malachite or bloodstone are great choices for high energy infusion. The quartz will amplify the healing effects of the malachite or bloodstone and intensify healing energy in the area.

♦ **To increase the flow of energy**—This increases the circulation of chi or prana along the internal pathways. Use at least four small clear quartz crystal points, each ½- to 2-inches long and ¼- to 1-inch wide. Place two crystals, one above the other, in a line pointed to the area in need of healing. Then, place two crystals below the area in a line with the tips pointing down or outward to carry energy away from the body. You can tape the crystals in place, even on clothing, provided you remember to remove them before moving around.

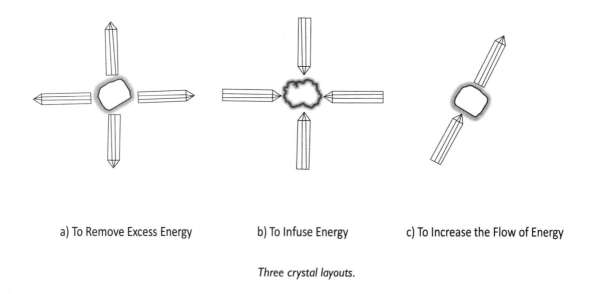

a) To Remove Excess Energy   b) To Infuse Energy   c) To Increase the Flow of Energy

Three crystal layouts.

Pain Relief

It is said that everyone deals with pain differently. So first off, try not to resist pain or any emotions that you might have about your pain. If you do, you are inhibiting subtle healing energy from reaching the part that needs to be healed. Shutting down your emotions over the long term might create lingering and chronic pain. When working with crystals, it's so important to keep that energy flowing!

Crystals for Healing and Chronic Pain

Crystal healing provides a holistic approach to pain; that is, it has the ability to help transform a person's attitude about the illness as well as the physical condition. There are many crystals available for healing. The following crystals, most are easily obtained, can help with chronic pain and other conditions—and with your state of mind, too.

Crystal	How It's Used for Healing
Amethyst	A master healer. Used for arthritis pain. Use surgical tape to hold the amethyst crystal over the area of pain. For deep pain, use two clusters of amethyst and place them on either side of the joint. For thyroid balancing, wear an amethyst crystal pendant at the heart chakra.
Clear quartz	A master healer. Place a clear quartz crystal of any size directly on the affected area. If it's too painful, gather several crystals around the area with the points facing outward to draw out the pain, infection, or inflammation.
Carnelian	Heals skin, acne, herpes, scars, and wrinkles. Either place it directly over the area or hold it an inch above the area and move it slowly in small circles for 5 minutes, repeat this twice a day or more.
Copper	Used for arthritis pain. Wear as a bracelet. Natural oxidation causes the copper to leave green marks on the skin. That's okay, just rub it off. Tape a small flat piece of copper over the afflicted area.

(continues)

(continued)

Crystal	How It's Used for Healing
Garnet	For correcting gynecological issues, PMS, or infertility. Wear it as a necklace or pendant, or hold or tape garnets over each ovary. Directions on use for fertility are featured later in this chapter.
Hematite	Use for pain in the legs, arms, or back or to increase circulation. Tape small ¼- to ½- inch pieces down the leg or spine and wear overnight.
Herkimer	Used for alleviating vertigo and dizziness. Keep a crystal diamond in each pocket or place one at the neck and one at the forehead for 5 to 10 minutes once a day.
Gold	Fortifies the energy fields to be more resilient to pain and increases pain thresholds. Gold also helps to boost immunity, reduce infection, and maintain physical strength.
Kunzite	Used for the prevention of heart disorders, for pain in the heart, and for post-operative recovery after heart surgery. Wear this crystal unpolished as a pendant at the heart chakra.
Turquoise	A master healer. It boosts the immune system and helps alleviate pain from digestive issues and sore throats. Wear as a pendant or chip necklace at mid-chest or at the heart or throat chakras.
Malachite	For the prevention of heart disease; wear it anywhere on the body.
Rose quartz	A master healer. Cools inflammation as well as emotional issues related to pain (for example, burns or trauma). Wear it as a chip necklace or tape a piece over the area overnight for longer-lasting effects.
Smoky quartz	A master healer. Draws out pain and releases negative emotions that might be causing physical pain. Place it over the affected area.

Be sure to cleanse your crystals regularly when they are used for healing purposes. For complete instructions on crystal cleansing, see Chapter 8.

Headache Relief

Sometimes excessive energy gets directed to the head area, probably to protect the brain from something such as a sinus infection, stress, or even an overactive imagination. Well, that excess energy needs a way out! The closest chakra to the brain is at the top of the head: the crown chakra. If the crown chakra is open, the energy can rise and dissipate. If it is closed due to energy blockages, the energy backs up and you get a headache or, worse, a migraine.

Imagine having a gentle, easy, drug-free approach to getting rid of a simple headache. I'm about to give you more suggestions! In the last chapter, I gave instructions on using a crystal wand to remove a headache. If you do not have a wand, use either a single-point clear quartz crystal or a single-point amethyst. A small, smooth, tumbled crystal in rose quartz, smoky quartz, or lapis lazuli can also be effective with the following technique that opens up the crown chakra and kicks that headache:

1. Take the crystal point and hold it on the top of your head in the middle of your skull with the point up.

2. Hold the crystal steady, touching your skull for a minute to gather the energies. You might feel some pressure. Energy blocked at the neck will begin to flow upward toward the crown chakra.

3. When you feel enough energy has collected, slowly raise the crystal 1 to 2 inches above the center of your head. You should feel all that excess energy being pulled up and out, directed by the crystal.

4. Breathe deeply to help channel the energy from the head. When you feel the headache is gone, lower your hand. To add a longer healing benefit, rub a drop of lavender oil on a massage crystal and massage your temples.

There are a couple of other ways to alleviate head pain. You can use an amethyst or a clear quartz crystal ball and roll it across your forehead and temples and back of neck. This will pick up excess energy and transfer it to the crystal. To ease sinus headache pain, place golden rutilated quartz crystals over sinuses (on your forehead and cheekbones) and lie down with the crystals on for 5 to 10 minutes.

Breathe a Sigh of Relief

In yoga, different breathing patterns are taught in order to control the internal energies of the body. For example, when you're holding a difficult pose, your yogi will tell you to expand your breath into your limbs to help steady yourself or lessen discomfort.

Just focusing your breath on a painful or troubled area provides additional energy for healing. When a crystal is added, the healing gets an additional energy boost.

One of the most frequent types of breathing used in healing with crystals is called a *circular breath*. This breathing pattern involves imagining that you're breathing into and out of the crystal.

Ready to give this a try? Follow these steps based on an ancient meditation:

1. Ground yourself. Relax and breathe regularly. Hold a cleansed and charged clear quartz or amethyst crystal that's 1 to 2 inches long to the area of discomfort.

2. Visualize the pain or discomfort as a mass of dark clouds over the area.

3. On the inhale, draw the dark clouds representing your pain or ailment into the crystal.

4. When you exhale, think of sending the clouds out from the crystals as white light.

5. Continue inhaling and exhaling for 5 minutes.

Cleanse and recharge your crystal afterward so it's ready the next time you need it.

Increasing Fertility

The pace of life seems to be quite a lot faster than nature intended and sometimes help is needed. There are financial, environmental, and health concerns for a newborn and a lot of competition to attract the right energies for a baby soul. Three karmic souls need to connect: the karma of the father, the karma of the mother, and the karma of the wee little babe who wants to come for an Earth visit on a lifetime visitor pass.

For a woman to increase fertility, she should wear the following two crystals:

♦ **Rose quartz**—It's called the *love stone* for a reason! It really tempers the heart and creates a full, loving aura around the expectant mother allowing a soul to enter. Wear this crystal continuously as a necklace or pendant at the heart chakra, even during the pregnancy, to send your baby soothing, calming, loving vibes. Rub a rose quartz or use a rose quartz facial roller over your face and body to increase circulation and to create a loving aura for a blessed spirit to find its new mommy.

♦ **Garnet**—This red crystal gathers the physical and procreative energies and should be worn near the ovaries. A small, flat, ½-inch piece of tumbled garnet can be taped at the sacral chakra, about 2 inches below the belly button. Wear during ovulation.

For a man to increase fertility, he can also wear garnet as noted above, as well as either of the following two crystals:

♦ **Green tourmaline**—Tourmaline provides electrical impulses and can be worn as a pendant to strengthen internal chemistry. Green is the color of the procreative life force. Wear continuously as a pendant at the heart or throat chakra.

♦ **Lapis lazuli**—This deep blue crystal opens the higher psychic centers to connect with the emerging soul energies and offers fatherly protection. Wear continuously as a pendant at the heart or throat chakra or as a large ring.

Also, the energy in your home is important to attract a newbie human. Think about this from the perspective of the baby soul who is looking for parents. He or she wants to come into a soothing, nurturing, loving environment (wouldn't you?). Use Feng Shui (see Chapter 15) to modify the vibrations in your home. Use crystals to calm your environment.

Timeline of Healing

When you first begin healing with crystals, you might actually feel worse. This doesn't mean the treatment isn't working—in fact, it indicates just the opposite! Energy is being released and is shifting around the body. This means it's working to find balance and then you will feel better, rebounding to a more harmonic state. A little crystal can go a long way toward improving health!

Crystals for Physical Healing

The following sections are arranged by an organ or a body part or condition. For body parts not mentioned, use the crystal for the chakra that is closest to the area. If you are uncertain, use one of the five master healers discussed in Chapter 9. Meditate and let your inner vision show you which crystal is needed. You can also use your pendulum by holding it over the name of each crystal until you receive a response.

Body Part or Condition	Crystal/How It's Used
Adrenal gland	Sugilite
Arthritis	Chrysololla (strengthens tendons and muscles)
Asthma	Fluorite (opens congested airways), rutilated quartz
Bladder	Bloodstone, rose quartz
Blood and blood disorders	Amethyst, aventurine, bloodstone (oxygenates), copper (for blood flow), fluorite (cleanses), garnet (circulation), gold (purifies), hematite (blood stream), jade (quality of blood), malachite, rose quartz, ruby, turquoise (immunizes)
Blood pressure	Amethyst dioptase, kunzite, turquoise
Blood sugar	Rose quartz, malachite, opal
Bowel troubles	Black tourmaline, red calcite (stops diarrhea)
Bone strengtheners	Calcite, fluorite, kyanite, lapis lazuli, selenite
Brain	Diamond, gold (balances left and right brain hemispheres), tourmaline (neural pathways), pyrite, rhodochrosite (improves memory), sugilite
Ears, eyes	Amber (pain), Herkimer diamond (balance), agate (soothes), jade, kyanite, opal. Hold against ears or on side of temples to warm and transfer energy
Female reproductive organs	Garnet, jade, rose quartz, rutilated quartz, smoky quartz

Body Part or Condition	Crystal/How It's Used
Hormones	Epidote (to offset a hot flash), labradorite (regulates metabolism)
Immune system revitalizers	Turquoise, amethyst, emerald, garnet, jasper, peridot, ruby, rutilated quartz, turquoise
Intestines	Pyrite, calcite
Inflammation	Rose quartz
Joints	Amethyst, chrysocolla, hematite
Lymphatic system	Fluorite, moonstone, rose quartz, sodalite
Lungs	Fluorite (colds/flu)
Heart	Malachite (cardiovascular disease prevention), bloodstone (strengthens the heart muscle), dioptase, emerald, jade, kunzite (a significant heart crystal), lepidolite, peridot, rhodochrosite, ruby, sugilite.
Kidney, pancreas	Amber, aquamarine, yellow or green calcite, carnelian, citrine
Liver, gallbladder soothers	Emerald, green fluorite, hematite, malachite (for detoxifying)
Spleen	Jade, jasper, malachite, peridot, rhodochrosite, rhodonite, rose quartz, smoky quartz, sodalite, sapphire, tiger eye, topaz
Lungs	Aventurine, turquoise, rutilated quartz
Metabolism	Apatite (suppresses hunger)
Muscles	Amber (pain), copper (rheumatism), hematite (increases magnetic activity), purple fluorite (for numbness)
Nervous system	Tourmaline, amazonite, aquamarine, azurite, dioptase, gold, rhodonite, selenite, sapphire, obsidian
Nose, throat	Celestite, kyanite, rhodochrosite (nasal tissues), turquoise
Pineal gland	Lepidolite, opal, clear quartz

(continues)

(continued)

Body Part or Condition	Crystal/How It's Used
Pituitary gland	Garnet, lepidolite, moonstone, opal, clear quartz, rhodochrosite, rhodonite, sapphire
Skin, tissue	Carnelian, gold, gypsum (wrinkles), peridot, rutilated quartz, sapphire, labradorite (emphysema)
Spleen	Bloodstone (strengthens), moonstone (calms)
Stomach, intestines	Chrysocolla (digestion), dioptase (nervous stomach), moonstone, obsidian, pyrite, tiger eye
Teeth	Fluorite, selenite
Thyroid	Amethyst, celestite, lapis lazuli, rhodonite
Urinary tract	Rose quartz, sodalite

Remember that your attitude, outlook, and determination are powerful tools in healing and recovery. When you're sick, it can be hard to muster up the energy needed for healing—that power is there; it's inside everyone of us, and we can use it to facilitate our own healing.

CARVED IN STONE . . . .

Always ask permission before giving healing and be gentle when you are using crystals for healing. You are among the very few who can step outside themselves to help another person. Give yourself a pat on the back for using your crystal healing skills and knowledge.

CHAPTER 12

Crystals for Emotional Well-Being

No doubt you have been stuck at some point with some feelings that you didn't want to express. Finding relief from negative emotions such as anger, grief, and jealousy can be a steep learning curve. It takes a lot of awareness and some help from our crystal friends to provide a way through our emotional experiences.

Crystals take us to a new emotional level where feelings about ourselves and others become lighter, transforming our moods in the process. The mind is cleansed, the heart is free, and we feel open to a whole new way of living!

Learn How to...

♦ Clear your anger, heal your wounded heart, and learn forgiveness.

♦ Attract love and joy for fulfillment.

♦ Use crystals to attract romance and deal with relationship issues.

How to Use Crystals for Emotional Clearing

You might have heard the quote "I think, therefore, I am," from Rene Descartes, the seventeenth-century French philosopher. That is so true! When you carry excess emotions such as anger or jealousy, biochemical reactions occur in your body that pump out more adrenaline, causing your heart to beat faster and nasty acids to churn in your stomach. So you feel bad in your head and in your body, and a vicious cycle begins.

Working with crystals gives your emotions a chance to restore balance before negative energy manifests at the physical level.

Clearing Anger

There is no greater poison than anger, says the Dalai Lama, the Tibetan Buddhist spiritual leader. Anger clouds your thinking and your ability to act in a reasonable way. You can also feel it physically as a raised heart rate, high blood pressure, and sour acids in your stomach. If we have an opportunity to consciously manage our negative emotions before they turn into anger or rage, our physical, mental, and social health will not suffer.

Anger acts as an energy blocker, usually at the solar plexus chakra. Blockages due to anger also often occur at the throat chakra, due to repressing words about feelings, and in the root and sacral chakras if you have suffered abuse. These chakras shut down their energy flows when affronted with negative energy to protect them from an energy overload. However, when chakras are in the "off" position, they don't let in much healing light and can block out love and compassion, the anecdote to anger.

Now you may think if your anger is really big, you'll need a really big crystal. In fact, even a small one about an inch in diameter will help. Try selecting a crystal from this list to help clear negative energy:

- ◆ **Hematite**—When you feel unsettled, hematite is a great grounder of emotions. Your anger will be more self-contained, and your thoughts will become gentler. Hold a tumbled piece 1- to 2-inches long in each hand. You might notice a feeling of heaviness as your emotional body sinks back into alignment and a sense of relaxation comes over you. You can move beyond your self-limitations.

- ◆ **Kyanite**—Do you get out of sorts with your thoughts and start to build a story that might or might not be true? Eventually even thinking about something you have little or no control over can lead to anger, but kyanite will cut through these mental illusions. Wearing a small piece as a jewelry item will help keep your mental fields aligned for a higher purpose.

- ◆ **Smoky quartz**—Wearing smoky quartz, one of the master healers, helps unblock and open chakras and absorbs negative energy. Its crystalline structure is able to take on the brunt of heavy emotions. However, it does absorb a lot of negative energy into its structure, so you will need to cleanse and recharge it more often depending on the intensity of your release.

If you find that you are truly having a hard time letting go of your anger, you might also want to try meditating with a love stone (discussed a little later in this chapter) or one of the Master Healers.

True Forgiveness

Forgiveness does not erase the wounds that have already occurred; it's simply a limit on punishing those who have hurt us. It takes effort and courage to let go. However, it's imperative that we do it. Hanging onto grudges kills the soul.

The shadow parts of ourselves are whatever we have shoved aside to either ignore or deal with later. By knowing ourselves better and embracing those shadow parts, we bring love and light into all dimensions of our being. It is from this enlightened space within us that forgiveness can be found and expressed to others. If you are not there yet and have some forgiving to do, a spiritual cleanse is a good way to prepare yourself. By cleansing yourself consciously rather than disassociating from the shadow, you will free yourself from negative feelings.

The following crystals are good to support a spiritual cleanse:

- ♦ **Blue lace agate**—A member of the agate family, the soft baby-blue color of blue lace agate will connect you with your spiritual gifts and provide nonjudgmental support and loving, unconditional energy.

- ♦ **Moonstone**—The ultra yin energy of moonstone provides motherly, unconditional love and acceptance. It is best worn at the heart or solar plexus chakra but can be worn anywhere else on the body.

- ♦ **Rhodochrosite**—This golden pink crystal with white banding provides renewal and a way to turn self-criticism, anger, and loathing into compassion, love, and self-acceptance.

- ♦ **Rose quartz**—This master healer is a heart chakra opener. Taken at this level of healing, rose quartz provides self-support and asks you to move forward, leave the past, and step into your spiritual glory.

- ♦ **Rutilated quartz**—This quartz crystal with its fine "angel hairs" breaks up old energy patterns and promotes clarity on issues. Rutilated quartz helps move you past outdated thought patterns so you can embrace new values.

- ♦ **Selenite**—Selenite is like frozen white light and will offer support and a sense of purpose from your higher self. It is best used overnight at the crown chakra so you can receive higher guidance without interference from daily distractions.

- ♦ **Sugilite**—If you are holding onto old judgments, sugilite helps you become more sensitive to higher spiritual values and will support your alignment with them as you develop more conscious awareness.

To initiate an energy cleanse, it is best to spend some quiet time away from others and begin by holding one of the suggested crystals in your left hand at your heart chakra. Focus on what you need to release as deeply as necessary, whether it is pain or anger. Continue to hold the crystal until you feel the energy clearing. If you experience a dramatic or sudden release of pent-up emotional energy—what we call a catharsis—do not be too concerned. Breathe deeply and rapidly and it will pass.

You will know that you have cleared what is needed when you feel a sense of peace and are more relaxed. The best compliment is from others who know you well and can observe your positive changes. Sometimes it takes a while for these changes to settle in and be integrated within yourself.

The 12 Love Stones

For centuries, both women and men have used gemstones and crystals to attract their love partners. However, when our love needs are not met, our expectations about life are left in an uncomfortable spiritual position. We begin to doubt, rather than be in wonderment about the process of relating to another person. If you exchange crystals with a friend, you will be forever connected to each other. So, to make that lifelong connection with someone extra special, choose one of the love stones!

Crystals have magical properties that break through personal barriers and help to attune oneself to a higher love vibration. The easiest way to get crystal energy is to wear the crystal as a pendant. The effects of crystal healing at the emotional and psychological levels are subtle. As your personal vibration changes to a higher, more positive outlook, you will attract your soul mate to you. If you already have a partner, your love relationship will deepen.

Some key crystals are useful in healing relationship issues. If you wish to combine a few of the crystals for help with multiple issues, you can combine three or four crystals—but no more because your heart will be busy enough as it is:

- ◆ **Amethyst**—Known to heal the heart at the highest spiritual levels, amethyst purifies negative emotions and promotes feelings of flexibility, cooperation, and peace. Amethyst provides protection and balance during major personal transitions and reduces feelings of being victimized by others. It also supports all aspects of spiritual growth with peace and calm to fulfill one's mission on Earth; it helps you love again and again.

- ◆ **Aquamarine**—Strengthens one's resolve to feel that life has purpose. This crystal is very protective and helps you remain centered through complex issues. Aquamarine is excellent for dispelling fear.

- ◆ **Bloodstone**—Dispels discouragement and gives strength and endurance to withstand endless difficulties. This crystal reduces stress and anxiety. Bloodstone revitalizes and encourages unselfishness in relationships.

- ◆ **Carnelian**—Eliminates feelings of inadequacy and low self-worth. This stone is especially good for recovery after rejection by your lover. It transmutes sadness in your heart into the initiative to do something positive about the problem. This crystal encourages enthusiasm and is good for giving vibrancy to one's sexuality.

- ◆ **Emerald**—A very ancient love stone, it helps soften arrogance and promote cooperation. Emerald dispels negative thoughts and helps you hold onto what is practical. It cools an angry heart and promotes divine love and peace. This crystal is excellent for preserving love that is maturing into a long-term relationship.

- ◆ **Gold**—Symbolizes the purity of spirit and activates one's highest potential. Gold promotes inner beauty and purifies negative energy. It can lessen the traumatic experience of learning one's lessons. Gold helps eliminate feelings of inferiority, depression, anger, and the sense of overwhelming responsibilities.

- ◆ **Jade**—Known as "a stone of fidelity," jade (jadeite) is soothing for the emotions and helps keep the peace in community and family relations. Improves self-worth and self-sufficiency; promotes peace, harmony, and tranquility through emotional detachment; and is excellent for recovery after an unpleasant experience (surgery, divorce, funerals, etc.).

- ◆ **Hematite**—Gives emotional support to a new love and protects the heart from small "love wounds." The shiny surface reflects back negativity and helps reduce stress to the whole body. Hematite also helps ground love energy so it doesn't fly away when challenged.

♦ **Kunzite**—Opens the emotional heart to the highest level. Because this gemstone has a high lithium content (used in psychiatric medicine), emotional stress and loneliness can be alleviated. Just looking at kunzite provides a sense of peace and stimulates sensuality. It allows you to surrender rather than resist.

♦ **Malachite**—Clears the heart of past experiences by unblocking and absorbing any negative energies. Malachite allows you to stay tolerant, loyal, and practical. It gives courage and helps dispel fear in the relationship. Malachite helps you break free of self-denial and repeating old love patterns and promotes responsibility and fidelity in partnerships.

♦ **Rose quartz**—The number one love stone, rose quartz opens the heart for love and gives love to the wearer who might otherwise have trouble giving love to himself or others. Rose quartz shows you the power of "love conquers all." This crystal brings softness to hardened hearts, teaching you to trust. It dispels negative emotional states, such as despondency and possessiveness, and promotes harmonious relationships. Rose quartz is very calming and loving.

♦ **Ruby**—Another ancient love stone that is still very popular today, ruby encourages romantic love and promotes the ideal relationship. This crystal brings focus to the heart and releases disoriented and trapped love energy. It protects the heart from unnecessary love-suffering and promotes the attainment of love objectives: health, happiness, wealth, and spiritual knowledge.

If you need to attract a new partner, to move on with a new relationship, or to help heal the one you have, read the descriptions again and then select the crystal that best fits your situation.

Opening Up to Joy

Many crystals will modify your mood and uplift your feelings. Some crystals seem so serious with their energy, focusing your mind on troubles, cleansing, clearing, and healing. Make a special "stress day" pouch of crystals to alleviate your mood. Pack a pouch with opal, rose quartz, moonstone, and citrine. Add a wrapped gummy bear candy to absorb the lovely crystal energies and eat it later when you need an additional perk!

Take a break once in a while and just feel really good and happy. Here are some more crystals to perk you up:

♦ **Clear quartz**—A clear quartz crystal with a rainbow is also a mood-lightener. The rainbow neutralizes and dissolves grief and other sadness and restores feelings of joy.

♦ **Herkimer diamond**—Glittery and seems to dance in the light, it brightens and enlivens your aura by clearing out stale energy. Even the smallest ones rolling around in your hand provide a sense of fun and adventure. It's like taking a train ride through Disneyland. You'll never want to get off!

♦ **Opal**—This is delightful for sour-mood interventions and provides a great display of colors. The colors in an opal brighten the colors in your aura.

With the play of light or luminescence, any crystal will generally light up your heart and open your third eye to the special pleasures of life. Open up your heart chakra and your eyes and look around at the gift of living at this very moment.

Lucky You!

There are so many crystals for luck, but in this part of the book, let's focus on wishing. You've heard songs about "wishing upon a star," and you can wish with crystals, too. It's actually a form of programming, but if you use the right crystal, your wish might come true. How, you ask? The crystal amplifies the thought energy and lines up the universal energy for wish fulfillment.

Which crystal is best to use for wishing? A double-terminated clear quartz crystal provides one end for giving and one end for receiving energy. After you have programmed your crystal for positive manifestation, hold it at the center of your heart chakra. Visualize what it is that you're wishing for. See the request going out as white light from your heart center through the tip of the crystal with your request. If the wish is your heart's highest purpose, you should see some results. How soon depends on how long it takes the universe to line up the energies.

Co-creating with the universe is tricky business, so be very specific about what you ask for. Your intention will be aligned with the universal laws of attraction. Here are some crystals that can be particularly useful in this regard:

♦ Rainbow moonstone has also been used for wishing. The colorful display looks similar to the energy glow from the aura around the human body. This energy charges your wishful intention. Place the crystal at your third eye and project the image of what you wish into the crystal. See yourself actually getting your wish fulfilled and then wear the crystal for 7 to 21 days to affect the change.

♦ Take any seven small crystals of the same kind, preferably Herkimer diamonds or another double-terminated crystal. Prepare each one with a prosperity wish programmed into each crystal. Wear these seven wish crystals in a pouch and hold them from time to time to reinforce the energy of the wish.

♦ A clear quartz crystal with a rainbow configuration, is helpful to manifest wishes. First, prepare your crystal by programming it with your wish. Then wear the rainbow crystal so your wish goes into your aura and attracts the wish to you. This technique of programming a rainbow crystal can also be used to attract a soul mate.

Granting a wish for someone else is easy to set up. Write the wish on a piece of paper and place it inside a special wish box with a lid. Place the seven wish crystals on top of the wish sheet in the box, close the lid, and leave it in place without disturbing it for three days. On the third day, remove the paper and burn it, sending the message and the accumulated energy into the universe for manifestation.

Crystals for Emotional Healing

It seems as though more and more people are suffering from deep emotional wounds these days. The prescriptions for antidepressants are skyrocketing, and we all have a friend or two who's down in the dumps. That's where crystals can really help, by gently releasing energy so it flows more freely in your subtle body. Crystals can help convert negative energy into positive vibrations, but they are not a substitute for treating more serious mental health issues. For severe depression or anxiety, seek professional medical advice. Remember that people will experience crystals differently. If one crystal doesn't work for you, go to another type.

The next time you're feeling blue, bring out some of these big guns:

♦ **Amazonite**—Soothes; is good for those undergoing emotional processes; and pacifies worries, fear, and aggravations. It's excellent for children, neurological problems, and nerves.

♦ **Amber**—Calms nerves, enlivens the body, and rekindles energy.

♦ **Amethyst**—Releases negative-thought programming, clears emotional blockages, moves you into cooperation with other supportive forces, allows you to use sensibility with your emotions, and moves you into a more conscious state to see the cause and effect of your emotional responses.

♦ **Apache tear**—Good for sorrow, grief, and forgiveness, it removes self-limitations.

♦ **Aquamarine**—Quiets fears, phobias, and anxiety; releases expectation; shields, stabilizes, and eases discomforts and hiccups caused by fear.

♦ **Aventurine**—Purifies the emotional body and tranquilizes nerves.

♦ **Bloodstone**—Grounds the emotional heart, alleviates distress and anxiety.

♦ **Blue lace agate**—Alleviates spiritual tension and emotional intensity.

♦ **Botswana agate**—Soothes repressed emotions and moves you beyond limits; it's excellent for smokers whose nerves are on edge.

♦ **Calcite (all colors)**—Clears chakras by color. Calcite is a gentle cleanser of emotional upsets, helps release emotional restrictions.

♦ **Carnelian**—Works with emotional states such as envy, fear, rage, and sorrow. Moves negative states into states of love; dispels apathy and encourages trust by connecting the lower chakras (base, sacral, and solar plexus) to the heart.

♦ **Chrysocolla**—Promotes emotional strength, stabilizes emotions, balances expression and communication, and releases distress and guilt.

♦ **Chrysoprase**—Used to alleviate alcoholism and ease feelings of depression. It allows you to take one day at a time and build on successes through small transformations.

♦ **Citrine**—Calms fears, promotes happiness, and frees energy for spontaneous expression of positive energies.

- **Clear quartz**—Unblocks and transmutes negative energy. Dispels negative dispositions.

- **Emerald**—An emotional heart soother, this crystal provides peace at the heart level, especially about matters that trigger anxiety.

- **Fluorite**—All colors of fluorite calm the emotional body. Purple fluorite helps to break up emotional blockages.

- **Kunzite**—With its high lithium content, it settles emotions quickly. Promotes feelings of well-being and peace.

- **Lapis lazuli**—Provides objective insight and mental clarity. Unblocks and releases emotions from the heart for self-acceptance. Reconnects the wounded parts to the whole.

- **Malachite**—Provides a strong release of negative emotions; best used in conjunction with rose quartz to bring peace after emotional release.

- **Moonstone**—Reduces emotional tension, provides missing emotional nurturing, and helps bring a sense of peace to the emotions.

- **Moss agate**—Soothes self-esteem, promotes positive traits and emotional strength; good for women's healing and nurturing.

- **Obsidian**—Powerfully releases negative emotions, overpowers old energy patterns by piercing any resistance, transmutes energy blockages into white light.

- **Opal**—Brightens negative attitudes and dispels dark moods. Helps to discern the truth and brings hope and happiness to the wearer.

- **Peridot**—Targets jealousy and releases self-centeredness. Restores inner balance that is overpowered by self-destruction.

- **Rhodochrosite**—A soothing emotional balancer used after a period of emotional stress. Works well to dissolve and transmute feelings of guilt.

- **Rose quartz**—Soothes and purifies all emotions. Provides loving energy and comfort to those with raw emotional states.

- **Rutilated quartz**—Pulls apart complex emotional issues and unblocks chakras to allow negative energies to dissolve.

◆ **Selenite**—Allows you to reach beyond your emotional state to higher psychospiritual centers such as altruism, compassion, and love.

◆ **Smoky quartz**—Excellent for stubborn people who refuse to let go of negative emotions. A powerful healer that dissolves and transmutes energy.

◆ **Sodalite**—Calms emotions and numbs mental chatter.

◆ **Tiger eye (yellow)**—Provides mental and emotional discipline for people who are unable to appreciate self-responsibility.

◆ **Tourmaline**—Green tourmaline keeps energy circuits open and energy flowing. Pink tourmaline activates and soothes the heart and prevents victimization.

◆ **Turquoise**—Provides emotional detachment and focus on self-accomplishment without entanglement with others.

Relationships

Relationships may seem tricky to master, especially as there aren't really manuals or guides written specifically for the people involved in the relationship. So, you may feel like you are on your own except remember that you do have your pals with you—crystals! They are a life saver when it comes to holding energy for relationships. They can keep you grounded and aware, dissolve anger, open your heart, sort out your thinking, and still give you lots of energy to have some fun! Let's have a closer look at the chief crystals for love-seekers:

◆ **Beginning a new relationship.** So, you are high on love (it's actually the dopamine being released from your brain). You can't focus on anything and you are waiting for the next text message. A grounding crystal can be helpful because you need to keep your feet on the ground. Try a bracelet of tiger eye, hematite, or malachite. If you need more self-confidence, wear carnelian. This is a great time to have a friendship ring before the diamond ring!

◆ **Challenges and struggles.** This is another stage in the relationship journey when the testing occurs. You check to see if the other is made of enough tough stuff to endure a longer lasting relationship. Keep the lines of communication open. Use crystals such as turquoise or smoky quartz to cool off your temperament and to open self-expression rather than buttoning-up your mouth. Use rose quartz liberally to keep the heart open for when you want to kiss and make up.

♦ **Partnering together.** This stage is finally where you each want to be. You worked together to arrive at a mutually agreeable place and have made commitments to each other to maintain the relationship. Add labradorite for perseverance of the spiritual journey, citrine for continued happiness, and pink tourmaline to keep the electricity of the relationship alive. Have you thought of doing a crystal healing on each other?

♦ **Mature relationships.** Did you forget something? Yes, sustaining your relationship is good but have you been helping yourselves grow spiritually, too? Add in lapis lazuli, larimar, blue lace agate, blue fluorite, and kunzite. Use clear quartz crystal balls around the room to help radiate your love and nurturing for each other. Use an aromatherapy diffuser to create a soft, loving vibration in the room.

♦ **Ending relationships.** Change happens, feelings get hurt, and then the crystals come out to ease the pain. Sometimes, a good grounding crystal like hematite works well. Zoisite helps you see where things went wrong and helps patch up those holes in your heart. A good protective crystal is rhodochrosite. It's pink and black and sort of looks like a hurt heart. However, its magic is that it will keep your heart open for more loving moments while stopping yourself from going crazy grasping for what must be released. When it's time to let go and move on, it's time to hit the "rhod."

CARVED IN STONE . . . .

Emerald: I activate your heart to follow love and compassion to its fullest. I provide self-acceptance. I ask you to surrender to divine love and feel the abundance of your true spirit.

CHAPTER 13

Crystals for Spiritual Healing

You've no doubt heard that crystals are great boosters in the search for spiritual wholeness. To gain insight, you must let go of any expectations and simply trust that you will encounter exactly what is needed for your own healing and growth at this time.

Think of crystals as a bridge to higher consciousness. They help you transcend the ordinary and enter a greater awareness about yourself. That awareness will take you to a higher level of consciousness where it is possible to be in direct contact with the sacred realms.

Learn How to...

♦ Connect and communicate with your crystal spirit.

♦ Access the crystal deva and the angelic realms.

♦ Use crystals for spiritual expansion.

♦ Talk with angels through crystals and receive special messages.

Deepening Your Spirituality

The microscopic details of a crystal are said to contain the same organization as the rest of the universe. Imagine being aligned with the same vibration as the rest of the universe. Suddenly, you realize that every cell in your body is in sync with all that is!

Spiritual development encourages manifestation, inner peace, connectedness to the awesome beauty around us, and an awakening of consciousness. You can no longer slumber through life. You are alive and pulsating with energy. You can use this awakened energy and knowledge for healing, for communicating with other realms, and for learning about yourself. The question is, how do we do all this?

To open a channel of communication within yourself, you must tune in to your energy and be open to working with the energy of the crystal. Tuning in to spiritual energy is similar to what happens when someone whispers. You have to become more alert and focused so you can hear. As our level of consciousness expands outward—like the universe—we are ready to take in more information about ourselves. Crystals help create an energy bridge that brings us into alignment with that universal vibration.

Spiritual energy can hold various vibrational levels. Some crystals are already tuned to help you access certain levels, such as when you want to access past lives or angelic realms. Some energies are so refined, though, that we are not even aware they exist! When we hold a clear crystal in our hands, it's as if we are holding a way to make that sacred connection within ourselves.

Many specialized crystals help support the development of our spiritual connection. These types of crystals tend to have a greater ability to hold lighter energy vibrations. When there is more light, there is more vibrational essence for bridging your consciousness to other realms.

Crystals used as "light tools," for spiritual attainment are often highly evolved. For a deep journey, meditate or sleep with a selected gemstone taped to your third eye or crown chakra at night. They will provide you with a pathway of consciousness. What you bring back from your journey is worth writing in your crystal journal.

Connecting with Crystal Spirits

The concept that there is spirit in all things is a belief shared by many faiths across the world. Among Native Americans, Inuit, First Nations, and other Indigenous Peoples there is a regard for the spirit in water, trees, rocks, animals—in all things. The realm or kingdom of these living entities is called a deva. Those divine spirits and beings form a collective of voices or a consciousness that is accessed through channeling with a spirit crystal. A spirit crystal is like a house that opens the door to channel the deva, the collective consciousness. Not all crystals are attuned at a high enough frequency to channel the deva realm.

I used one of my Himalayan clear quartz spirit crystals to contact and channel the deva. I held the spirit crystal in meditation and when I asked, "What is your purpose?" the deva's response was as follows:

> I am all of that which matters to you on this plane. I open the centers from the heart to the throat chakras so you can speak the beauty from your heart. I provide a light blue colored ray to your third eye to open your awareness to higher planes and to infuse this color into your aura for protecting the vibrational spectrum.

You might be offered a devic name by the spirit crystal, which is the name of the group consciousness coming through that special spirit crystal. That is very good news because now you are the proud owner of a spirit crystal. You might hear the name pronounced inside your head, or it might come spontaneously from your mouth. Use the name to summon the deva (the collective voice) by holding the spirit crystal calling the devic name three times before using the crystal. One of my spirit crystals has a protrusion that looks like a small whale-like fin. It gave me its deva name, Orca. This spirit crystal provides a channel to communicate information about the bodies of water on the earth and about water in the body.

Asking an Angel for Advice

Making contact with an angelic presence can be a beautiful and uplifting experience. When you have spiritual validation from a source outside of yourself, your faith—if it was shaken—can be restored. Your heart is wide open to give and receive love and compassion.

Many world faiths believe in a guardian angel, a protector who is assigned to you at birth. If you have been aware of the presence of an angel, consider yourself fortunate because the channel to the angelic realm must have been opened at that time. Working with crystals can help you keep the channel to that realm open.

Here are a few crystals that help access the angelic realms:

- ♦ **Angelite**—This light blue crystal holds angelic energy and provides a shield of light around the wearer. It can establish a telepathic portal to the angelic realm.

- ♦ **Celestite**—Light blue and transparent, it opens clear communications with the angelic realms to provide guidance, especially when you dream.

- ♦ **Aura quartz**—A lovely crystal that compels angelic forces to attend when called. The surface gleams like the light from the angelic realms and, like a moth is attracted to light, the angels will come where there is angelic light. Be sure to get genuine aura crystals.

- ♦ **Clear quartz**—Use a channeler crystal—the clear quartz configuration with the seven-sided face—to access the secret angelic realms

- ♦ **Selenite**—A crystal that increases intuition and psychic awareness of the mystery realms. A certain formation of it is called *fishtail* but looks more like a pair of angel's wings. When meditating with selenite, ask to be given access to the angelic realms.

When you are looking for additional crystals to help you gain access to the angelic realms, ask the angels that walk with you to guide you to specific crystals. Many crystals that facilitate opening of the third eye and crown chakras also facilitate telepathy and clairvoyance—both skills that are helpful in communicating with angels.

To make a "phone call" to the angelic realm during meditation, use a cleansed and fully charged clear quartz channeling crystal. Program the crystal with this affirmation: I, [your name], am open and clear to receive communication from the higher angelic realms. I am surrounded by light and love.

Get grounded by visualizing roots growing from under your feet into the ground to anchor your energies. If you need to move around during the meditation, move slowly and gently so as not to shock the connection to the more subtle angelic energy realm. Then follow these steps:

1. Hold the crystal at your heart chakra and place your right thumb on the face of the channeling crystal. Relax your mind and your body. Regulate your breath so it's deep and evenly paced. Visualize white light coming in and out of the crystal into your heart chakra.

2. Now visualize white light coming in and out of your third eye and crown chakras. This helps open the higher centers for communication.

3. You might feel some tingling at the top of your head and maybe some warmth at the heart. That's okay because it signals that your heart and crown chakras are activated and that you are ready and open for communication.

To capture the attention of a specific angel, try singing very sweetly. Let's say you wanted to call Gabriel, the Messenger Angel who is often depicted with a trumpet. Using your voice very lightly, sing sweetly calling the name Gabriel in long tones, "Gaaaaa-briiiii-ellll…."

Call several times and then stop and listen for a response. Then meditate, leaving your mind open to see images or hear messages. Do not be afraid to ask for your angel to provide you with something, such as comfort and advice or healing. I've heard it said that if you ask three times, you cannot be refused.

If you receive the name of an angel from the other realms, the two of you are bound together, and you can call on this angel again when needed!

Spiritual Healing

All crystals can provide an increase in awareness, healing, meditative peace, the release of energy blockages, and so on. By selecting crystals for spiritual healing you can find it easier to move through life's obstacles. The right crystal can ease your distress and help you move past the sticky places. When others need your help, distance healing using crystals can also provide some comfort.

Crystals for Distance Healing

Two methods of working with crystals are simple and effective for distance healing. One is passive using the photo of the individual who needs on-going healing; the other method works actively with the person.

Place a photo of the person who has consented to distance healing on a shelf or table where the picture can remain for up to three days or longer. If there are other people in the photo, take a piece of paper and cover their images. This will help you focus better on the person receiving healing energy. Distance healing should be attempted only when you have been given permission to do so. If distance healing is against the will of the other person, regardless of your best intentions, you'll run up against a closed energy field.

Select up to three crystals, depending on the illness, the body part, or the chakra that needs healing. Put these crystals aside. You'll also need six to eight small cleansed clear quartz or amethyst crystals (master healing crystals) to arrange in a circle around the photo. Hold all the crystals in your hands and program them with the following affirmation. "These crystals are now activated at highest intent to provide distance healing for [name of the person]."

If you want to include the specific healing issue, you can either write it on a piece of paper and place it under the photo or simply state it as part of the affirmation. Hold the crystals and meditate, thinking of the person and her healing needs.

Smudge the area and the photo, then place the clear quartz or amethyst crystals in a small circle around the photo with the tips pointing in toward the picture. (If you are using tumbled crystals, just arrange them in a circle.) You can tape the crystals onto the photo directly or to the glass in the photo frame.

Leave the crystals in place for a few days and check in with the person to see how the distance healing is working for her. Once a day, you might like to sweep your crystals with some incense or smudge to clear any accumulated negativity. At the end of the healing period, cleanse and recharge all your crystals.

Healing Is in the Air

For the second method of distance healing, you will coordinate a time to send healing to the person. The other person will need to remain quiet or sit in meditation for at least 10 minutes while you send the crystal healing energy.

Use a cleansed and fully charged clear quartz or amethyst transmitter crystal at least 2 inches long, programmed with the same affirmation outlined in the previous method. At the appointed time, ground yourself and hold the crystal in both hands with the tip pointing up. Visualize the "target" person inside the crystal. See that person receiving healing. While visualizing, direct your breath into and out of the crystal. This will help build up the energy charge in the crystal and to direct your healing intent.

Continue to focus and use circular breathing into and out from the crystal for about 10 minutes. It can seem like a long time, but it's worth it to send the highest form of vibration to a loved one.

Don't forget to write in your journal what time your healing started and ended and note any thoughts, messages, or images you might have received while sending distance healing. Check in with the other person to see how she is feeling. You might find some interesting similarities of observations!

Crystals for Spiritual Expansion

A crystal can provide healing at physical, emotional, psychological, and spiritual levels. Like veils removed from your mind, crystals clear your consciousness so you can see truth and reality more clearly. They allow you to communicate better, whether it is through mental telepathy, by speaking passionately about a topic, or by producing something creative like music or a drawing. They also provide deeper meditation where you will be less distracted and will find yourself immersed more deeply in the experience of emptiness.

In selecting a crystal for spiritual expansion, try to find one that is excellent quality; in other words, look for a crystal that has good color and is attractive in its shape and size. Keep in mind that sometimes a uniquely shaped crystal can provide direct access to information on past lives, future events, and metaphysics. These oddly shaped gemstones hold a lot of power!

In general, the following crystals for spiritual expansion are used for meditation while holding them in your hand, wearing them, using them for the suggested chakra, or including them in crystal layouts. Give yourself lots of time to work just with one crystal, and remember to record your experiences in your crystal journal.

- ♦ **Amethyst**—A major crystal that is used as a crown chakra opener. Amethyst facilitates expansion of the third eye and expands psychic abilities by connecting intuitive receptors to the crown chakra, which provides a link to higher states of consciousness. Use amethyst on any chakras to unblock and remove limitations to spiritual growth and awareness.

- ♦ **Apophyllite**—This crystal is an awesome opener of the third eye and crown chakras. Apophyllite facilitates astral travel and initiates a person to new levels of intuition. This crystal acts as a bridge to cross-time dimensions. Astral travel (also called an out-of-body experience) is an event marked by your subconsciousness leaving the physical plane and traveling to a nonphysical astral realm where you can visit loved ones who have passed on, talk with spiritual teachers, and enjoy countless other freedoms.

- ♦ **Azurite**—Provides an opening to a deeper level of consciousness and cleanses and prepares the mind to work at a higher spiritual level and to find deeper understanding and acceptance. It works with the throat chakra to purify the intent behind one's spiritual activities.

- ♦ **Azurite/malachite**—This crystal is a blend of two types that often grow together; they provide an integrated energy with a powerful sense of getting to core matters by probing and penetrating past. The truth is exposed by unlocking the past. Use this crystal at your third eye or throat chakras for a more intense experience by moving past your intellect and opening you to embrace trust and intuition.

- ♦ **Bloodstone**—This crystal provides grounding for going deeply into spirituality and mystical matters without getting lost. Bloodstone is a great anchor or safety net and can be used with other crystals to preserve your subtle energies. Hold this crystal in your hand or place it at your solar plexus chakra.

- ♦ **Blue lace agate**—This crystal helps you to speak your truth, to channel your higher thoughts, and to express your spirituality. It is very calming during spiritual expansion. Wear it as a necklace or place it at your throat or third eye chakras.

- **Calcite**—Pink or white calcite opens the higher chakras where a direct channel is needed for communicating with your highest self. Use it in your hand during meditation or place it at your throat, third eye, or crown chakra.

- **Carnelian**—Restores trust to spiritually jaded people and helps keep the focus on a higher level rather than at the physical or emotional levels. Wear this crystal at your heart chakra or hold it in your hand during meditation.

- **Clear quartz record keeper**—The little triangular bumps on the face of the record keeper crystal may contain past life information for yourself or others. When in meditation, rub the triangles slowly to release their energy. Inhale deeply to bring the energy into your conscious awareness.

- **Celestite**—Used at the throat, third eye, and crown chakras, it provides a pathway for consciousness to enter the higher realms.

- **Charoite**—This ray of purple light dispels fear of the unknown and connects the third eye to the mental plane to help loosen attachment.

- **Citrine**—Its golden rays provide a complex energy structure that energizes the crown and sacral chakras and protects the aura. Use it at your heart chakra or hold it in your hand during meditation.

- **Diamond**—Provides spiritual confidence and activates the crown chakra. The brilliance of light from a diamond dispels brain fog and gives clarity to meditation.

- **Dioptase**—This brilliant green crystal provides attunement for the third eye. It can be a wake-up call for those still so attached to worldly problems that entering into higher states of consciousness is impossible.

- **Emerald**—Balances the heart and crown chakras. It provides peace and calms the emotional heart for higher spiritual attunement.

- **Golden topaz**—This builder of faith is also a crown chakra activator and helps to recharge it with golden light. It opens and reconditions the third eye to see at a higher level.

- **Iolite**—Provides an ability to open the third eye for clarity of visions and other intuitive work. It protects the holder when entering higher states of consciousness and generates feelings of unconditional love.

- ◆ **Kyanite**—Initiates the movement of energy in the upper chakras to more subtle levels of awareness; it helps you see how spiritual and physical bodies reflect each other's needs for healing.

- ◆ **Labradorite**—This crystal operates on and unifies the upper chakras (heart, throat, third eye, and crown). It helps with detachment from situations so clarity of spiritual purpose can be achieved.

- ◆ **Lepidolite**—An excellent crystal to reach past lives, it improves intuition and helps with the perseverance of one's spiritual journey.

- ◆ **Moldavite**—A major transforming crystal and tool of consciousness. Wearing even a small piece will augment your abilities for interdimensional communication. It provides a channel for other light beings to contact you.

- ◆ **Purple fluorite**—This crystal holds intense white light and activates the third eye and crown chakras. It clears out what is not needed for your highest good and provides clarity and understanding.

When you select your crystals for spiritual expansion, look for lighter or transparent crystals with good structural shape because these relate most often to the higher chakras. You can always use your pendulum to check out the use of crystals or contact the deva of the crystal for more information.

Pineal Activation

The pineal gland is very small and is located inside the center of your brain, above and behind the pituitary gland. It must be very important for this gland to be surrounded by a mass of soft tissues and a hard skull casing. So why is there all this security? This tiny gland is a connector to higher consciousness. The pineal gland is very sensitive to light, to sound vibrations, and to the subtle vibrations from crystals. The pineal gland is also sensitive to electromagnetic energy and to spiritual vibrations sensed through the third eye.

The pineal gland is like a dimensional doorway to higher states of consciousness and to self-actualization. When the pineal gland is activated, there is increased support for expanding perception and developing psychic abilities such as clairvoyance, seeing auras, and communicating in angelic realms. You can see why the pineal is important for spiritual healing work.

The pineal gland is also responsible for regulating the sleep cycle through the release of melatonin. Melatonin is a hormone that helps us sleep and adapts our wake-sleep (circadian) cycle to seasonal and time changes. Exposure to light helps determine the release of melatonin.

All-night gamers and text kings or queens, pay attention! Do you remember the warnings to reduce your cell phone use at night? The light of a cell phone, called *blue light*, actually mimics full-spectrum sunlight. The light is received through the eyes and a signal through the optic nerves is sent to the pineal gland where it interprets what's going on out there. If there is light, we stay awake and alert.

The Flow of Fluoride

It is important to keep a pure body for optimal activation of the pineal gland. Sometimes, the pineal gland is weakened by excess toxins in the body, including fluoride. Fluoride is not the same as the healing crystal named fluorite. Fluoride is the ionic form of fluorine and is used in a stable form for industrial purposes. When the pineal gland encounters too much fluoride, it calcifies as brain sand, known as *corpora arenacea* (mineral deposits of calcium and magnesium).

Municipal water systems often add fluoride to reduce tooth decay. If you want your pineal gland to benefit right away, you can limit your exposure to fluoride in water and toothpaste and keep your pineal active.

Let's go through some ways to activate your pineal gland:

- ♦ Harmonic resonance is helpful. Search YouTube for some sounds at 936 hertz (Hz) to activate the pineal gland. I have a special pineal-activation tuning fork that I activate by tapping the fork against a crystal, and then hold it near my head for about 30 seconds.

- ♦ Tapping the forehead gently with your middle finger is a simple way to send a vibration to the pineal gland. Avoid tapping your third eye.

♦ Singing to your pineal gland is also an activator. Taoist chi master, Mantak Chia, provides instructions for activating the pineal gland through breathing exercises and sound. (See Appendix B for more details.)

♦ Crystals that activate the pineal gland include aura quartz, apophyllite, Herkimer diamond, fluorite, and selenite.

Try taping a small ½-inch piece of one of the pineal-activating crystals listed above on your third eye at night. Do this every night for a few weeks and see if you sleep better. You might also increase your telepathic abilities!

CARVED IN STONE . . . .

Celestite: I give you clarity of communications from your heart, from your mind, and from the divine source. I increase your awareness of higher realms. I provide optimism and energize your spiritual path.

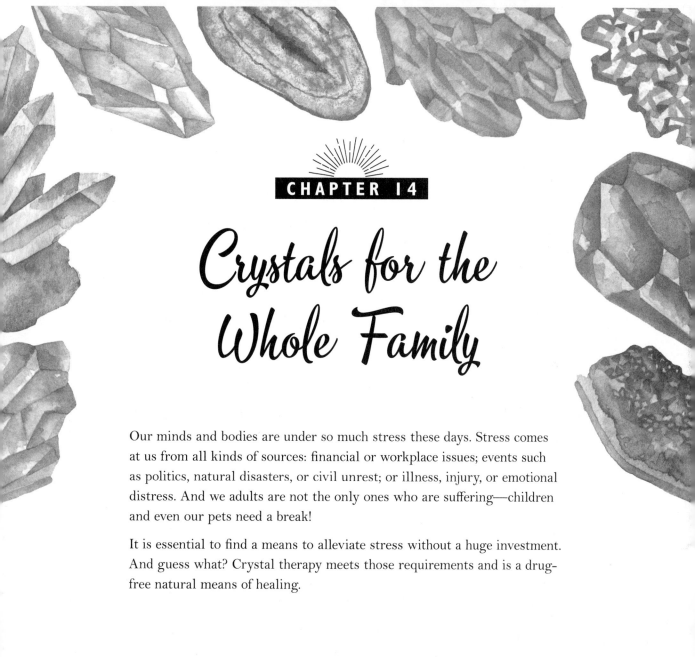

CHAPTER 14

Crystals for the Whole Family

Our minds and bodies are under so much stress these days. Stress comes at us from all kinds of sources: financial or workplace issues; events such as politics, natural disasters, or civil unrest; or illness, injury, or emotional distress. And we adults are not the only ones who are suffering—children and even our pets need a break!

It is essential to find a means to alleviate stress without a huge investment. And guess what? Crystal therapy meets those requirements and is a drug-free natural means of healing.

Learn How to ...

♦ Increase self-growth and further development with crystals for men and women.

♦ Help teenagers improve their study habits and reduce their stresses.

♦ Respond to the spiritual needs of children with crystals.

♦ Use crystals for healing pets and animals.

Even Tough Guys Need Healing

Crystals and gemstones have often been worn by men as jewelry or decorating formal suits to signify their official or regal status in society. If you are a man in an urban setting, you might feel awkward about wearing crystals dangling down in front of your chest in public. If you are not inclined to look like an "urban shaman," here are some suggestions:

♦ Wear your healing crystals in a medicine pouch (a pouch on a string) tucked inside your shirt. Try to select crystals that are relatively flat, so your pouch will go unnoticed. Place your crystals into your breast pocket to help heal your heart, either physically or emotionally.

♦ For the office or workplace, leave your stones out as decorative objects. If anyone asks, you can say you are a mineral collector, or you are buying stones for your kids as part of their geology class!

♦ Keep your crystals loose inside your front pants pockets, and hold them in your hands several times during the day.

♦ At night, leave the crystals next to your bed or under your pillow while you sleep. Remember to cleanse and recharge your crystals at least once a month.

♦ Go for a scheduled crystal healing. Let the crystal energy therapist place crystals on you to clear and balance your energy during a session.

The following crystals and gemstones are useful in healing men's issues. Some of these issues address reducing stress, improving health, increasing power, strengthening self-esteem, and improving communication skills. Of course, these crystals can be used by anyone with those issues:

◆ **Amethyst**—Also called the "royal stone," amethyst is not only a master healer but its most noted healing quality is its ability to purify and transmute all forms of negativity. Get a large amethyst crystal cluster for your home or office to protect yourself from hostile energies around you. Consider a large, well-set amethyst gemstone ring to enhance your personal magnetism and provide mental clarity. Amethyst is also helpful to connect to one's spirituality for guidance.

◆ **Jade**—Known as a "crystal of tranquility" and the "sport stone," jade promotes agility and swiftness. Many men from the Far East know the benefits of wearing jade. It soothes emotions and provides emotional detachment and restoration after various traumas such as minor surgery, divorce, funerals, or job loss. Some say jade is for good luck. Jade is easily obtained and can be worn as a pendant, bracelet, or ring.

◆ **Labradorite**—This surprisingly powerful stone lends terrific force to self-empowerment, brilliance in thoughts and actions, and transformation. It's a great leadership stone that creates change around you and gives you strength for enduring partnerships. It can break up old worn-out patterns and support your creativity to see situations with new logic and outlook.

◆ **Lapis lazuli**—The "stone of the pharaohs," lapis lazuli is well known as a favorite stone used in the courts of ancient Egyptian kings. This deep blue stone stimulates mental strength and intellectual precision. Lapis is a consciousness elevator, raising one's awareness to new heights and to greater expansion; it intensifies psychic power. It brings feelings of success, connectedness, and protection.

◆ **Malachite**—A "man's stone," its deep forest green is symbolic of the deep healing and cleansing this stone provides. It aids in breaking old patterns, whether emotional (stuck patterns of behavior) or physical (tumors, swollen joints, muscular, and so on). Malachite promotes successful business relationships and the increase of wealth by removing obstacles to one's growth. The most important aspect of this crystal's healing ability, however, is preventive health of the physical heart and liver. If you are attracted to this crystal, chances are you have a family history of heart-related problems and probably need a heart check-up.

♦ **Moonstone**—The "feminine balancing crystal," moonstone provides depth of perception, feelings, discernment, creativity, intuition, and self-expression. This crystal is used to soften and balance dominant male attributes. Other properties of moonstone include increased awareness and focus, rejuvenation of the skin and hair, and protection for travelers by letting them see possibilities ahead.

♦ **Rose quartz**—The "love stone" is a master healer that specializes in transmuting emotional negativity at all levels. It enhances one's ability to give and receive love by opening the heart chakra and stimulating flexibility in communications. It mellows out a reluctant heart, provides peace in relationships through harmony, and supports mental tranquility. It can heal a broken heart.

♦ **Smoky quartz**—The "emotional balancing crystal" is another master healer and is a very specialized crystal for negative emotional energy. This crystal is excellent for mood swings, aggressive actions, ill tempers, and generally nasty thoughts. This stone is helpful to ease burnout, fear of failure, reluctance to take risks, as well as to lessen tendencies to overeat, smoke, or drink due to stress. It helps you accept responsibility for yourself and broadens your capacity for effective communication.

If you have reservations while wearing (or using) gemstones, set them aside, just for a few weeks or so and see what happens. I'm willing to bet you'll be singing a different tune in four weeks' time! Your system will be asking for them. Next time, try a different selection of crystals for your specific needs and see if you get different results.

Crystals for Women's Health

Crystals can be used to assist women of all ages at all stages of healing. The awakening of the self to a spiritual journey is not an easy task. It can demand time and resources to achieve self-development and growth. Some choose not to undertake the risks and perils of peeling off our defenses to become fully human and to experience the full wealth of life.

Crystals provide protection and give sanctuary for the deep healing a woman does within herself. The inner journey becomes sacred to those who can withstand the intensity of full consciousness.

The real healing comes from the heart level, so wear your crystals as a pendant at the heart chakra or as a necklace surrounding the heart chakra.

The following crystals and gemstones are useful in healing women and in addressing women's issues:

♦ **Amber**—A "gentle stone," it is very soothing and calming to the nerves. It can uplift a negative disposition and encourage you to take life less seriously. It promotes fidelity in relationships. Amber guides the emotions toward a clearer mental outlook and encourages greater responsibility for one's choices in life. It is also excellent during post-operative care.

♦ **Amethyst**—A master healer, it purifies and transmutes negativity and provides protection and balance during transition periods. It reduces the feeling of being victimized, giving you a spiritual perspective on life's circumstances. A lavender-pink colored amethyst will open and lighten up a betrayed heart, healing the sense of lost life and innocence. A blue-red colored amethyst promotes a deep spiritual connection between one's self and life's challenges giving patience and calmness despite overwhelming odds. A chevron amethyst (banded white and purple) helps peel away old karmic patterns to promote self-love and the ability to get along with others, especially with one's soul mate or family members.

♦ **Apache tear (obsidian)**—Known as the "grief stone," it allows tears to be shed, stimulating emotional spontaneity and the release of barriers that prevent you from experiencing deep sorrow. This stone is excellent for transmuting one's own negativity in stressful situations. An Apache tear is a dark black obsidian that when held up to the light appears transparent. However, it has been noted that the grief one feels goes into the stone and can turn it opaque.

♦ **Jade**—The "crystal of tranquility" soothes emotions and helps keep the peace in community relations. It provides a sense of self-worth and the capability to deal with any situation. It promotes harmony, balance, and tranquility through emotional detachment. Like amber, jade is excellent for recovery after an unpleasant experience (minor surgery, divorce, funerals, job loss, and so on). Jade can change color depending on the health of the person.

♦ **Jasper**—Known as the "nurturing stone," it makes it easier to use one's own power and to know that it cannot be taken away. It calms aggressive energy and facilitates safety and protection during recovery from stress, operations, and other life traumas and change. Red jasper provides lively fresh energy and reduces feelings of being victimized. Yellow jasper balances hormones and protects the wearer during travel. Green jasper restores energy and focus when recovering from burnout.

♦ **Red coral**—Known as a "woman's stone," it calms emotions and dispels feelings of despair and despondency. It encourages passionate energy and stimulates and strengthens female reproductive organs through tissue regeneration. This stone relates well to the spleen meridian for blood circulation and purification of the kidneys and bladder. Red coral is considered to be the blood of Mother Earth by Native Americans and is considered particularly precious by Tibetan women for menstruation, fertility, and blood disorders.

♦ **Rose quartz**—The "love stone" is a master healer and transmutes emotional negativity at all levels. It enhances healing by balancing energy and hormonal fluctuations. Rose quartz embodies the expression *"love conquers all."* It is excellent for calming the heart and solar plexus chakras after emotional upheaval, chaos, trauma, or crisis. Rose quartz allows love to come to wearers who have trouble finding love within themselves or to give to others. This is also a great friendship stone to give to someone.

♦ **Smoky quartz**—Another master healer, the "emotional balancing crystal" clears and transmutes negative emotions. If you need a crystal to ease the monthly physical and emotional tension that accompanies PMS, smoky quartz is it—it also works well to quell general crankiness and stress! This crystal does an excellent job of stabilizing mood swings and grounding all kinds of negative energy. Smoky quartz reduces the fear of failure, unblocks self-limitations, and lets you risk trying some new experiences.

♦ **Sodalite**—The "stone of peace" helps alleviate insomnia caused by overactive mental chatter. It provides mental focus, and maintains logical reasoning when faced with emotional upsets. Sodalite promotes trust and enhances companionship and common goals with others. It is excellent for women who need to mentally relax.

Health, harmony, and hormones all in balance … you can't argue with that! Just be sure to use your chosen crystals with consistency and intention for best results.

Health and Harmony for Teens

Teens might need some healing tools to deal with certain issues that are relevant to their personal health and harmony. Here are six issues common to teens and some suggestions on how to use crystals for each issue. (Adults, children, and even seniors might also benefit from these crystals, too.)

- **Trouble sleeping**—Sleeplessness often comes because our minds are troubled by what has happened during the day. Crystals help regulate mental activity and calm excess mental energy and anxiety. Place the crystal on your chest for about 10 to 15 minutes before sleeping.

  Recommended crystals: sodalite, blue lace agate, rose quartz, amethyst

- **Unsettled or off-center feelings**—Feeling weird or unbalanced is not uncommon among teens due to hormonal fluctuations and new experiences. The teen brain goes through many changes. Teens often need to center themselves and ground their energies so they can be more effective in day-to-day living. Wear one of the recommended crystals by itself at the heart chakra for best effect.

  Recommended crystals: lapis lazuli, selenite, Herkimer diamond, clear quartz cluster, double-terminated clear quartz crystal

- **Fears**—There are many types of fears such as fear of being in a closed space (claustrophobia), stage fright, fear of failure, fear of rejection, and fear of the unknown. Crystals can help reduce the severity of fears or nervousness. Wear the crystal for several days before engaging in an event that is known to scare you. Hold the crystal in your hand for deeper effect. Put your fears into the crystal and let the crystal's energy work with you.

  Recommended crystals: petrified wood, aquamarine, jasper, sugilite, sodalite, amber, Apache tear

♦ **Self-esteem**—Low self-esteem is caused by thinking of yourself in a negative way, such as being a failure or having doubt in your own abilities. Orange carnelian is an especially powerful crystal for self-esteem. It is also good for skin complaints such as acne and rosacea. This crystal is best when worn at the heart chakra to provide nurturing to a depleted energy system. Others might notice your brighter outlook even before you do!

Recommended crystals: carnelian, amethyst, aventurine, rose quartz

♦ **Memory and logic**—Who wouldn't want a crystal to provide improved mathematical abilities and increased memory? The recommended crystals help provide precision, the ability to see relationships between things, and a coordinated response to problem solving. The best way to use these crystals is to hold them in your hand and gaze at them, sleep with them near your head, or keep them on your desk when you study to enhance your recall of information. The crystals will help declutter and restructure your left brain where logical abilities reside.

Recommended crystals: pyrite, purple fluorite, geodes, double-terminated clear quartz crystal, selenite

♦ **Bullying and intimidation**—Bullying serves no aim other than to position the victim as inferior to the bully. Crystals are able to project positive energy around the wearer for several feet and anyone nearby will pick up the vibration. The crystals will help you feel protected, grounded, and self-confident. They are marvelous tools.

Recommended crystals: red or green jasper, labradorite, hematite, malachite, lapis lazuli, tiger eye, aventurine, carnelian, garnet

You can't skip through the teen years, but the right gemstones can make them a heck of a lot easier for both your adolescent and you!

Crystals for Children

Crystals are truly gifts from the earth. Children seem to have a natural attraction to any kind of stone or crystal. They pick them up and fully explore them. They are curious to know how a crystal smells, and what sounds it makes when the crystal drops on the ground or plops into water.

Some children suffer from different physical ailments as they grow up. Having a crystal such as amethyst can help remove pain when properly directed. At the emotional level, there are crystals to help with feeling afraid or lonely, such as rose quartz, turquoise, or sugilite. Some children seem to be spiritually advanced and need to have a crystal like lapis lazuli that protects their energy fields or their minds from the thoughts of others. Children are part of the mosaic of Earth and can't always speak up about their spiritual needs because they lack an adult vocabulary. That does not mean, however, that they don't have spiritual needs. They do.

Children can respond very quickly to the healing energy of crystals. However, please consult the best available, qualified medical help to care for your children, and use your common sense regarding your children's health and wellness. As a reminder, don't let children or pets put crystals into their mouth; some, like malachite, contain high levels of copper that can harm their health.

The following crystals can help your child's healing at the physical, emotional, and spiritual levels. Let your child carry the crystal in her pocket, or place one or two in a small medicine bag around your child's neck. Let your child sleep with her special crystal.

- **Amethyst**—Helps children in transition, whether it be a minor event like a growth spurt or a major disappointment such as failing a grade, or the devastating news of divorce or death in the family. Amethyst accepts all negative emotions and provides comfort through spiritual acceptance. For children with various physical or emotional disabilities, an amethyst cluster in the room will help clear unwanted discharged energies and bring the room back into a balanced state. For pain on the body, hold an amethyst directly on or over the area for up to 20 minutes.

- **Aventurine**—The "leadership stone" strengthens and restores heart energy, providing a balance of male and female energies. This crystal is green, loving, embracing, and protective of the heart. Many children who are shy, timid, or suppressing their leadership qualities need a crystal like aventurine. This stone helps the individual to become active and initiate action on his or her own accord.

- **Carnelian**—The "self-esteem crystal" is used to dispel feelings of inadequacy and low self-esteem. The deep orange colors relate to strengthening and blending the first, second, and third chakras, promoting self-security and self-love. The pinker shades enhance love between child and parent through self-acceptance. This crystal is great for dermatological ailments such as acne. Hold the stone over the skin and move it in circles for several minutes several times a day.

♦ **Lapis lazuli**—A "psychic balancing stone," it is an incredible stabilizer for children who show psychic gifts early in life. The deep blue color stimulates expansion of consciousness in a supportive way, promoting purification and clarity of spiritual insight. Lapis lazuli provides self-acceptance of one's given gifts and encourages openness of one's spiritual awareness. This stone is highly prized for its protective powers and stimulation of all psychic senses.

♦ **Pyrite**—A "protection stone," iron pyrite comes in many shapes, from sun discs to cubes. Children are attracted to its shiny brassy surfaces. Pyrite is like a small mirror; negative energy is reflected away. The terror of feeling unprotected is reduced. There is also a feeling of physical empowerment, that life in the physical form is perfect, and love is abundant.

♦ **Rose quartz**—Another terrific general healing crystal for children, especially for those who have a lot of hurt feelings or aggressive tendencies. For hyperactive children, it soothes erratic emotional states, such as anxiety, fear, and impulsiveness. For young hearts, rose quartz helps keep the heart chakra open, vital, and protected.

♦ **Tiger eye**—A "grounding stone" that when rocked back and forth, reflects light as if a tiger were winking at you. Let your children explore this fascinating stone, and help them find the flashing tiger's eye. This stone is excellent for grounding psychic energy and providing security to open up the psychic centers. Sometimes children get carried away and become lost in their dream worlds. Tiger eye helps pull them back into their bodies after astral travel. Perhaps every parent needs one for their child before trips to the shopping mall!

You can encourage children's interest in the mineral kingdom. Let children pick crystals for themselves. Often, they will select a crystal that is helpful to their healing process.

Healing Animals with Crystals

Using crystals for healing pets and animals can produce quick results. Healing animals requires the healer to have a strong and centered mind. An animal's mind is not like a human's. Humans *relate* to pain; animals *react* to pain.

In other words, when you work on your pet, know when enough is enough. When the healing is good, the animal will show signs of comfort and affection, such as drooping eyelids, drooling, softening of muscles, and sighing.

Healing Pets

The following are some suggestions to help your animal friends be more comfortable. It is not intended that this information replace the advice of a professionally qualified veterinarian. As always, seek the best available competent medical advice for your pet or animal. For best results, remember to use fully cleansed and charged crystals and cleanse them after each use:

♦ Place amethyst or rose quartz underneath your pet-friend's bed or pillow for up to 2 weeks. Be cautious of sharp edges on the stones, and position them to be comfortable and safe for your pet. If the crystal energy is too intense, your pet will be agitated and might not want to rest in his bed. If your pet likes the crystals, you will see an improvement in his disposition and health within a few days.

♦ Choose a crystal from the list in the next section. Hold it in your hand, and starting a few inches away from the affected part or injured area, rotate the crystal clockwise. Take your time, go slow, and breathe gently and evenly. Animals express their emotions with movement, so watch to see if your pet wants more or tries to move away.

♦ Get a small pouch that can attach to a collar, and place up to three small crystals inside it. Be careful that the pouch does not interfere with your pet's movement or can become caught on anything. Detach the pouch when your pet is not supervised.

For additional healing, you can fill the water bowl or bucket with gem water (see Chapter 19).

Crystals for Animals

The following is a list of generally available crystals and gemstones and their associated physical healing focus.

♦ **Amethyst (master healer)**—Use for all healing: pain, fear, disorientation, and the head area.

♦ **Calcite**—Skeletal strengthening and bone mending.

♦ **Carnelian**—Skin, boils, lesions, and scrapes.

♦ **Clear quartz (master healer)**—Effective for all conditions.

♦ **Coral**—Kidneys and bladder.

♦ **Fluorite**—Use blue for bones; blue-green or clear for respiration; green for blood purification; and green-yellow for digestion.

♦ **Garnet**—Reproductive system and physical stamina.

♦ **Hematite**—Muscular system and for reducing pain.

♦ **Kyanite**—Alignment of all chakras (yes, animals have chakras, too!), tendons, and bones.

♦ **Malachite**—Blood and liver cleansing, heart problems, and liver detoxification. (Malachite should only be used externally because the high copper content is poisonous. Do not permit your pet or animal to lick or eat this crystal! Even consuming small amounts can lead to serious or fatal blood poisoning.)

♦ **Rose quartz (master healer)**—Use for injuries, for wounds, and to reduce stress.

♦ **Smoky quartz (master healer)**—Nervous system, swelling, and hostility.

♦ **Sodalite**—Calming nervousness, and for settling down during travel.

♦ **Sugilite**—For comforting a lonely or dying pet.

♦ **Turquoise (master healer)**—Use for digestive healing and protection from illness.

Crystals tend to amplify effects, and you need to be cautious until you determine how your pet will react.

CARVED IN STONE . . . .

Jasper: I provide integrity to all pursuits, whatever you turn your mind toward. I provide an anchor for your day-to-day living. I awaken your awareness of the beauty that surrounds you.

CHAPTER 15

Multipurpose Crystals

Believe it or not, you can use crystals in almost every aspect of your life to provide a little boost here and there. The use of crystals in everyday living provides a continuous field of energy that can help keep you aligned to your highest vibration, at home, at work, even when dreaming!

Whether you want to balance your body, your unconscious mind, your appliances, or your home, there's a crystal that can get the job done.

Learn How to...

♦ Use crystals around your house and office.

♦ Select jewelry to balance your subtle body.

♦ Improve your luck with crystals.

♦ Enhance your dreams.

Daily Crystal Use

Just as there is a crystal for every illness, there is a crystal for every situation—and I mean *every* situation, from studying to increasing lottery luck to harmonizing your home!

All crystals will provide some level of healing. You will get the best results from particular placements of crystals on your body and in your home and that's what you'll learn in this section. Let's get started with something anyone can do.

Crystals for Learning

Many types of crystals are useful for students. A clear quartz cluster or amethyst cluster on your desk will help your focus and concentration. Or bring a double-terminated quartz crystal to an exam and gaze into it when you need your mind to be clear.

Got a big test coming up and need to memorize lists, names, and dates? A lapis lazuli, tiger eye, clear quartz window crystal, or green tourmaline can help get your mind in gear. Tape the crystal onto your third eye to reduce fogginess while you study or wear a crystal head-band. (Something you'll learn to make in the next section.)

Crystals on the Brain

To increase your intuition and open higher chakra centers, glue or tape a crystal such as clear quartz, lapis lazuli, celestite, or Herkimer diamond onto a stretchy headband. Wear it at your third eye in the center of your forehead and slightly above the eyebrows. You can also sleep with your headband at night to increase dream clarity. The crystal energy goes right through tape and cloth without altering its signal.

Crystals for Computers, Cars, and Coffee

Placing a crystal, especially black tourmaline or shungite on or near electromagnetic equipment (computers, large appliances, and car engines) will help regulate subtle energy fields and dampen electromagnetic fields (EMFs). Ongoing use of crystals with appliances will promote a longer lifespan with fewer breakdowns. You will definitely want a crystal for your coffee machine!

Adorn Yourself with Crystals

The extraordinary actress Elizabeth Taylor was well-known for her collection of exquisite jewelry and had some of the biggest and purest gemstones. She not only knew that they truly belonged to the earth, but also knew of their power to heal, to soothe, and to boost energy. Of course, not everyone has a budget to purchase the rarest gemstones, but you can benefit from more reasonably priced crystal jewelry. Just be sure they are genuine, quality gemstones to get their maximum healing power.

Wear Them

The easiest way to benefit from crystals on an ongoing basis is to wear them. Activate the lower three chakras (base, sacral, and solar plexus) by wearing rings, bracelets, and belt buckles or by slipping them into your pockets or a purse. See below for activating the upper chakras (solar plexus, heart, throat, third eye, and crown). When it comes to jewelry, the bigger the crystal, the more powerful the effect because a larger crystal often stores more energy than a smaller one does.

Here are a few guidelines to follow:

♦ To soothe or activate the solar plexus chakra, use a crystal in a pouch or on a necklace that reaches your abdomen.

♦ To activate the heart chakra, wear a necklace or pendant on a chain that is at least 18- to 22-inches long.

♦ For the throat chakra, wear a choker, a necklace that is 12- to 16-inches long, or a gemstone pin to provide more direct healing.

♦ The third eye and crown chakras respond well to crystals in earrings, tiaras (just like royalty or a pageant queen), headbands (on the forehead or crown), or hats and scarves with gemstone pins.

Conductive Crystal Energy

Metals provide electrical conductivity for the energy of the crystal, but each metal transmits crystal power differently. This means that some will feel right for you, while others might be unbearable.

Here are some general rules when it comes to choosing metals to use with crystals:

♦ **Gold**—It is the master of all metals. Gold emits solar, fire, yang, and masculine energy, and enhances intelligence and the higher mind. Gold gives a sense of power and absolute purity as well as a connection to great strength. Gold can link with a matrix of other crystals and is an activator of their electrical circuitry.

♦ **Silver**—Its qualities are feminine, cooling, yin energy, and the moon. When silver is worn, energy is retained and circulates throughout the subtle body. Silver also provides a balance when used with other crystals. It is the metal of choice for many jewelers for gemstone wrapping because silver does not block the energy of the crystal.

♦ **Copper**—A conductive material that can pass electrical pulses along its matrix without interference, copper is a servant to other energies, both human and crystal, by stabilizing energy transfers.

♦ **Platinum**—This expensive metal is perfect for seers and seekers. It provides clairvoyance, specifically hindsight and foresight. It will keep your crown chakra free of debris.

♦ **Titanium**—This metal is biocompatible, meaning your body is unlikely to react or be allergic to it. This is a metal that supports communication from outer space and can be used for interstellar communication.

There are quite a few people who have metal allergies. Most often the toxic effects come from nickel allergies. As a reminder, to avoid metal toxicity, do not put jewelry in your mouth.

As you continue to work with crystals, your sensitivities to crystals *and* metals may change. This is a positive marker of your deepening connection. It gives you something to look forward to.

Rings on Her Fingers, Rings on Her Toes

When looking for a ring, find the right balance between the quality of the gemstone, a size that fits your body type and personality, and your budget. Some jewelry needs to be highly functional for everyday wear. A ring that would suit an office worker might not be the best choice for a landscaper, for example.

After you've chosen the metal and a gemstone, think about the shape of the stone. Each shape has a story:

- ♦ **Circle**—A symbol of wholeness, completeness, and unity. Energy circulates and is renewed by a circular stone.
- ♦ **Oval**—An oval stone keeps the energy of both the sky (spirit) and the earth (groundedness) flowing throughout the subtle bodies.
- ♦ **Triangle**—A triangular stone represents the sacred trinity, a pyramid to focus energy for visions, dreams, and goals in life.
- ♦ **Square**—A square stone aligns and structures energy to provide stability and security.
- ♦ **Emerald**—The facets on an emerald-cut stone produce a mirror-like quality of eternal light representing the highest level of truth.

Deciding on which finger to wear your crystal ring is significant and can influence your energy and luck. Rings will open the energy in your fingers and hand chakras. Use the following illustration to figure out which crystals suit you best.

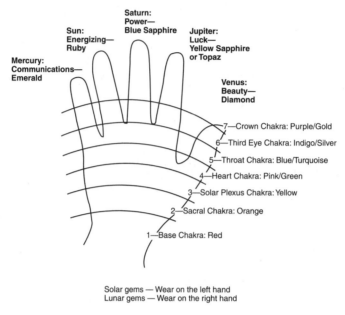

Chakras, planets, colors, and gems related to hands.

Lunar gemstones activate benevolence, gentleness, and creativity and should be worn on the left hand, which is the receptive side. If you're a person who angers quickly or who might be a bit arrogant or rash, consider wearing a lunar crystal on your left side to tone those qualities down a little bit. (Really, just a little. It's for your own good.)

Wear traditional lunar gemstone rings on the Mercury (emerald), Jupiter (yellow sapphire or topaz), or Venus (diamond) fingers.

Solar gemstones activate wealth, fame, friendship, and health, and they should be worn on the right hand. Wear traditional solar gemstone rings on the Sun (ruby) or Saturn (blue sapphire) fingers.

Bracelets

The ever-popular chip-stone bracelet is easy to wear, inexpensive, and provides some crystal benefits as your body picks up particles of crystal energy and distributes it through-out the body and aura by following the meridians and other channels of energy. However, this is not very focused energy. Think about it: your hands are waving around all day and are never stationary long enough to get good saturation in any chakra. If you want to get more concentrated crystal energy, remove the bracelet and place it on top of a chakra, or place the bracelet on your belly button to balance your energy.

You can also find ceremonial bracelets that combine powerful crystals and metals made by artisan healers. These specialized bracelets provide a shot of energy—think of Wonder Woman and her magic bracelets that she used to deflect flying bullets! Bracelets provide significant energy coming into the body if worn on both wrists.

Pendants and Earrings

Earrings are worn close enough to activate the throat and third eye chakras and will also influence the crown and heart chakras. If the earrings are long and dangly, the crystal energy will circulate in the aura. You might be more sensitive to crystals worn closer to your head. If you feel dizzy and disoriented, remove your crystal jewelry, sit down, and drink water to ground your energies. Breathe deeply, relax, and allow the energy to dissipate.

Pendants are usually worn at the throat, heart, or solar plexus chakras. When wearing a crystal pendant to activate or reenergize the solar plexus or heart chakra, choose a crystal that's at least a half-inch large. Anything smaller is not going to be very effective. If the chakra is burned out, overworked, and lacking energy, a larger restorative crystal such as rose quartz can be very soothing.

Pouches of Power

Crystals can be placed in pouches and worn at the heart or solar plexus chakras for long-term intensive healing. Sacred items such as animal fur, shells, bone, and other natural objects that have ritualistic significance may also be placed in the pouch.

Leather and silk are the best materials for making a pouch because they allow the energies to circulate unimpeded. Use a leather string to maintain the energy transference. If you are vegan or an environmentalist, hemp or bamboo are suitable alternative materials. As a reminder, never touch someone else's sacred pouch without permission! Getting into someone else's space and energy uninvited might cause an energetic mishap for you and the pouch-wearer.

Increasing Prosperity and Luck

You can program your crystals for an unlimited increase of wealth and prosperity. Think big! Ruby and citrine are good crystals to use for attracting wealth. To magnify your money, put a small piece of each crystal in your purse or wallet next to your money. If you have a cash register, drop a citrine in there, too. Before buying a lotto ticket, rub your crystals in your hands to activate their energies and think of winning the prize and then select your ticket.

If you would like to program several small crystals or gemstones at one time, slip them into both hands and hold them in front of your nose before expelling your breath to program the crystals. During programming, ensure that all the crystals make contact with your breath. Then place them on top or around a symbol of your goal, such as a map of Europe if you want to travel there or around the photo of a friend you want to connect with. Leave them in place for seven days for the energy to line up and manifest the wish.

Feng Shui

Feng shui is the ancient Chinese art of placing things in the environment for harmony. Feng shui has grown in popularity with its wider introduction to the West. It's related to the principles of yin and yang—the feminine and masculine in balance.

Feng shui is a complex field of study, but the results are so powerful that a business using feng shui principles can augment its sales rapidly. Consequently, some of the more famous feng shui masters in Asia are booked years in advance and command significant fees. In the West, feng shui has become more popular but is used mostly in residential settings. Crystals are used in feng shui to provide balance to the environment.

What's a Bagua?

A *bagua* is a tool used to determine areas in your home or work environment where there might be an energetic imbalance. It's a diagram of eight symbols used to represent different directions, yin-yang principles, seasons, elements, and family members. Each section of a home, a garden, or other area maps to one of the eight segments in the bagua. By using different cures or remedies in the segments, imbalances in the environment and home are influenced and balance is restored. Crystals can be used to adjust these imbalances when you understand the bagua and a few other concepts.

A bagua is used in a room or house by laying an 8-segment grid over the floor plan. The bottom segment, the Career segment, is aligned with the entrance to the front door of the house or the entrance to a room. To the immediate left of the door is Knowledge including courses, books, and training programs. To the immediate right of the door is Helpful People, such as friends and others who help us. Travel is also included in this segment.

Opposite the door is Fame or Rank. Fame is what you are best known for, what you are good at, or what you are certified to do. To the left of Fame is Wealth. Wealth can include possessions or things, such as an heirloom stuffed Labrador duck worth $10,000. (Really, there is such a thing called a Labrador duck.) To the right of Fame is Relationships (shown in the illustration as Marriage), which includes partnerships and anything that takes two or more people for wholeness to be accomplished.

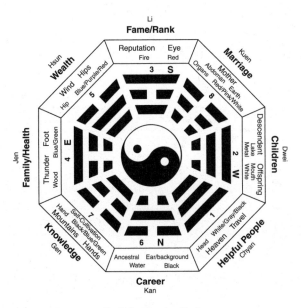

Align the front door along this plane

The bagua and its corresponding elements, body parts, colors, and life situations.

The left middle side of the room is Family/Health and our ancestors who provide continuity of wisdom. (Even those who don't have known family can still use the wisdom of their ancestors, real or imagined.) To the middle right is Children, who provide inspiration and creativity. (Even those who don't have children can imagine the energy of being a child with great imagination and the freshness that unimpeded joy and creativity brings.) The center of the room is called *Tai Chi* and represents you in total harmony with all that is. The symbol of Tai Chi, the balance of yin and yang energies, is shown in the illustration by a circle with a black and white motif in the shape of the number 69. There is a drop of yin in the yang and a drop of yang in the yin. When chi is balanced, there is health and harmony.

Too Much, Too Little

To harmonize a segment of a room, take a look at your life and where it is now. In the following table, place a check mark in the column that you think best represents what you'd like to improve and make more active or tone down by making it less active so harmony and balance are restored. If you feel a segment is just right, you can check that column, too. Life can change; therefore you should keep track of what you did and didn't change so you can continue to make effective adjustments.

Segments to Harmonize

Segment	More Active	Less Active	Just Right
Career	❑	❑	❑
Knowledge	❑	❑	❑
Family/Health	❑	❑	❑
Wealth	❑	❑	❑
Fame/Rank	❑	❑	❑
Marriage	❑	❑	❑
Children	❑	❑	❑
Helpful People	❑	❑	❑
Tai Chi (yourself)	❑	❑	❑

Now select the type of crystal needed for the segments you would like to enhance from the following crystal bagua chart. Next, select the shape of crystal needed to either make that segment more energized or to tone it down.

Crystal Bagua Chart

Wealth & Prosperity	Fame & Fortune	Love & Relationships
Element: Wood	Element: Fire	Element: Earth
Color: Purple/Red	Color: Red	Color: Pink
Amethyst	Garnet	Rose quartz
Purple fluorite	Carnelian	Pink tourmaline
Ruby	Fire agate	Kunzite
Sugilite	Peridot	Rhodachrosite
Geodes	Your "personal" crystal	Pairs of crystals
	Pyramids	
Family & Health	**Tai Chi–Self**	**Children & Creativity**
Element: Wood	Element: Earth	Element: Metal
Color: Blue/Green	Color: Yellow	Color: White
Malachite	Citrine	White calcite
Chrysocolla	Yellow fluorite	Selenite
Petrified wood	Clear quartz	Hematite
Amber	Yellow calcite	All metals
Crystal wands and tall,	Sulpher	Pyrite
square shapes	Crystal balls	Crystal clusters
Knowledge & Wisdom	**Career & Life**	**Helpful People & Travel**
Element: Earth	Element: Water	Element: Metal
Color: Blue/Brown	Color: Black	Color: Black
Turquois	Black tourmaline	White
Chrysocolla	Opals	Agate
Azurite	Pearl	Marble
Lapis lazuli	Coral	Granite
Sapphire	Black onyx	Round or oval crystals
Jasper	Crystal egg	
Pointy shapes		

Changing the Energy

If you want to have more time to spend in other areas of your bagua, tone down the overactive segment by selecting a shape for a less active crystal. To activate a sector, select tall, pointy, shiny shapes such as pyramids and spires. To tone down a sector, select crystals that are short, rounder, and have soft edges such as crystal balls or geodes.

For example, if you want to increase the energy in your career segment, you might select one or more black crystals. Place a black obelisk for decoration in this segment or even tack a photo or postcard of opals on the wall. You might find your career gets launched or that you have become more noticeable at work.

Now you are ready to purchase the appropriate crystals, if you don't already have them, and place them where you can see them in the identified segment of the home. The crystals can go on the floor, on a table, on a book shelf, or anywhere visible. Be sure, however, that your crystals are safe from children and pets.

In a few days, the subtle energies will ripen and blend with your surroundings, and you will see the results. A powerful shift can occur as you are altering the subtle energies of your environment and your subtle body. Make minor adjustments, as needed, by adding more crystals or moving them into different sectors to achieve balance. Keep track of the results in your crystal journal.

The Art of Bagua Maintenance

If you are using crystals in the bagua over a long time, remember to cleanse and care for your crystals. Monitor the energy generated from the crystals in each segment to ensure you haven't over activated the sector. Cleanse the area with smudge and refresh the crystals, or replace the crystals with new or different crystals. Let the crystals recharge in the sunlight or moonlight occasionally.

To clear environmental energies, program a smooth, polished clear quartz crystal to clear unwanted energies and toxins. Hold the crystal in an upright position in the middle of the Tai Chi (center) of your home. Holding the crystal at the base, slowly rotate the crystal to the right, visualizing white light streaming out and consciously clearing out all negativity in all segments.

You can also use some of these techniques to create a crystal bagua in the form of a crystal grid. (Find out more on this in Chapter 18.) I did say that crystals were multipurpose!

Dream Enhancement

Sleeping with crystals can encourage both dreaming and recalling those dreams by providing increased clarity of mind, mental recognition of the dream state, and awareness of your own consciousness. Wearing and using crystals throughout the day will also increase awareness when you are in a dream state.

There are three aspects of dreaming to program into your crystal. First, you need to direct yourself to actually dream. Next, your program should direct you to remember the dream. You have to store the information in your brain as a function of memory. Part of this memory will be patterned with the crystalline energy of the crystal and your bioenergetic systems. The third part is to recall the dream. Your mind has to retrieve the information from memory storage.

When you wake up in the morning, see if you can recall the dream. If you need a little help, hold your crystal near your third eye and remain still for about 5 minutes. If you still can't remember your dream, that's all right. Get up, and get on with your day, but remain receptive to recalling your dream. You might be sitting eating breakfast when the dream will suddenly come to you.

Crystals for Dream Enhancement

Just about any crystal will help you connect within your dream state. However, some crystals have a particular mission. Try these crystals for different experiences:

♦ Amber, jade, and aventurine all soothe emotions and quieten very active dreams.

♦ Blue tiger eye is a real eye-opener—of the third eye, that is. Use this crystal to go deeper into your dreams.

♦ Celestite keeps your crown chakra active for receiving messages from subtle spirit energies who use the dream state to teach us.

♦ Herkimer diamond produces memorable dreams, sharpens your memory of them, and provides healing at the mental and spiritual planes.

♦ Labradorite and moldavite produce spacy, prophetic, visionary dreams.

♦ Moldavite provides a powerful connection for communication to the stars and our extraterrestrial friends.

♦ Mookaite, the Australian dream stone, is a form of jasper and is great for accessing dreams and protecting the dreamer as entering into other states of consciousness.

♦ Moonstone is protective for astral traveling. It softens difficult dreams and nightmares.

Your dream crystals can be tucked into your pillowcase overnight to prevent them from rolling around. You can also just hold them in your hand or tape a small piece of crystal onto your forehead between your eyebrows with white surgical tape to intensify your dream state. If you find you are awake all night, remove the crystals or switch to a less active crystal.

CARVED IN STONE . . . .

Sodalite: I can calm and strengthen a troubled mind. I expand consciousness with clarity and increase powers of the third eye. I provide mental serenity and insight. I help you accept the truth without judgement.

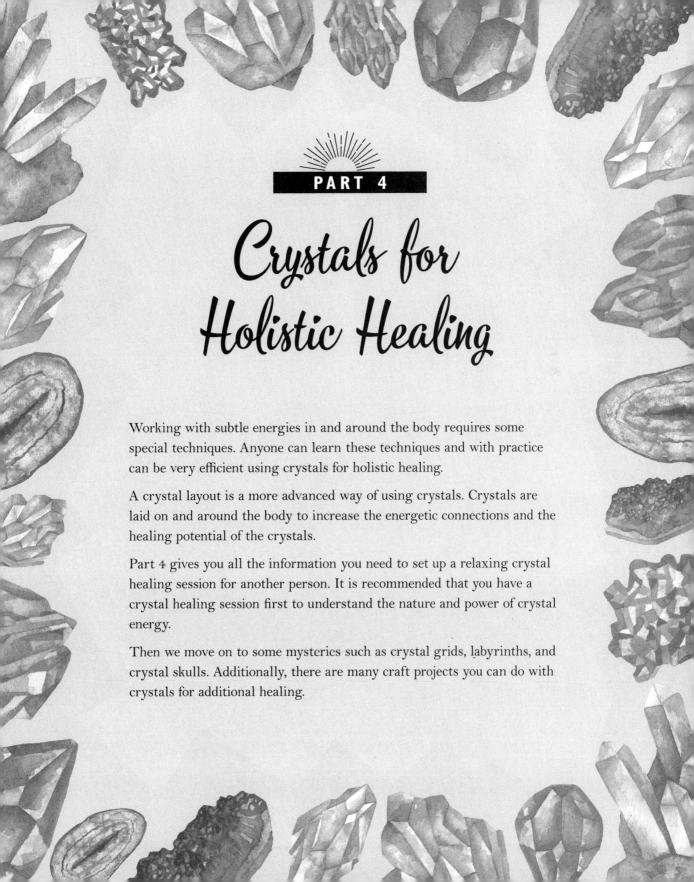

PART 4

Crystals for Holistic Healing

Working with subtle energies in and around the body requires some special techniques. Anyone can learn these techniques and with practice can be very efficient using crystals for holistic healing.

A crystal layout is a more advanced way of using crystals. Crystals are laid on and around the body to increase the energetic connections and the healing potential of the crystals.

Part 4 gives you all the information you need to set up a relaxing crystal healing session for another person. It is recommended that you have a crystal healing session first to understand the nature and power of crystal energy.

Then we move on to some mysteries such as crystal grids, labyrinths, and crystal skulls. Additionally, there are many craft projects you can do with crystals for additional healing.

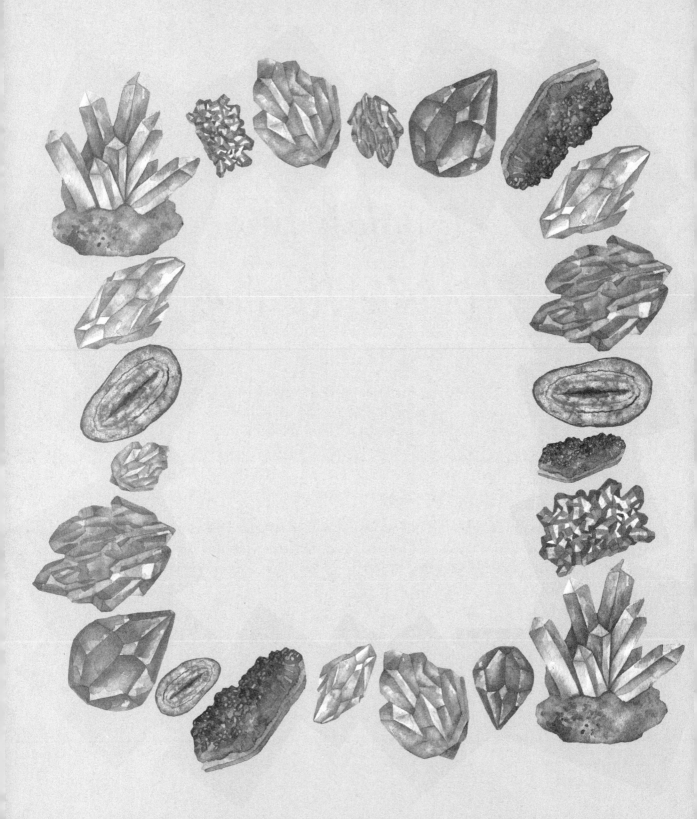

CHAPTER 16

Crystal Layouts

Crystals are beautiful to look at on their own, but when you start putting them into geometric layouts, not only does their appearance become even more dazzling, but their power also magnifies!

Layouts have been used for thousands of years and, as such, are obviously nothing new. We can't be sure what our ancient ancestors used these techniques for, but *we* can use them for meditation, healing, or connecting with the spirit world. Anything is possible when crystals start communicating with each other!

Learn How to ...

♦ Use sacred geometry on and around your body to enhance healing.

♦ Place crystals in a layout for meditation and dimensional healing.

♦ Activate your layout.

♦ Prepare for more crystal grid work.

Patterns of Power

In this chapter, you're going to learn how to lay crystals on the body for optimum healing power. But why, you might be asking, do gemstones have to be positioned in a pattern? How does this affect their healing power?

Sacred geometry and the use of stones in special geometric patterns is as old as the hills. Sacred geometry refers to formations used in the construction of sacred architecture and in the design of sacred art. Actually, ancient civilizations were building structures like the famous Stonehenge, near Amesbury, England, earlier than 3,000 B.C.E. These types of formations seem to amplify energy and healing and provide a gathering point for people to access higher states of consciousness.

When crystals are laid out in a pattern, they also start to speak energetically to each other. The crystalline resonance is amplified by the pattern, making it possible to enter into a higher state of awareness. Maybe when creating your own crystal geometric patterns, you'll rediscover an ancient secret!

Crystal Geometry

In Chapter 3, we talked about Platonic solids and sacred geometry and how these concepts relate to the idea of crystal healing. The harmonics and proportions of geometric designs are thought to be a means to communicate with the sacred and to provide the powers of healing through their mathematical significance in relation to the laws of the universe. Although geometric designs can be intricate and artistic, there's much more to them than beauty. When certain crystals are laid on or around the body in a very specific manner, they begin to resonate with each other and connect inter-dimensionally.

A crystal layout is a geometric arrangement of crystals placed either around or on the body to create or augment crystal resonance for meditation and healing. When you sit or lie in a *crystal layout*, it becomes a living *mandala* of energy where your mind becomes more focused for dimensional access, subtle energies are invoked, and healing is more effective. A *mandala* is a geometric pattern symbolizing the universe and the cosmic order of all things.

A Crystal Crown

Need more intensity in your meditation sessions? Want deeper interpersonal communications? A crystal layout called a *crystal crown* is just what the crystal healer ordered! This is a nice beginner layout, and the suggested pattern works well to provide relaxation (because you will be laying down) and an opening of the crown chakra for spiritual expansion. Crystals in a layout should not actually touch your body. That way, you are getting subtle energy directed for spiritual expansion rather than for direct physical or emotional healing.

A crystal crown layout.

To set up your crystal crown, select some of the spiritual expansion crystals listed in Chapter 13. Try to use two of the same type of crystal because you'll put one on each side of the head to balance the left and right brain hemispheres, as well as create a yin-yang balance within the subtle energies.

To balance the upper and lower chakras, you'll need extra grounding. This time, as well as the visualization of roots growing under your feet for grounding, you can also place a dark crystal 2- to 4-inches long, such as black tourmaline or obsidian, about 6 inches below your feet to anchor you to the earth. Set this grounding crystal in place before you lie your head in the crown.

> You'll need an affirmation for programming the layout. Here's one suggestion for general use: I, [your name], am able to receive and accept all that is.

Now we're ready to get down to work! Set up the following pattern of crystals in a semi-circle on the floor; then gently lay your head inside the semicircle. If you want to align the crystals on top of a bed, gently place a pillow over them and then lay your head on the pillow or tape them in place. You will be staying in the crystal crown as a meditation for about 10 to 20 minutes.

Layout your crystals for the crystal crown like this:

♦ At the side of each temple, place a 1-inch piece of sodalite to provide stress reduction and to calm the mind.

♦ On each side of the throat, place a 1-inch piece of azurite, lapis lazuli, or dioptase to release worldly concerns and enter into a deeper level of awareness.

♦ At the top of your head (about 2 inches above the center), place a large amethyst with the tip pointing away from the head. The crystal will provide protection as well as a crown chakra opening.

♦ On each side of the amethyst, place a piece of clear or white calcite or selenite. This will open the communications channel for telepathic messages and images.

♦ Place a third eye crystal such as topaz or lapis lazuli on your forehead. This will expand your awareness and provide mental clarity.

♦ At the heart chakra, place a crystal such as rose quartz or kunzite to balance the physical, mental, and emotional levels and to open the heart chakra for healing.

After the basic layout is set up, you can hold additional crystals in your hands. For extra focus, you can listen to a meditation tape. If you have some healing to do, focus on that area and the crystalline energy structures will work with you on the problem.

If you want to set up this type of layout for a partner, have the person lie down first and then place the grounding crystal, then crystals around the sides and top of your partner's head.

Now you are all set to breathe deeply and relax your body. Activate your third eye by focusing on the middle of your forehead. The crystals at the crown will make a connection with the third eye as they open the crown chakra. You can direct your own visualization or meditation or simply ask for a healing and see what happens.

Some people report seeing images and even colored lights in the room as their upper chakras open. The important part is to not fall asleep while you are in an energy circle or other layout so you can be conscious of the energy shifts. When you are aware of what you see through the veils of time and past the material plane of existence, there are lessons to be learned. If you are asleep, there is little value to these lessons. You are training your mind to see to other parts of the cosmos. Holding on to your consciousness takes time to develop.

When you have completed your meditation, disengage your energy by mentally projecting the word *release* to cease all energy connection between you and the crystals. Take off your heart crystal and dismantle the crystal crown layout. Write any thoughts or inspirations you have in your crystal journal. Cleanse your crystals and tuck them away. Try a different assortment of crystals for your next crystal crown layout.

Here's a story about how the crystal crown layout created a connection to the angelic realm for a female client. The crystals used during this healing session were alternating clear quartz and amethyst points around the head. In the crown chakra was a 4-inch piece of celestite. Blue lace agate was placed on her throat chakra to help give voice to the subtle energies of the higher realms. The client meditated as the crystals were placed around her head. She verbally requested access to the angelic realm on a personal quest to find out what she needed most at this time and to get some personal direction. Some ethereal music played softly in the background and the lights were dimmed to help create a relaxing mood.

The crystals helped the client to see that her way of living life, so packed with self-directed activities, was keeping people away. By being task-oriented, she was concerned mostly about accomplishing *things*, at the expense of developing deeper relationships with *people*. The crystal crown helped her to connect with her angels, who left her with clear messages on what activities were to be saved and to be let go. The messages gave the client a new path and objectives. As the messages came from her own conscious connection, she trusted them to be true. The client was excited and happy to have found the answers she needed most at this time.

Angels are universal. Have you talked to them recently? Maybe they have a message for you, too.

A Ring of Crystals

Why do we wear rings (wedding rings), put things in a ring (a circus ring), and see rings (ring around the moon)? Well, for one thing, rings can contain things. A ring is a circle and can rotate in any direction. It represents perfection and the blissful void. It is the beginning and the end. Rings are also an alchemical sign of completion and wholeness. When crystals are arranged into a circle, we are containing the energies of the crystals and can direct that energy for healing and meditation. If this is your first time in a circle of crystals, you are in for a treat!

One of the first crystal layouts I tried was a basic circle. I gathered every crystal I could find in the house—all 34 of them. After cleansing them, I took them outside and put them in a wide 5-foot circle in the grass to soak up the sun's rays for recharging. Later that afternoon, I entered the crystal circle and sat in meditation for what seemed like hours, connecting with the earth, the crystals, the lovely welcoming energy, and my inner spiritual place of joy. It was a wonderful initiation, and I recommend it for anyone who has more than a few crystals or for someone who is developing a crystal toolkit and wants to establish a connection with their crystals.

How do you make a perfect circle of crystals? Don't worry—you don't need to acquire a huge compass or the equipment that roadside surveyors use. All you need is a length of string and an eye for detail:

1. Place a heavy crystal in the middle of the floor or ground where you want to make your circle.

2. Cut a length of string that will be one half the diameter of the circle you want to make.

3. Attach one end of the string to the crystal in the center, and stretch out the string to the edge of the circle. Place a quartz crystal at the end of the string.

4. Position the crystal with the tip pointing in toward the center of the circle. (If you are using a tumbled crystal, just place it according to your intuition at the end of the string.) Swing the string to the next position a few inches from the first crystal, and place the second crystal.

5. Continue to move around the circle following the length of the string. Each crystal will be exactly the same length from the middle of the circle.

If you have only 4 crystals, they can be placed using the string length at north, east, south, and west positions. If you have, say, 12 crystals to use in a layout, place the first 4 crystals in each of the four directions, and fill in the remaining space between the 4 directional crystals with the other 8 crystals.

The most important part is to stand back from the circle and ensure that you see good alignment and spacing between your gemstones. Read the section about activating the layout later in this chapter, and you'll be all set for a new experience every time!

The best use of a ring of crystals is to sit in it. Before you enter the ring, remember to activate the layout (as described later in this chapter). As you step into the circle, visualize a ring of white light rising up like a column around you, enclosing you. Once you feel this powerful energy connection, you can direct healing to areas of your body or to emotional issues. You can also hold the thought of sending healing to a person. When you are surrounded by crystals and are making that crystalline connection, you are linked with all things. Saying a prayer or a positive affirmation is very beneficial, as it will be amplified and transmitted by the ring of light.

When you have completed your healing or meditation session, disengage from the energy by mentally projecting the word *release*. This will cease all energy connection with the crystals. Gently get up and step outside of the ring. You do not need to dismantle the ring and can reuse it later. However, you should clear the energy by smudging the area with sage or incense. You can also add a small bowl of dry sea salt to purify the circle while you are away. You can use the ring up to three times before cleansing the crystals in salt water and recharging them for the next session. Also, you might want to keep track of the number of crystals you've laid out by taking a photo. I've lost a few to the vacuum cleaner from carelessness!

Animals seem to benefit from circles of stone, too. While traveling in Nepal, I came across a street dog that had been in a fight and was a bit banged up, bleeding and limping. The villagers thought I was crazy when I directed the dog back to my room. The dog waited outside while I got some crystals and set up a circle of quartz crystals around his body, putting an amethyst cluster under his bleeding neck. He stayed there for over an hour and then left of his own accord. The next day, the dog seemed perfectly fine.

Star of David

The Star of David is an ancient symbol that is rich in symbolism. It consists of two inter-locking equilateral triangles forming a six-point star. In Judaism, it was used by kabbalists for protection against evil spirits. In Hinduism, it is called the *Shatkona*, representing the union of Shiva and Shakti, godlike energies that form all of creation. The Star of David crystal layout is used for unifying and integrating energy. It's a terrific layout, but it can be a little tricky to get the crystals aligned properly.

To build the Star of David layout, set up two triangles of crystals with 3 crystals for each triangle.

The first triangle is the Shakti triangle pointing down (female energy). First, put a crystal as a marker in the center of the area where you want the layout set up. Using a length of string, measure the placement from the central marker directly below, in a southern direc-tion. Place a crystal there, pointing toward the center. For the second and third crystals, use the string above the marker to place a crystal in the northeast and one in northwest directions. Point the crystals toward the center.

The second triangle is the Shiva triangle (male energy) with the point of the triangle facing up. Use the string to position the first crystal directly above the center marker to the north. This crystal should point towards the center. For the second and third crystals, use the string as you did for the first triangle and place a crystal in each of the southeastern and southwestern directions. No crystals are laid at the eastern or western sides.

For the Shakti crystals, you can use the yin crystals mentioned in Chapter 7 such as moonstones. For the Shiva crystals, the layout will be more powerful if all the crystals are the same type such as tourmalines.

Stand back and ensure that each crystal tip is aligned and pointing to the center. If not, adjust them. Now you have two triangles in union and can remove the center crystal. Read the section later in this chapter on activation of the layout, and you're good to go!

When you enter the Star of David, try to think of the formation as two interlocking three-dimensional triangles and that you are going to sit in the middle where they lock. This sacred geometry will provide a gentle alignment to your subtle energies that will open your energies for higher meditation and communication with the cosmos. Ask for a chakra alignment or an alignment for your highest good.

Try boosting the energy flow of the Shiva-Shakti or Star of David layout by holding a clear quartz crystal in your left hand with the tip point inward and a clear quartz crystal in your right hand with the tip pointing out.

The Obliging Oval

The alignment of crystals in an oval pattern is the most versatile of layouts. An oval doesn't take up much space; any size crystals can be used; and the layout is effective for chakra balancing, physical healing, and past-life recall. Ovals help contain energy, provide protection to the aura, and aid in the circulation of energy throughout the subtle body.

For the oval layout, you'll need six large clear quartz crystals. If you can, find some crystals that are 3- to 6-inches long and 2- to 4-inches wide; they carry the right type of energy to hold the dynamic geometric structure together. Try to select ones that feel heavier than they look. Remember that the larger the crystal, the more energy it can hold. The placement of the crystals is as follows:

- ◆ Place one crystal at the head, pointing up, and one at the feet pointing down.
- ◆ Place one crystal pointing up on either side of the body at the lower hips to catch energy for balancing the lower chakras.
- ◆ One crystal on either side of the body at the upper arms to catch energy for balancing the higher chakras.

Oval layouts feel protective and provide a deep meditative experience. Don't forget before you enter the oval to activate the layout (described later). You can ask for communication with a spirit guide or with angels while in this type of layout.

If you are working on physical healing, place additional crystals on your body while in the oval layout. You can add more crystals—at the third eye and heart chakras, for example—to boost the subtle energies. After the session, smudge the area and cleanse and recharge your crystals unless you are reusing the oval for another meditation. Write any impressions in your crystal journal.

Your crystal layout can remain on the floor to reuse at a later time. Use a silk cloth to cover the crystals for dust protection and to help retain the energy of the crystals.

Activation of the Layout

Just setting out the crystals will provide some energy connections between the stones. When the crystals are properly aligned, the crystalline structure actually takes its shape from the geometry of the layout. To realize the dynamic energy activation of the layout takes a further step.

You can activate the layout simply by using your intent. Visualize the layout as a three-dimensional structure. In a circle layout, for instance, think of a ball of light. In an oval, think of an egg-shaped light structure.

Adding a further ritual to the activation creates a sacred space for the layout and protects it from vibrational intrusions. Using strong intent and visualizing the three-dimensional structure of the layout, point a kyanite wand at the center of the layout for at least 21 seconds. This will allow time for the structure to adjust and to align on the subtle side of things. You will use this same technique later on for aligning a crystal grid complex.

You might like to experiment with various types of layouts, such as a spiral of life. The spiral of life is made of a line of crystals that spirals toward a center. The right-handed spiral (a spiral rotating to the right) is considered sacred. Walk gently, following the spiral. You can stand at the center of the spiral and feel a wave of energy rushing toward you. Breathe this energy into your body, focusing on the chakras or any areas that need healing. Consider investing in a 1- to 2-pound bag of smaller, 1-inch crystals to use in more complex layouts. Cleanse and charge them before placing them into a layout.

Crystals can also be selected and added as part of a crystal layout for a specific healing event, such as one on the following list. Even if you only had one or two of each crystal and some clear quartz crystals to put in the layout, it will be enough to activate the energies.

- ◆ **Forgiveness:** rose quartz, blue lace agate, kunzite, sugilite, amethyst, selenite, rhodochrosite.
- ◆ **Rebalancing energy:** use 4 double-terminated clear quartz crystals at each of 4 directions around the body. Place a double-terminated crystal at the heart chakra to balance the upper body and one at the solar plexus to balance the lower body.
- ◆ **Physical healing:** hematite, malachite, calcite, coral, turquoise, rutilated quartz.
- ◆ **Mood lifting:** citrine, amber, jade, lepidolite, tiger eye, tourmaline.
- ◆ **Mental relaxation:** azurite, carnelian, fluorite, lapis lazuli, moonstone, sodalite, peridot.
- ◆ **Game changing:** moldavite, rhodonite, tourmaline, rutilated quartz, smoky quartz.

You will find a lot of crystals have multiple meanings. When they are placed together in combinations and amplified within a crystal layer, they help direct and focus your thoughts towards your goal or intention. It's great to try them out. Draw a diagram of each layout into your crystal journal and write up your experience.

Prepare for Crystal Grid Work

If you have followed these chapters consecutively, you've noticed that each one takes you progressively into more detailed use of crystals. It's like getting a whole course on healing with crystals. However, knowledge can fade if unused for too long. To keep your enthusiasm and knowledge alive, continue to wear your crystals, visit rock shops, and use your personal crystal for meditation. When you are surrounded by crystals, it's like getting a crystal healing session. After a trip to my local rock shop or gem show, I feel quite invigorated wearing my new crystals.

Another great way to keep your new knowledge alive is to work with a smaller cosmos of crystal grids. Everything you have learned up to this point can be combined using sacred geometry. Use your knowledge to construct and to activate a crystal grid. Take what you've learned about cleansing and programming crystals to prepare the crystals for grid work. By now, you have an understanding about each crystal and its meaning. In this chapter, you learned how to activate crystal healing layouts and will use the same methods for activating your crystal grid in Chapter 18. See? It's all coming together now.

There are advantages and disadvantages to using a full crystal layout over a crystal grid. For one thing, in a crystal layout, your whole body and energy field is completely within the field of crystal energy activation. Layouts are very powerful. However, a layout is not something that is easily transportable, especially if you are using large heavy crystals or many smaller crystals as part of it.

In the next chapter, you will learn a method of doing a full crystal healing session using layouts on the body. When you want to move some serious energy, a crystal healing session with a layout can be an intense experience. To sustain the healing energy after a session and especially for chronic issues, wearing your crystals is a perfect way to maintain your connection to the energy.

CARVED IN STONE . . . .

Kyanite: I open the dimensional portals. I provide the connectivity between different energy sources and etheric layers. I unify the frequencies for communications and I direct energy flows.

CHAPTER 17

Become a Healer!

By now you know that crystal healing is a versatile form of cleansing and shifting energy, whether that energy is in the air, in your mind, or in your body. You've come a long way in a short time, and you might want to try what you've learned in a full healing session with a partner, either a friend or a client.

Before you begin, you'll need to cleanse the working area, arrange your crystals, and decide which of the gemstones you'll be using. We'll cover all the groundwork in this chapter.

Oh, just one more thing you'll be needing for this session: confidence!

Learn How to …

- ◆ Set up your healing space and assemble your crystals.
- ◆ Analyze your partner's healing needs.
- ◆ Prepare yourself for healing.
- ◆ Conduct a crystal healing session from beginning to end.

Clearing the Space

When you prepare an area for a healing session, you need to take great care to prepare a sacred and clean space. Why? When you purify the environment using a room clearing technique such as smudging, you are changing negative emotional residues back to white light, which is what you want surrounding you and your partner during a healing session. Here are some more ideas for room clearing.

Singing Crystals

What the heck is a singing crystal, you wonder? Does it perform at Madison Square Garden with backup dancers? Hardly! *Singing crystals* are long, tapered pieces of clear quartz that chime when tapped gently with another crystal. To clear a room, tap the crystals together while walking around its perimeter. The crystal resonance is released into the room to disperse negative energy. You can find singing crystals in metaphysical shops or online.

You can also use singing crystals to clear a chakra. Simply hold the crystals over the energy center and tap gently. The first time you try this, you'll notice that the first few taps aren't particularly melodious. This is because the sound is meeting a discordant energy. Continue to tap gently until you hear a pure sound.

Ting Cha Ringtones

As mentioned in Chapter 8, Tibetan chimes, called *ting cha* or *tingsha*, look like two small 4-inch metal cymbals. Ting cha are traditionally made from gold, silver, copper, brass, nickel, tin, or lead. Ting cha are rung at the beginning and end of meditation sessions and during other practices in Buddhist temples. Ting cha help to clear energies, to pacify local spirits, and to return the mind to a meditative state.

To clear crystals of unwanted energies and refresh them before a healing or meditation, set your crystals out. Ring the ting cha about 4 to 6 inches away from the crystals, imagining the sound waves washing over each crystal and purifying it. Imagine the sound going through each crystal, aligning its internal crystalline structure. Ring the ting cha seven times without letting the sound fade away. This will sustain the clearing vibration.

To clear a room of unwanted energies before a crystal healing session, seat yourself in the middle of the room and ring the ting cha at least seven times until you note a change in tone that signals clarity. Wait until each ring has faded completely before striking the ting cha again. Anything in the room will be cleared of negative energy, including other crystals. If your crystals have been programmed, the ringing will not affect the programming.

If you're looking to purchase ting cha, you'll find them in a Tibetan arts and crafts shop or on the internet under "Tibetan chimes" or "prayer chimes."

Salt Water Bowl

In Chapter 10, I talked about using a crystal to pull negative energies from the chakras and flick the energies off the crystal. Although you can certainly let that energy dissolve into the air as white light, you can also flick it toward a salt water solution, which will absorb the energy in a more visual way.

Set up an 8- to 10-inch bowl of salt water to absorb negative energies. When flicking unwanted energy off the end of your crystal, simply aim toward the bowl. A bowl of dry salt can also absorb unwanted energies in the room. Add a few teaspoons of lavender and sage to the bowl to keep it fresh for a week at a time. However, do not reuse the salt water or the dry salt because it will be filled with negativity. Pour it into the drain or into the earth and be done with it.

Aromatherapy

A great way to prepare the healing space is using an aromatherapy diffuser to release essential oils into a room and disperse unwanted energies. See Chapter 20 for more ideas on using diffusers and crystals.

My favorite cleansing blend of essential oils is frankincense, rose, and orange. The frankincense oil grounds unwanted energy; the rose oil transmutes negative energy to a higher vibration; and the orange oil imparts an uplifting vibration to the room.

You can pick up a prepared mix of aromatherapy oils, or locate an aromatherapist who can prepare a blend just for you and your specific needs.

Assembling Your Crystals

Although you might have many crystals—too many to keep track of, you might think—it's important to keep them protected, especially after they have been cleansed. Keep them in tip-top order, cleansed and ready for use during any healing session.

It's worth taking the time to learn your crystals by name and to memorize their healing powers. Although you'll prepare before a healing session to have a good idea of which gemstones to use, you don't want to be searching for a crystal you didn't think you'd need! Having your gemstones handy and arranged for practical use will save you time and frustration.

"Old Pal"

After your crystals have been cleansed and charged, they should be kept separate from gemstones that are not cleansed and may still carry negative energy. That's where a toolbox or tackle box comes in handy. I have a plastic box with various compartments—interestingly, it has a curious sticker on the outside that says "Old Pal." I find that very fitting—certainly crystals are some of my best old pals! Keeping them all together means the crystals will resonate and learn from each other's experiences and vibrations. Do they actually speak to each other? Well, you might not hear actual voices coming from inside the box, but their various resonances certainly do affect each other!

Because crystals can get heavy, select a sturdy box with a handle for easy transportation. You should be able to safely pick up the box and set it in the sunlight or moonlight to recharge all your gemstones at once. Now isn't that convenient? To protect your crystals' tips when storing your crystals in a tackle box or toolbox, stuff cotton batting at the ends of each compartment to prevent crystals from knocking against their storage units or each other.

Tools of the Trade

After you have selected a toolbox, consider how to arrange the crystals inside of it. Here are some suggestions:

- Chakra tune-up kit (see Chapter 5)
- The five master healers (see Chapter 9)
- Layout crystals (see Chapter 16 and this chapter)
- Grounding crystals, such as black tourmaline
- Kyanite, selenite, or clear quartz wands
- A place for your crystal pendulum

Keep aromatherapy bottles and supplies away from crystals because they will absorb the various scents. This can be a serious issue when using the crystals near the eyes as they may be sensitive to volatile oils. Additionally, the chakras will pick up unpleasant vibrations, and if they are stale or impure, the chakra will shut down.

Protect your healing crystals from EMFs. Keep your crystal toolbox away from sources of electromagnetic fields such as TVs, computers, radios, wiring, microwaves, and other home appliances. These can cause crystals to absorb their energy vibrations. When this happens, you might notice that your crystals are not working like they should or like they used to, even after a thorough cleansing and charging as their natural resonance is altered.

If you are still learning which crystals are which, label the sections in your toolbox. If you forget the name of a crystal, create a mystery section and take these gemstones to someone who can identify them for you such as a gemologist, geologist, or jeweler.

Crystal Analysis and Selection

Seeing the effects of crystals on someone other than yourself makes working with a partner fulfilling. Still, it can be overwhelming to research hundreds of crystals. Start with just a few crystals in your toolbox, such as the master healers and the chakra tune-up kit, to develop some healing skills.

Having a system handy will save you time and reduce the chaos of determining which crystals to use. A system provides an approach to analyzing which crystals might be needed in a session with a partner.

When you are first working with a partner, don't just dig into your crystal toolbox and start choosing gemstones for her. It's much better to take the time to find out about what she'd like to heal during the session. Really get down to the core of the issue, if you can. Ask probing questions that can help you determine which crystals to use. For instance, if someone is feeling uncertain about her job, is it because of a mean boss, new responsibilities, or a general lack of passion for the work? The specific information you glean could mean the difference between using a carnelian in the sacral chakra for self-esteem issues or a lapis lazuli at the third eye chakra for clarity on seeing her spiritual direction!

Have your partner intuitively select a few crystals to which she is attracted. Interpret the crystals for her, telling your partner about the uses of the crystals she's chosen and why she might have chosen them. Use them during the session at the appropriate chakra. Record any responses from your partner about these crystals in your crystal journal.

Music is an important part of the healing session to relax, soothe, or energize your partner. Allow your partner to choose from your selection of healing music. Crystals will also resonate to the music.

Ask your partner to intuitively select any essential oils to be used at the beginning of a session to create a relaxing environment or at the end of the session to help integrate all the healing energies. Some good choices may include the following:

♦ **Clary sage**—clears the aura and grounds energies

♦ **Frankincense**—purifies and removes negative influences

♦ **Geranium**—creates a sense of joy and happiness

♦ **Rosemary**—refreshes and re-energizes

♦ **Rose**—opens the heart chakra and soothes emotions

Next, use the following analysis worksheet to collect information from your partner for a crystal healing session. You might want to make several copies of the worksheet so you'll have a blank one handy.

For general physical health, record what the person says about her current health issues; this provides indicators for selecting additional crystals and a way to measure progress when following-up after the session. For general emotional and psychological health, ask what's been on her mind or what has been causing her stress. For psycho-spiritual issues, ask who or what has been spiritually inspirational and where she could use more peace in her life. Remember, your own intuition is important in this process. The crystals you sense are needed will be very helpful to the healing process.

For chakra analysis, determine which chakras are blocked by noting any ailments near the location of a chakra. You can ask your partner if she feels blocked anywhere in particular, or you can ask your pendulum which chakra to work on. Examine the crystals your partner selected to help you determine which chakra she seems to be targeting.

You can also record any affirmations you programmed into the crystals.

Analysis Worksheet for Healing Session

Name of client/partner: _____

Selected music: _____

Essential oil(s): _____

General physical health
Crystal(s) selected: _____

General emotional health
Crystal(s) selected: _____

General psycho-spiritual health
Crystal(s) selected: _____

Chakra analysis
Crystal(s) selected:

   1 Root _____

   2 Sacral _____

   3 Solar plexus _____

   4 Heart _____

   5 Throat _____

   6 Third eye _____

   7 Crown _____

Supporting affirmations

_____

General notes: _____

_____

_____

_____

Putting Your Lessons to Use

Before beginning work with a partner, ensure that the room where you will be working is cleared of negative energy (as described earlier in the chapter) and that your crystals are cleansed and fully charged. You can use soft music, candles, flowers, and aromatherapy to energize the room and to provide a pleasant and relaxing atmosphere.

You learned how to cleanse an aura in Chapter 10—that's a great place to start. Make note of the areas on your partner's aura that seem "sticky" so you can follow up during the session. Using the analysis worksheet, select the crystals you will use during the session, and put them on a nearby table so you can access them easily.

During your first session, finding your way around so many crystals might seem awkward and you may not know where to start. That's where taking a crystal course helps. You can practice in a classroom and use techniques on another student. During a course, you will also receive a crystal healing and learn what to expect. Putting it all together is what makes a crystal healing session so special.

In this session, we focus on the steps for completing a crystal healing with a partner: grounding, putting crystals on any areas of concern for your partner, and clearing and balancing the chakras. It will take about 30 minutes. How's that sound? Let's do it!

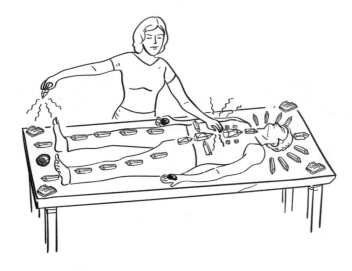

A crystal healing layout.

1. Have your partner lie face up on a massage table or on a comfortable mat on the floor. Place a dark grounding crystal, such as obsidian or garnet, 4 to 6 inches below your partner's feet, if he is lying on the floor. If he is lying on a table, place the crystal between his feet at the ankles. You can say a protection prayer and go through your own grounding exercise. (See the Crystal Healing Layout diagram.)

2. Consult your analysis worksheet; if your partner has any physical, emotional, or psycho-spiritual symptoms to be addressed, bring out the crystals you selected for those issues and place them at the correct points on the body. Don't forget that you can also tape them onto your partner's clothing so they don't slide off. (Review Chapter 11, Crystal Selections, for techniques used for physical healing, such as infusing energy.)

3. Gently place the chakra crystals you selected onto each chakra. You can also add a crystal crown layout around the head as detailed in Chapter 16. Use the techniques for clearing chakra congestion as outlined in Chapter 10.

4. Use your kyanite wand to center and balance each chakra. See Chapter 10 on aligning chakras in seconds.

   So far, you've placed crystals for the physical system, for the emotional and mental subtle energies, and for spiritual guidance or chakra healing. You've been busy programming, placing crystals on and off and doing some clearing, and chakra balancing. Now it's time to let the crystals do the rest so you can take a break.

5. Leave all the crystals in place on your partner and leave the room or sit quietly at least 3 feet away from your partner to allow all the healing energies to integrate. This last step is important to affect a healing response. It is also a time when your partner might seem to take a nap because he is so relaxed.

6. After about 5 minutes, rouse your partner gently and remove the crystals. (See the following closing section so you don't damage subtle energies when you remove the crystals.) Put your crystals aside for cleansing. Let your partner get up when he is ready. Offer him some water for grounding.

Congratulations! You completed your first crystal healing session. The debriefing with your partner after a session is important. On your analysis worksheet, write notes as a record for following up later if needed.

Closing the Session

Ending a session takes finesse and skill. You don't want to suddenly cut off the lovely flow of crystal energy by yanking the crystals off your partner and telling him to get up. There should be no sudden movements, nothing that will startle the other person out of his blissful state. Instead, gently remove the crystals, one at a time. Remove the grounding crystal last. Remember that the crystals have been sitting there for a while and the energy structures are still in place around your partner. Removing crystals too rapidly can cause discomfort or leave tears in a person's energy fields. Place the crystals aside to cleanse them properly later. Your partner might need some help getting up. Tell your partner to take his time because the subtle body energy will need a moment to get resettled after they are up. Ask your partner about their experience with the crystal healing and write up the results and impressions in your journal.

CARVED IN STONE . . . .

After a crystal healing session, you'll notice the person looks more relaxed and has an interesting glow of light around the face. Keep a mirror handy for your partner to see ome of these facial changes. This is the power of crystals, for relaxation and for the connection to sacred healing.

CHAPTER 18

Transformational Tools

Do you want to ask more about the mysteries of crystals but are afraid to ask? There are many people all over the planet who work in exceptional ways with crystals, as Earth keepers, Earth healers, crystal guardians, gatekeepers, crystal healers, crystal technologists, and crystal engineers. It's wonderful that crystal energy unifies so many who are engaged with the planet and its natural forces. Some might want to go further in these studies. For now, feel the energy of the macro-cosmos by using a crystal labyrinth for mindfulness training or experiment by setting up a crystal grid to bring sacred geometry into your life and into your living room. Experience the vibration of crystal singing bowls to harmonize and balance your body and mind.

This chapter includes some transformational tools to use on your journey. The way you use crystals will change the way you see things, feel things, and connect to your spirit. We will explore the mysteries of crystal skulls. Who doesn't want to know more about crystal skulls and how to connect to their wisdom?

Learn How to ...

♦ Create an effective crystal healing grid.

♦ Walk a labyrinth for mindfulness.

♦ Talk to your crystal skull.

♦ Listen to the music of crystals.

Crystal Grids

Crystal grids are a great way to pull in massive amounts of potential crystal healing energy. You might use all your crystals to create your grid or select ones for a special purpose. A crystal grid provides a structure using sacred geometry to create a dimensional space. This space creates a container to focus energy for a specific healing purpose. The use of a template to lay the crystals on helps with the precise geometric alignment and to focus your intent.

What is the difference between a crystal layout and a crystal grid? A crystal layout is the placement of crystals on and around the body for a meditation or healing session. A crystal grid doesn't use your body or anyone else's body for that matter. In a grid, crystals are laid out in a geometric pattern to integrate and focus energy for a specific goal or purpose. Through intent, that energy is focused to heal yourself or someone else or to help something manifest.

How to Create a Crystal Grid

Following my simple method, you only need a few components to create a crystal grid. The grid will remain in place for at least a day or more. The longer the grid is left in place, the more intense its effect; however, there is a point where you need to dismantle the grid since it has done its job or needs to be cleansed and recharged. If this is your first grid, you may be quite excited to see what it will look like.

State your goal. Write down your intent on a piece of paper as clearly as possible, include any timelines to help manifest your intent. For example, "I will find my soul mate within three months." Sure, why not, but be prepared to leave your grid out for three months to let the magic happen. You can also write a longer manifestation letter containing your hopes, wishes, and desires.

Program your focus crystal. A focus crystal is a crystal that you program with your intent and meditate with before adding it to the center of the grid. You will also work with this grid crystal daily to maintain and manifest your intent. The focus crystal can be a crystal cluster or a crystal pyramid, but an even stronger crystal to select is a single transmitter crystal of clear quartz or amethyst. Transmitter crystals are designed by nature specifically for the purpose of focusing and sending out energy and messages. You will place your intent or manifestation letter under the focus crystal. If you have a photo of a person that will benefit from the intent, place both the photo and the letter under the focus crystal.

Pick your crystals. Bring out your crystals and lots of them. You can use all your crystals in some way for your grid, or you can select only those that address your goal. Refer back to your intent: finding your soul mate, for example. For this intent, select love and relationship crystals (rose quartz and rhodochrosite), but also select crystals that enhance communications (moonstone, azurite, and sodalite) and grounding (turquoise, which doubles for communications, or smoky quartz), so the love of your life knows you are a good thing. Selecting crystals is like a narrative of how you want things to go; just match up your intent with the best crystals to support that intent.

Using a kit containing preselected crystals, instructions, and a printed grid template is an easy way to get set up quickly. Just be sure to cleanse and charge your crystals before setting up your grid.

Pick a spot. You need to select a place to lay your grid that will remain undisturbed for at least one to three days or even more. You can lay out your crystals following a prescribed template like the ones described in Henry M. Mason's book *Crystal Grids*. Later in this chapter, I've included the Flower of Life grid that you can copy, or you can find and download a free image of a grid from the internet. If you don't want the crystals to move about, you can tape them to the grid, but know that the crystal resonance will be confined by doing this.

Design your crystal grid. Now the fun part begins. Use your selected crystals to design your grid. To begin, place the programmed focus crystal in the middle of the layout with the written intent under the crystal. Next place crystals in a ring surrounding the focus crystal; these crystals provide the strongest intent, so they are placed closest to the focus crystal. For our soul mate example, these are the love and relationship crystals—rose quartz and rhodochrosite. If you're using a template, lay them on the grid lines, or just evenly space them around the focus crystal. Use four to six crystals or more if they are very small. It's okay to alternate different types of crystals.

Continuing with our soul mate example, the next ring of crystals is for communications—to get to know one another. You can use moonstone, azurite, and sodalite. Place these crystals on the energy lines following the template or place them free form, but try to align them into a geometric pattern. You can be more specific later. The universe knows what you are doing.

The third ring out from the focus crystal is for the grounding crystals. In our soul mate example, these are turquoise and smoky quartz. Align these crystals following the grid lines or follow your inner geometry teacher and go freely with the energy.

You can also place additional small quartz crystals to draw out the energies into the room and into the cosmos for creation. Remember the diagram in Chapter 11 that shows three crystal layouts to direct energy for healing? These techniques can also be used to lay out your grids; to remove excess energy, to infuse energy, or to direct the flow of energy.

Just think about what you are doing and why. There's no right way of doing this—there are many ways. Follow your intuition and be creative with the universal energies.

See the following figure as a rough example for our love grid. The image on the left illustrates an amethyst focus crystal, six surrounding round crystal shapes representing the love stones, six darker transmitter crystals used for grounding, and some smaller thin crystals to draw the energy from the love stones outward. There's also a tiny moonstone crystal in between each thin crystal to further align the energies to the moon goddess who governs the coming to fullness of all things and who is associated with the mysteries, psychic development, and fertility. The image on the right shows just a portion of the many energy lines that link the crystals in sacred geometry.

 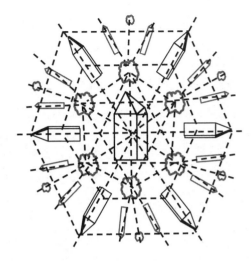

Crystal Grid and Energy Lines

A crystal grid and energy lines.

Activate your grid. Now that you have created the grid, activate the energy lines using a crystal wand. A kyanite wand is best because its natural purpose is to align energy structures. Other wands that are good for this task—a quartz crystal (great), a long quartz crystal wand (better), or a selenite wand (perfect)—can be used to draw energy lines between crystals to align their crystalline structures. Start by pointing your wand at the focus crystal. Then, while moving your wand, visualize an energy line being drawn from the focus crystal to each stone. Just be sure you have one line drawn from the focal crystal to each grid crystal to activate the connections. The crystals will then link their energies to each other.

This is the sacred geometry being activated in your crystal grid. It's quite complex, and when the energy settles in, creation starts. Sometimes manifestation can happen quite quickly.

Meditate with your grid. Now that the grid is set up, meditate with the intent set in your mind for a few minutes and then just let the intention go into the grid. You may feel a glow of energy from the grid. Stay with the glow for as long as you can to receive healing benefits, too.

Maintain your grid. If you can, make a daily routine to sit and reflect on your intent to help sustain the manifestation using the grid. You can also reactivate the energy of the focus crystal. (No, it didn't fall asleep, but it can become dormant if you ignore it.) Gently tap a few times on the crystal's tip with your middle finger—that's your fire finger in some systems, ether or space in others. Tapping it will send an electrical impulse through the crystal to reenergize it.

Here's a shortcut—use four pieces of kyanite as part of the grid to help maintain the structural integrity. You can say a dedication prayer for the grid. Add in a prayer of protection to help maintain the energy of the grid, and ask for special spirit guides or angels to stand watch and contribute their energy. If you have some carved stone angels, they can face outward to protect the grid.

You may want to swap out crystals or substitute newly charged ones to boost the energy. Remember to redraw the energy lines and smudge after.

Dismantle your grid. Stand in front of the grid and give a short verbal command to the energy structure of the grid. Say "release" and then, starting from the outside and working inward, pick up each crystal and put it aside. Remove the focus crystal and burn the piece of paper you wrote your intent on to release the intent. Cleanse all your crystals and recharge them to restore their strong yang energies for use in a new grid.

Flower of Life Grid

The Flower of Life grid is an extraordinary tool used to understand life. The symbols contain the fundamental forms of space and time. The image can be found in many places around the world, including the ancient Temple of Osiris at Abydos, Egypt, on a mosaic floor in Ephesus, Turkey, and in China. Thus, it must be important because of its presence in so many ancient places. When we tap into the ancient symbols, we can transcend our ordinary restrictions and access dimensional healing. The image encapsulates sacred geometry, light energy, and the expansion of dimensions. The teachings are quite deep and require some guidance. The image should be seen as three dimensional.

The Flower of Life.

The information about the Flower of Life really belongs to ancient mystery schools teachings about the secret of life. There are many who believe the image is a template from which all life springs. The structures for each of the Platonic solids is contained within the Flower of Life. You may recall that the Platonic solids represent each element that makes up our universe.

The Seed of Life and the Tree of Life are also embedded in the image. The Tree of Life is formed by joining the centers of the Flower of Life. It is an ancient Judaic-Kabbalah symbol representing the mystical interpretation of nature and is used for the purpose of explaining the relationship between the eternal infinity and the mortal finite universe.

There is also Metatron's Cube embedded in the Flower of Life. This cube is named after the archangel Metatron and is thought to be formed from his soul. The center of the cube is called a *star tetrahedron*, a three-dimensional tetrahedron of two intersecting tetrahedrons representing spirit and matter. In Egyptian mysteries this is called the *merkaba* (mer-ka-ba), meaning "light" (mer), "spirit" (ka), and "body" (ba). The merkaba is the form of the divine light body used in ascension to higher realms and as a bridge between the spirit and body to move from one dimension to another. All this sacred geometry is breathtaking, isn't it?.

These powerful symbols can be activated with further knowledge and training. As beginners, for now your crystals can be used on the Flower of Life grid for alignment and symbolism and to focus and increase the healing power. If you use the Flower of Life, you will connect with every type of grid. The important key is to see it dimensionally as a cosmic whole. You will need lots of crystals to use the Flower of Life. Look for smaller thinner crystals to fill the grid with interconnecting crystals. Once set up and activated, it can be left out or covered with a cloth for protection when not in use.

There are other formations that can be used for grids. Create your own—maybe a heart-shaped one using a heart-shaped rose quartz and other love stones. Put a picture of your sweetie in the middle with a special crystal to send some love.

Here are some crystal grid suggestions to help your manifestations:

♦ **Health and wellness:** green fluorite, sodalite, amethyst, jasper, aventurine, gold, turquoise, calcite, malachite, and quartz crystal points.

♦ **Wealth and abundance:** citrine, garnet, ruby, aventurine, sunstone, and pyrite. Place your prosperity grid in the wealth sector of your home (see the Feng Shui section in Chapter 15) or in the southeast corner of your home.

♦ **Emotional balance:** kyanite, rose quartz, rhodonite, sodalite, jasper, carnelian, lepidolite, double-terminated quartz, amethyst, and tourmaline.

♦ **Mental alertness and mindfulness:** lapis lazuli, sodalite, tiger eye, purple fluorite, and selenite.

♦ **Psychic development:** celestite, tiger eye, selenite, apophyllite, topaz, and Herkimer diamond.

Crystal Bagua

If you read how to use feng shui to create balance and harmony in Chapter 15, you **might** have figured out that the bagua is a type of grid. The meaning of each sector has already been determined over the course of many centuries. It's probably something you won't need to change. There is one aspect, however, that you can change, and that is to work the bagua in miniature instead of placing the crystals throughout the house. Here are two versions of a crystal bagua you can try:

1. Print out or draw the bagua chart found in Chapter 15. Place the bagua in the center of your home and orient the bottom to align with your home's main entrance. You will place the crystals on this bagua. Select crystals to place on each sector, determining which crystals will bring that sector into balance and harmony. Since the crystal bagua is located in the center of the home, the energy will radiate and balance each sector throughout the house. As a small note, you don't need to place crystals in all sectors, only the ones that need rebalancing. If you aren't too sure, use your pendulum to help you identify which sectors to work in. Hold your pendulum in each sector and ask, "Does this sector need to be realigned?" If yes, then use your pendulum to determine which crystals to put into what sectors. Keep a record of your formation by taking a photo or drawing the crystal bagua in your crystal journal.

2. Create a dream board using light Bristol board. Draw the 8-sided bagua in the center with spokes for each sector radiating out. Cut and paste an image to enhance each sector. For instance, for your knowledge sector add an image of books or an educational certificate and paste a photo of a crystal such as a crystal geode for enhancing the knowledge sector. Or, you can use a hot glue gun to affix small lightweight crystals to the board. The universe understands what you are doing and will help align the energies to your goals. Keep the dream board visible to keep your goals foremost in your mind and to give power to your intention.

Mindfulness Healing

Maintaining awareness from moment to moment enables you to stay present for what is happening right now and prevents you from making up things. Conceptualizing about what's happening can lead one to false conclusions or to misinterpret what is happening. In fact, when you stay in the moment, you can actually relax! Research has shown how mindfulness training reduces stress and anxiety. Studies on mindfulness have also shown other beneficial results, such as reduction of inflammation, increased antibody production, and other health benefits. Classes in mindfulness are usually around eight weeks in length and may be hosted by hospitals, community groups, yoga studios, spas, retreat centers, or private instructors. To compliment your journey in healing and wellness, there are also some additional supports for your mindfulness practice. Of course, crystals have become mainstream for their benefits in harmonizing the body-mind connection.

There's another step both beginner and intermediate mindfulness seekers can take with their crystals for healing, and that is using them in a labyrinth walk. Labyrinths are used for walking meditations, spiritual contemplation, religious reflection, and mindfulness training. First, learn more about the labyrinth and then add in crystals for even more healing benefits and self-transformation. Ready? Here we go!

Labyrinth, a Circle of Healing

Who doesn't need some stress relief? Labyrinths have been used in meditative walking and for ceremonial use for thousands of years. A labyrinth is a symbol of spiritual renewal and healing for the body, mind, and soul. For mindfulness, the labyrinth provides an exquisite opportunity for a journey to inner knowledge and peace. In fact, there are experts trained as labyrinth facilitators to help you with your labyrinth experience. If you are new to labyrinths, try meeting up with a group to get an overview of how to approach and work with labyrinth energy. To amplify the effect, crystals can be used as part of the labyrinth journey to heighten your awareness considerably. Your mind will be clearer; you will feel a sense of peace; and you may find a deeper sense of healing.

A-mazing!

You may be interested to know that there is a difference between a maze and a labyrinth. A maze is a puzzle, a riddle, or something to be solved; it contains complex path constructions that require choices to be made about direction. The design of these branching paths is called *multicursal*. The objective of a maze is to get to the center, but more importantly, to get out! Some mazes include dead ends and can have one or more entrance and exit points. Some may lead you on a wild goose chase and you might find yourself in one of many dead ends. Mazes are a wonderful way to exercise the left side of the brain and involve logic, memory, and strategic thinking.

While a maze is multicursal, a labyrinth is unicursal, meaning there is only one path and this path does not branch out. There's only one way in and the same way out—you end up where you started. A labyrinth is used as a symbol of meditative contemplation symbolizing the journey into ourselves and back out into the world. Its history is rich among many civilizations: the Vikings used images of labyrinths carved into stone; the mythical monster, Minotaur at Knossos in Crete was trapped in a labyrinth; Romans inscribed coins with labyrinths; and the image has also shown up in Peru among other countries. In the modern era, labyrinths are used in hospital settings, correctional institutions and jails, spas, religious and spiritual retreat centers, and city parks. So why is the labyrinth so important to so many different cultures through time? Simply, the journey into the mind never really stops.

Common between both a maze and a labyrinth is a center point—a place to be reached. Isn't that a bit like getting into our minds and finding the source of a problem or finding the key to knowledge? Maybe getting to the center is like finding the god-source within ourselves? There's no doubt working with a labyrinth is a mystical journey and can illuminate your spirituality.

Labyrinths have been found on the floors of many cathedrals across Europe. The most famous is in the Chartres Cathedral, built in the early thirteenth century in Chartres, France. It's large, measuring 42 feet across, and if unraveled, would be 858 feet long. (See the Chartres labyrinth figure.) Some labyrinths are much larger and can take more than 30 minutes to walk through. Where can you find a labyrinth? There are public labyrinths all over the world and directories can be found online. Veriditas and the Labyrinth Society are two major organizations that provide directories on their websites. (See Appendix B for more details.)

As we twist and turn inside the labyrinth, it's like getting into the recesses of your mind. Once you arrive at the labyrinth's center, you arrive at your answer and have the revelation you were seeking. A pause for quiet reflection will help the accumulated subtle energies settle. Let the insight manifest as an awareness in your mind, like an idea becoming stronger and stronger. As you gently make your way back out of the labyrinth, bring this new insight with you. It may develop further on your journey back to the entrance, a return to the outer world where you can manifest your revelation.

There are some great healing benefits from walking a labyrinth. The Labyrinth Society reports, "For a majority of walkers (66% to 82%), labyrinth walking increased levels of relaxation, clarity, peace, centeredness, openness, quiet, and reflectiveness, and reduced levels of anxiety, stress, and agitation. The experience of labyrinth walking supports recovery, renewal, integration of the whole person, and facilitating a sense of harmony."

Chartres labyrinth.

The labyrinth provides a mental and spiritual journey following life's twists and turns from the beginning of life to death and then rebirth. This simulation achieves a dynamic psychological journey, a blend of the real physical world with the inner world. The symbolism of the Chartres design is intricate, mystical, and illuminating. It is a spiritual teaching tool, and if you connect with a qualified teacher of the labyrinth, your journey will be quite powerful. However, if you aren't able to go to these beautiful labyrinths, you can use your fingers or an even better tool, a crystal, to trace through one on paper.

Crystal Healing with Labyrinths

As a transformational tool, walking a labyrinth provides an opportunity for an inner connection that is helpful to initiate dream quests, trance and channeling sessions, and other modes of introspection and spiritual renewal. When you add crystals to a labyrinth walk, you'll enhance your experience with a clearer mind and become more aware. It can be as simple as having crystals in your pocket or holding one in each hand as you walk the course. You may find a labyrinth made of crystals. What an exciting experience that would be.

Your approach before the walk is important. Use a consecration or dedication ritual before you start your journey. The intention is to receive something back—a message, a lesson, or insight about yourself or a matter that needs to be addressed. The alternating patterns going back and forth create a balancing effect, harmonizing within our bioelectric circuitry. Carry a crystal programmed with your intention in a bioenergetics circuit to help manifest the program. Which type of crystal should you carry? As this is a personal experience, the first-time through, use your personal crystal. You're already bonded with it and you trust your crystal. The labyrinth experience will only add more to the matrix of the crystal. You'll carry the labyrinth with you as part of the energy signature of the crystal and can tap into it during a later meditation away from the labyrinth.

As you circulate through the labyrinth, there will be an increased refinement of your subtle energy. Your crystal will be alert and will help carry out your intentions and hold the energy for you as you shift your consciousness. The crystal acts as a bridge between your consciousness and the higher levels of consciousness. The labyrinth is the transformational tool to help you shift your energy, your thinking, and your way of being. The crystal is a partner in this transformation. Both the crystal and the labyrinth are transformational tools.

Remember to bring a journal in which to write your impressions. It might seem like a lot to process. The journey is up to you. There are no wrong turns in a labyrinth.

Finger Walking

Maybe you can't get out to a large outdoor labyrinth. Why not try a finger labyrinth to achieve peace and serenity in your own home during a work break. You can start with the Chartres image, using your finger to slowly follow the winding path as you would if you were walking it. Go smoothly and gently, watching your breathing as you do. You will find a sense of peace. You can also use carved labyrinth boards that have a groove for your finger to run in. Some labyrinth boards have both a left- and a right-side labyrinth. Run a finger from each hand through the labyrinth to balance the left and right sides of the brain.

These finger boards are often used in hospitals and clinical environments as part of wellness programs. Finger walking helps to relax the mind of stress and anxiety, and it also focuses you on what you're doing rather than becoming caught up in other things. Go at your own pace, and stop when you want and rest.

This seems like a good time to add in your crystals. You can use a smooth crystal such as a tumbled carnelian (for energy), rose quartz (for love and compassion), moonstone (for sacred journeys), or bloodstone (for grounding). You can also use the smooth-end of a crystal wand or crystal massage tool. Program the crystal with your intent. Place the crystal at the entrance to the labyrinth and slide the crystal slowly through the labyrinth. Corners might need more awareness, but relax and you'll make it through without much thought. You may find this a very powerful way to shift energy. You may feel unwanted energy being released. Go slowly and breathe because the crystal healing will be highly activated with the sacred geometry of the labyrinth. Use different crystals to experiment with left- and right-brain activation (analytical and creative sides, respectively). Write your experiences in your crystal journal. By the way, a finger board makes a really nice gift for any occasion. Children also love to follow the lines of a finger board.

Crystal Skulls

A crystal skull is a quartz crystal carved in the shape of a human skull. Crystal skulls have such a fearful mystery and so much misinformation surrounding them, it's no wonder we don't feel too comfortable with them. An amazing amount of folklore with various stories of intrigue and warnings abound, meant to scare us off a bit and rightly so. We are looking at our own impermanence—our own mortality.

Crystal skulls are amazing tools for connecting you to a higher energy that can help you achieve your needs, such as a need to be healed. That makes them powerful, indeed. When you understand how they are used for healing, you may find it reasonable to look into having one of these beauties for yourself.

Crystal Skulls for Healing

The famous Mitchell-Hedges crystal skull was found in 1924 by Anna Mitchell-Hedges when she was a child during one of her father's archaeological excavations in Belize. Despite misadventures and many claims the skull may have been from Atlantis, scientific analysis shows it isn't of great antiquity. Yet, it has been guarded very carefully through the years. Many consider it to be one of the 13 ancient sacred skulls that when joined will reveal messages for humanity.

I sat in meditation with the famed Mitchell-Hedges crystal skull in Anna's home prior to her passing. During this meditation I found a rare clarity of messages coming into my head telepathically. The teaching was quite clear and amazing! Skull meditators have seen holographic images, heard bells, or felt the presence of beings. One researcher found that, in itself, the Mitchell-Hedges skull did not have any direct powers, but he did feel that the skull was an amplifier of one's own psychic centers and that brain waves trigger a crystal resonance or wave from the skull. Does that sound similar to the science of crystal resonance mentioned in Chapter 2?

The crystal reflects that signature wave back and stimulates the psychic centers. Perhaps that's why some crystal skulls seem to work for some people and not for others. The energy of the crystal needs to match and resonate with the person. You are its guardian, its custodian, and will look after it for a long time. Let's have a look at how to acquire a crystal skull for yourself and use it for healing and meditation.

Selecting a Crystal Skull

Imagine selecting a friend. It's a very personal experience. Finding a skull is similar. You can leave it up to intuition but do cover the basics. Look at the crystal first before you look at the skull's formation. Is it sitting flat on an even surface? Is it well polished? Next, ask if it is a good skull? Does it have two eyes, a jaw, teeth, and other skull details? One of my wholesalers has a shelf full of crystal skulls at eye level and as you walk into the room, they are all looking at you! What an amazing and awesome experience! It's like trying to pick out your own puppy from many different litters. How do you make up your mind? They all have a voice, but which one is the one for you? I like to select one that pushes me a bit to grow.

Sometimes as soon as you touch a skull, you know it's right. You may feel a sense of joy, a special familiarity and excitement. Look no further, the choice has been made. The skull has picked you! If it takes a bit longer to find a skull, put the crystal skulls that you are attracted to out in a row, and use your pendulum to select one. It's best to walk around to detach a bit and to ground yourself and then come back to them and let yourself be guided. Pick the skull that you feel the strongest vibrations from or attraction and keep this one as your own personal skull. You can purchase the remaining skulls if you feel you would like to pass them along to others or will use them later on for yourself.

A crystal skull is a portal. The third eye and crown chakras become activated just by holding and looking at a crystal skull. My friend, Skully, says it is an aide "to opening communications within yourself to reach other dimensional beings—to receiving their teachings to develop your intuition and understanding of self and others. To develop compassion for all things as there were others here before you and about leaving it for others after you." Other cultures use skulls a symbols of rebirth and renewal, not death.

As a skull is such an amazing, powerful communications and transformational tool, it needs to be kept away from negative or overpowering energies. A few words of advice—avoid putting your skull behind glass, such as in a glass bookcase or in a glass jar. Avoid covering it up or tucking it away. Skulls want to be out in the open. I asked an expert if a skull would be okay in a pyramid, and sure enough, it's okay for recharging but don't leave it in there for long. Just one more item for you to be aware of: the eye sockets are energy portals, and as such, avoid poking them.

Skull Components

There are many different styles of skulls. There are 22 bones in the human skull that are immobile and one that is mobile, which is the mandible or jaw. Often, skulls are carved as one piece and include facial bones that form the upper and lower jaws, nose, orbits, and other facial structures. When you look at many skulls, they may appear like they are mass produced. However, consider this: each skull is carved from crystal and is hand finished. Traditionally, the eyes are carved last to open the energy of the skull. Some skulls are more detailed than others, but that doesn't mean they are less effective. People are drawn to different styles, and each crystal skull is completely unique.

Some skulls seem contorted or stretched. These elongated skulls are called *comets*. I have seen skulls with hairstyles that look like Elvis's hair wave or a feathered headdress. Some are special for interdimensional access, ascension support, and access to alien beings, star beings, extraterrestrials, Atlanteans, Lemurians, ancient Peruvians, and Ascended Masters—the works! There are even dragon skulls that serve as a bridge between nonhuman dimensions for elemental work. You might like to delve into these different skull types right away if you are attracted to them or go for a more conventional look. What matters is that you "trust what you are drawn to" say the experts at crystalskulls.com.

Cleansing and Recharging the Skull

Crystal skulls are crystal and as such, you need to follow the same guidelines for them as for all crystals (as mentioned in Chapter 8). Be mindful of the skull's composition and cleanse it appropriately with smudge. Recharge it in sunlight or moonlight or lay the skull among other crystals, such as selenite, for recharging. If you are really in touch with your skull, it will tell you what is best for its health.

Welcoming, Activating, and Naming Your Skull

Observe all the physical aspects of the skull. It's part of the bonding process to admire all the skull's nooks and crannies. Hold the crystal and talk to it. Let your voice resonate in the crystal. Find out where your skull wants to reside when it's not with you. Mine are lined up and like to be in a particular order, and some don't like to be placed next to others. They can be bossy and even humorous, but really all they are trying to do is get into a spot where they can be in their best energy.

To turn on the energy of the skull, you can go through the crystal activation in Chapter 8, or do a crystal blessing exercise or skull dedication. To activate, use sounds such as those from a ting cha or a tuning fork. You can also bathe your skull with a homeopathic solution made from another ancient skull; or with the crystal vibration from another skull, or from an ancient skull that might be touring your area. The activation of a skull is to wake up the skull's consciousness and to open the consciousness within yourself. The clearer the connection, the more active and energetic the skull will be. In addition, it will expand over time and with increased usage.

You don't actually name your skull. The skull will give you its name when its ready. Once named, however, you can't really sell it. It's yours to keep. Remember, you are its custodian.

Maintaining and Working with Your Skull

If you must, keep your skull in a velvet bag to protect it from scratches. Talk to and touch your crystal skull. As its caretaker, you must keep it safe and should not abandon it. It will change the energy in your home. Note: A skull isn't a pet. It likes to be appreciated. Listen to it.

Take your skull with you to sacred sites to gather up the energy. Place it on the ground or near special features such as altars. Dip it into sacred water. It's especially important that it meets other skulls and has download and upload sessions. Have a picnic and put the skulls together in a meeting place. It's okay to add a crystal skull to your bagua, specifically in the Ancestors sector, as a connection to the past. If you wish to use the skull as a symbol of transformation, add it to one of the other sectors.

Types of Skull Crystals

Not all crystals can be made into skulls. They not only need to be hard enough to carve without falling apart. They also need to reflect the healing energies of each type of crystal. With more sophisticated manufacturing tools and artisans, skulls have been made from crystals where a part of the crystal skull, usually the top, has another crystal as part of the same skull. The secondary crystal is left untouched in its natural form, and it can be a thing of beauty to see the natural crystalline material as part of the skull. A more brittle crystal can be left untouched and supported by the skull. An example is a stick of green-blue tourmaline laying on one side of a quartz crystal skull. These are unusual pieces and make a special addition to any collection.

Over the past few years, many different types of crystals have been made into skulls due to demand. Everything from amazonite to zebra stone has been used to make skulls, and some are very pricey because they require expert handling. In fact, noted celebrity Victoria Beckham carries a black tourmaline crystal skull wherever she goes to keep her mind positive and to protect against negative energies. I have many favorite skulls such as a labradorite skull and a lapis lazuli skull. My friend Skully says that smoky quartz skulls are particularly worth having and to look for those with veils as they are best for scrying and seeing past and future events.

Communicate with Your Crystal Skull

If you remember from Chapter 5, you entered into the crystal to get in direct communication with it. When the crystal is dense, black, or opaque, getting inside a skull you can't see into is a bit difficult. However, you can imagine an opaque crystal skull as having a large chamber inside its cranium, and once inside, you can speak directly to and communicate with beings. You can touch the walls for information, visions, and messages.

Crystal Skull Meditation

Setting time aside to meditate with your skull can be very interesting. Sometimes the skull will not want to connect on your time and may appear later in the dream state. Be sure you have your skull fully activated and then you can proceed with a deeper meditation with your skull. The mark of successful meditation with your skull is when you receive messages, healing energy, and other communications from it. The skull may be obvious in its messages, or it may work quietly in the background in your dreams.

Sit quietly with your crystal skull in your hands, rest it in your lap, facing up toward you. Gaze gently into its eyes. Try not to blink. This is a form of scrying, discovering hidden knowledge. Just breathe gently and allow whatever sensations arise to evolve. If you get further instructions from the skull, such as to close your eyes, then try it. The skull may want you to see something and to go deeper inside. Stay in touch with the skull during your meditation session, and when finished, thank it and place it down safely. You may then want to shake out your hands to disconnect from the energy.

Crystal Singing Bowls

Another great transformational tool that's very popular with healing studios, meditation centers, and even among musicians is the crystal singing bowl. These are made from crushed quartz crystals that are heated and formed into bowls. When tapped with a gong, the bowls emit a very long natural resonance. Its tone is dependent on the size of the bowl and the material it's made from. It's an electrifying feeling, a pure sound vibration that resonates right through you. As our bodies are mostly water, the crystalline sound energy aligns all our subtle energies, our chakras, as well as our organs, tissues, bones, and brain.

Scientists and technologists (the new alchemists) have added even more healing to the bowls. Additional crystals, such as ruby, and metals, such as gold and platinum and tanzanite, can be added together to create a pure vibration. One such company, Crystal Tones in California, makes Alchemy Crystal Singing Bowls. The sound from these bowls can create a deep relaxation response, accelerate healing, and initiate shifts of consciousness. A healing session with the bowls is a truly transformative experience. If you can't find a therapy session using crystal singing bowls, check out videos on YouTube.

If you can, attend a live concert of crystal bowls or even organize such an event; it will be very beneficial to your health, your mind, and your community. (Bring your crystal skulls, they will love to come too!)

CARVED IN STONE . . . .

Are you a Seeker on a quest for knowledge and learning about the sacred mysteries? The veil between your consciousness and those of other realms is much thinner at various times of the day and night, during rituals and ceremonies, and at special times of the year. The truth always been there for you to find.

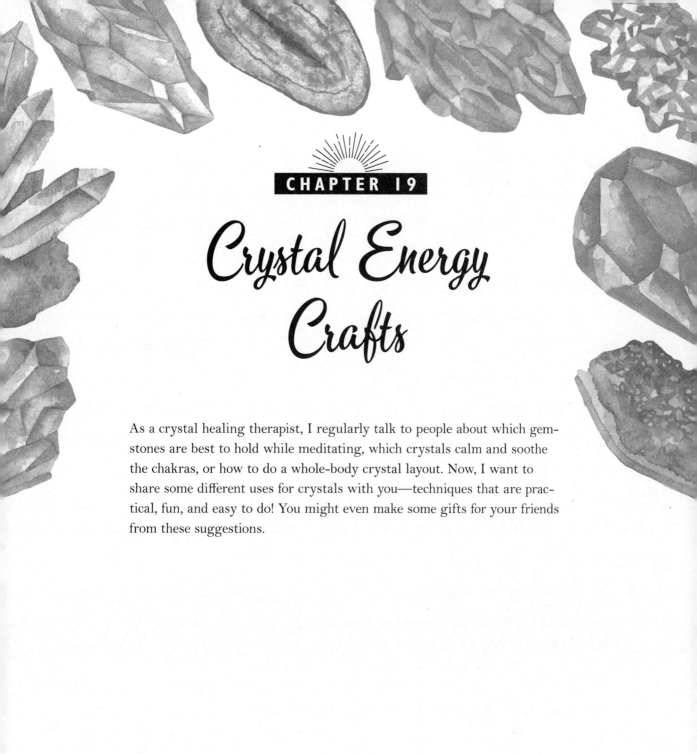

CHAPTER 19

Crystal Energy Crafts

As a crystal healing therapist, I regularly talk to people about which gemstones are best to hold while meditating, which crystals calm and soothe the chakras, or how to do a whole-body crystal layout. Now, I want to share some different uses for crystals with you—techniques that are practical, fun, and easy to do! You might even make some gifts for your friends from these suggestions.

Learn How to ...
- ◆ Make gem water.
- ◆ Fashion power packs.
- ◆ Create dream pillows.
- ◆ Make a money tree.

Healing with Gem Water

No doubt you have heard of special places where you can drink natural spring water that comes from a sacred site like Lourdes or from the holy wells in the United Kingdom. There are many claims of healing from drinking sacred water. These healing waters are available throughout the world.

When water travels underground, it becomes electromagnetically charged by piezoelectric energy emanating from the crystalline bedrock. The water also picks up an energetic field unique to its location. When we drink this water, we are actually getting crystal-charged water!

Because our bodies are approximately two-thirds water, the electrolytes contained within each cell can be manipulated and changed by the crystal-charged water. Electrolytes are responsible for carrying nerve impulses and muscle contractions, so if they are out of balance or in poor condition, the ramifications could be quite serious.

When we drink crystal water, the crystal energy works its way into each cell and transfers light in the form of ions to the body's systems. An electrolyte conducts electricity and works with piezoelectric energy introduced from a crystal. So, just as we can program a computer and make it faster and stronger, we can program the crystal water through intention to create healing energy structures. Imagine that!

Mixing Up a Batch of Gem Water

The traditional way to create gem water from gemstones is to place a few cleansed crystals, such as clear quartz or rose quartz, in a clear glass jar and fill it with spring water.

Why spring water, you ask? Well, spring water already carries a universal life force and electromagnetic properties. When this combines with the power of the crystals, you have a regular life-sustaining elixir on your hands!

As a reminder, malachite, also known as *copper carbonate*, has a high copper content and reacts with acids, so it should not be used for making crystal water and should not be given to animals, especially. Also, avoid azurite, orpiment (contains arsenic), and cinnabar (contains mercury) when making gem water. Commercially prepared essences of gemstones or homeopathic doses that use dilution methods are generally safe.

To infuse your spring water with crystal power, place the crystals in a jar with a clear glass lid and set the jar in direct sunlight for 4 to 7 hours. (Be sure the jar is in a safe place and won't be hidden by an approaching shadow.) After crystallizing the water, remove the crystals using a slotted spoon, and transfer the crystallized water to an airtight bottle. Drink the water within a few hours because the potency decreases rapidly over time.

When you sip your crystal-infused water, you will find that the plain old spring water has changed its quality. It will feel different, more full or thick in your mouth, and less watery. This is because it has started to take on the properties of the crystals and may even feel heavier.

What kind of benefits can you expect from drinking gem water? They're similar to wearing crystals, except you will feel them at a subtle level within your body tissues and cells as the chi or prana gets reenergized. If you are sensitive to your energy body, you might also be aware that your chakras and aura is brightening.

You can use different combinations of crystals in your water for special concerns. For example, tiger eye and lapis lazuli help you to focus on school studies. For skin issues such as eczema or rashes, infuse the water using an orange- or amber-colored glass with carnelian and opal to help rejuvenate the skin.

Because the gem water has to be consumed within a rather short period of time to receive its benefits, I recommend using a smallish jar to steep it in. Another nice thing about this process is that you're getting double benefits—making a wellness energy drink for yourself while recharging your crystals in the sun. There are a number of new products on the market that feature clear glass water bottles with a crystal or gemstones sitting in a well inside the bottle. You never need to clear or clean the crystals. The water gets charged without direct contact with the crystals. Try drinking the gem water three days in a row for amazing results.

Moon Juice

As mentioned in Chapter 8, you can charge your crystals in moonlight, so why not set out your crystals for both moon bathing and making gem water. Soak cleansed crystals in a bowl of spring water in full moonlight, and pour off the water to drink in the morning. Add a few drops of dew water if you can get it. It will have been blessed by the fairies.

Other Uses for Crystal Water

Remember that crystal water must be used within a few hours or be disposed. If you happen to have some crystal-infused water left over, or you want to find more uses for this amazing liquid, here are some ideas for putting the extra to good use:

♦ Pour any remaining water into your flower pots to energize your plants. Crystal water is excellent for seeds and starter plants. If you have an ailing tree or shrub, pour a circle of crystal water around its base a few times a month.

♦ Use natural fabric, such as cotton, or a sea sponge to soak up crystal water, and then place the damp cloth on sore muscles or on the forehead for headaches and sinus issues.

♦ Pour the water into a plastic spray bottle, and spritz the room and your bed linens. Add a few drops of essential oil to the water and increase the subtle effects. Geranium, mandarin orange, and peppermint oils create an uplifting and joyous environment. Try combining crystals and essential oils, such as amethyst and lavender, for peace and relaxation prior to meditation or yoga. Spray the mixture into the air and then walk into the mist to fluff up your aura with an energizing vibe.

♦ My favorite room-freshening blend of gem water is rose quartz, amethyst, and blue lace agate with a combination of clary sage, lavender, and orange essential oils. The room becomes warm and welcoming, imparting a brighter, lighter, and higher vibration in the therapy room.

♦ Use gem water in your bath water.

♦ Spritz yourself, too, and be sure to get a little dab in each chakra.

The Healing Power of Gem Essences

Have you ever wondered why there are so many different types of medicines to do the same thing? Well, what works for one person doesn't necessarily work for someone else. Each one of us may need a different type of medicine for healing. The same is true to some degree with crystals because each crystal is different and so is each person's energetic field.

What if there was a method of getting a standard dose of crystal healing power? There is! A *gem essence* provides the same jolt of energy to everyone because it provides the same vibrational essence of the gem. It's a homeopathically prepared solution made by using sunlight to infuse spring water with the characteristics of specific crystals. This method is used to preserve the special essence of the gem.

Our human systems accept gem essence and can fully integrate it as part of our own energy. The practice of using this subtle material healing is called *energy medicine*. This healing restores balance to the body's energy field to bring about health and wellness.

A gem essence is like gem water, except it has longer-lasting healing power. You create gem essence the same way as you make gem water, but to hold the gem essence so it can be stored for a longer time, you add alcohol produced through a distillation process (usually brandy) to stabilize the energetic properties. It's a common process for stabilizing homeopathic solutions. There's very little alcohol in a drop of the finished essence. Here's how to make a gem essence:

1. Place a few cleansed crystals, such as clear quartz or rose quartz, in a small- to medium-size clear glass jar, and fill it with spring water. Place a clear glass lid over the top. (You can also use a quartz crystal singing bowl to make the gem essence so there are no energetic obstacles.)

2. Set the jar in the sun and ensure it is exposed to full sunlight during the peak hours of the day when ultraviolet light is at its strongest.

3. If you can, stay by the water jar or bowl and soak up the sun for a little while, focusing on positive thoughts, praying, or meditating; this helps to bind the pattern for healing in the water. Remember Emoto's findings about the water crystals being structured through thought from Chapter 3? Your prayers and focused intent will be magnified by the crystal and the water will take on the healing properties of the crystal and your positive thought.

4. After 7 to 9 hours of sun exposure, pour the water into a sterile pitcher without touching the water to keep the gem essence pure. You can use another crystal to prevent the crystals from falling out as you pour.

5. Using a syringe, fill a sterilized 2-ounce amber-colored bottle with a glass dropper, halfway with gem water. Fill the remainder of the bottle with brandy. Use a good brand of VSOP (Very Special Old Pale) brandy to stabilize the gem essence. Use of the amber bottle prevents contact with sunlight, which can definitely decrease its potency over time. Shake the bottle 32 times to disperse the alcohol and activate the ingredients homeopathically.

6. Label the gem essence with the name of the crystal used and the date it was made. It's best used within six months while its potency is at its highest.

The usual gem essence dose is two to four drops, three to five times a day as needed. A course of treatment should not exceed six weeks because as the energy is integrated, sensitivity to the formula decreases. There are no known toxic effects to gem essences. However, you might notice some positive effects over the first few days of taking the formula. You can also add up to eight drops to plain bath water to soak your entire body (and chakras!) for 20 minutes in the gem essence.

Like gem water, some gem essences can be applied topically for physical healing. Add four to eight drops of gem essence to an 8-ounce bowl of water. Soak some cotton balls or pads in the solution and apply the gem essence externally for 10 minutes. Here are some suggested gem essences for topical application:

- **Amethyst**—To ease headaches or stress, apply to the forehead and temples.
- **Carnelian**—For skin complaints such as rashes, pimples, or redness, apply over the area.
- **Hematite**—Apply to sore muscles and painful joints and bruises.
- **Rose quartz**—To alleviate inflammation in the joints, place cotton soaked in essence over the joints.

- **Tiger eye**—Apply to the stomach area to calm a stomachache and to aid the digestive organs.

- **Turquoise**—To cool a fever, apply to the forehead; to reduce a sore throat, apply over the throat.

Crystal Power Packs

Small crystals have great benefits when grouped together in a bag. You can create your own power pack of crystals from gemstones or crystals that are chipped or are too small for big healing issues. Instead of restringing a broken gemstone necklace for instance, remove them from the string and reuse them in a pack. Remember that *all* crystals, regardless of their size, have piezoelectric characteristics.

Here are some ideas for using the power of many tiny crystals:

- Find or make a little drawstring bag—cotton, silk, or another natural fabric—and place your crystal pieces inside. Place the bag in the refrigerator and use it to cool irritated muscles, ease sinus pain, and relieve headaches.

- Place a crystal pack at the top and bottom of a bone (for example, at the wrist and elbow or at the knee and hip) for 3 to 5 minutes to help clear the meridians of stagnant chi.

- Add some herbs to a crystal pack, such as lavender for relaxation or peppermint to perk up your energy. (It is not recommended to use herbs in crystal eye packs because dust and particles from the herbs can cause eye irritation.)

- Enhance dreaming by making a dream pillow using rainbow-colored crystals. Select some brightly colored crystals, but limit the crystals to seven types; otherwise, your head will be too "buzzy" to sleep. Place the crystals in a silk bag and then tuck it under your pillow. If your body needs to relax, place it on or under your belly to absorb the energies. Some crystals that enhance dreaming are mookaite (the Australian dream crystal), labradorite, and moldavite. Check out Chapter 15 for more types of crystals used to enhance dreams.

♦ For a younger sleeper, make a baby dream pillow to place under a baby's bed (it's safest there!) and help her relax and align her subtle bodies as she goes through rapid growth. Some calming and soothing sleep crystals that babies and young children like are rose quartz, sodalite, amethyst, amber, aventurine, and moonstone.

I mentioned a crystal power pack in Chapter 12 for your "Stress Day" consisting of opal, rose quartz, moonstone, and citrine. Here are some other power pack combinations to help you through life's highlights:

♦ **Improving communications, attention, and focus**—turquoise, lapis lazuli, tiger eye, smoky quartz, and clear quartz

♦ **Calming fears and emotions or post-traumatic stress disorder (PTSD)**—kunzite, aquamarine, amethyst, fluorite, citrine, and a self-healed clear quartz crystal

♦ **Attracting prosperity, wealth, and abundance**—jade, aventurine, citrine, Herkimer diamond, gold, ruby, sun stone, and tiger eye

♦ **Peace and calm**—sodalite, sugilite, larimar, agates, blue lace agate, celestite, and rose quartz

♦ **Energizing, increasing luck**—garnet, green tourmaline, double-terminated clear quartz, amethyst, Herkimer diamond, citrine, pyrite, aqua aura quartz, and tiger eye

How about some special help for insomniacs, those of us who are so plugged into work and other stresses that at the end of the day nighttime relaxation is all but impossible? A different kind of sleep pack is helpful for chronic restlessness and anxiety. Try these ideas:

♦ **Hematite**—It's physically and mentally calming and helps to deflect and transform unwanted energies into universal light. If you're physically uncomfortable at night, tape pieces onto your body at the joints or around sore spots.

♦ **Kunzite**—It has a high-lithium content and helps a whirling, neurotic, or obsessive mind calm down and relax. Wearing the crystal at the heart chakra throughout the day provides the most help. For people who wake up earlier than expected without full rest, you can use this crystal to reduce anxiety over not getting enough sleep! Many people sleep less than five hours a night with no ill effects. In fact, I sleep less than six hours a night surrounded by many crystals. They provide me with energy and help me maintain a higher vibrational rate.

◆ **Lepidolite**—It can be used during the day to help offset the build-up of muscle tension so you are more relaxed by bedtime. If you wake up during the night, you can use it to settle an overactive mind and reduce a build-up of physical tension. Holding one loosely in each hand will help you drift back to sleep.

◆ **Moonstone**—It's a very old remedy for calming the emotional distress that activates insomnia. It helps reduce emotional tension. Moonstone is feminine yin energy that helps to stimulate self-composure and self-confidence. I keep pieces of moonstone by my windowsill during the full moon to absorb the lunar rays. When needed, place the crystal on the solar plexus or heart chakras against bare skin and focus on the crystal to activate it before sleeping.

◆ **Sodalite**—It's a crystal of peace that helps to calm mental chatter and confusion. Putting the crystal under your feet will calm your whole body. Placing the crystals around your head or in your pillow at night will promote mental relaxation. You can also program the crystal with an affirmation such as, "I am now fully relaxed and sleepy."

You can also try a layout of the above crystals around your bed on the floor, taped under the bed sheets, under your pillow, in your pillowcase, taped onto your chakras, or on your night table. Maybe you can think of some new ways, too.

To cleanse a crystal sleep pack, smudging is best. When you are finished using your pack, recycle the crystals by giving them a good cleanse in salt water and letting them recharge for at least a few days in sunlight or moonlight.

Other Crystal Crafts

When you incorporate crystals into crafts, you're getting more bang for your buck, so to speak. First, you're creating something that's lovely to look at or that has a specific use; second, you're harnessing and using positive energy in a new, fun way! If you happen to be very crafty and need lots of gemstones to work with, you can buy crystals in bulk. Ask your local gem seller for assistance. They may even have crystals for craft items at a discounted price.

Money Tree

My grandmother had a money tree made from the leaves of jade. Each crystal leaf was hand carved and attached to a wire frame that had other small gemstones covering the branches, trunk, and base. It was so beautiful. When a breeze came through the room, the crystals would tinkle lightly, their sounds crisp, calling the wealth and abundance gods to come.

You can make your own, too, and place the money tree in your home using feng shui principles to place it in the wealth corner of your bagua. Each time you go by the tree, lightly brush the leaves to activate its wealth energy and wish-fulfilling power. Here are two suggestions for making your own money tree:

1. Thread small crystals that have eyeholes onto a wire frame tree. Make the wire tree from copper wire as it is easier to bend and more conductive for the crystal energy. Affix the tree to a wooden stand to carry the weight of the crystals. Smudge your crystal tree and invoke the money gods.

2. You will need a wire-framed tree, some crushed crystals, and glue that dries clear for this money tree. To make a tree branch, pour a small amount of glue (2 teaspoons) in a 1-inch oval on a silicone-lined sheet. While the glue is still wet, drop crushed gemstones into the glue. Repeat for each additional branch. Allow them to set thoroughly, overnight is best. Peel the disc off the sheet, apply a drop of glue to the underside, and place on a branch of the wire tree to simulate leafy branches. Fill your tree with either all the same color crystals or make a rainbow tree for wishes to come true.

Crystal Kits and Gifts

All kinds of science kits are available for people of any age. Crystal growing kits are especially popular, providing all the materials needed for homegrown crystals, usually from chemical reactions. They are a lot of fun.

If your youngster needs a science project (or just wants to learn more about crystals), you can easily put your own crystal science kit together. Use a plastic tray with multiple sections, and add a card with the name of each crystal, where it was found, and any other details such as its lattice structure.

You can build a collection of stones and crystals representing each of the igneous, sedimentary, and metamorphic rock classifications we talked about in Chapter 2.

How about creating a chakra crystal kit with a crystal for each chakra? A rainbow pack of crystals for enhancing the aura or stress pouch along with a gift certificate would also make a lovely gift.

For someone who could use some healing, it's easy to put together a healing kit as a gift in a smart-looking box. Here's a sample "prescription" or Rx crystal healing kit:

◆ Hematite (muscle pain, liver cleanse)

◆ Malachite (internal organs, heart)

◆ Rose quartz (reduces inflammation)

◆ Carnelian (skin ailments)

◆ Calcite (bone)

◆ Green fluorite (digestion, colds)

◆ Amethyst (headache)

Add some instructions on how to use the gemstones, such as placing the crystal on the afflicted area for up to 10 minutes or taping the crystal on the area overnight. You can also create a kit for increasing romance and another kit for spiritual attunement perhaps including a crystal angel or an animal totem. Personalize the kits with a special selection just for the recipient—one for a coworker for his work stress, one for your sister to help with her pregnancy, and so on.

Crystals help stimulate creativity, so I'm sure once you get going, you will think up some more ideas on how to use crystals!

CARVED IN STONE . . . .

Crystals are all around us. Their crystalline structure binds the earth together and us along with it. Spiritual growth, healing the inside and out, and consciousness raising are all helped when we interact with crystalline structures. Crystals are truly a gift from the earth. There are few things on this planet that haven't come from this planet, except for moldavite and a few other meteorites to give us a needed boost of energy and healing.

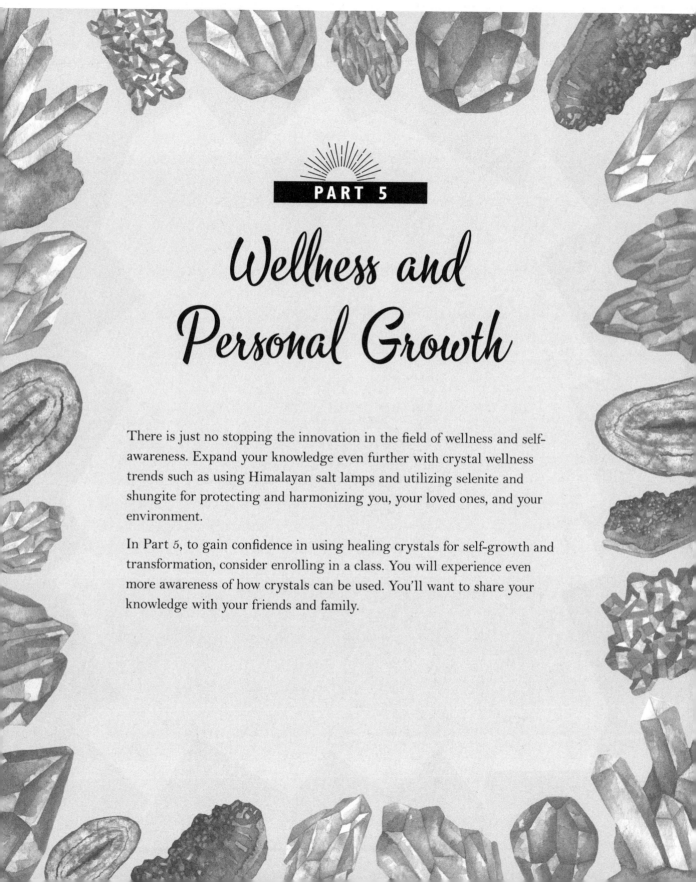

PART 5

Wellness and Personal Growth

There is just no stopping the innovation in the field of wellness and self-awareness. Expand your knowledge even further with crystal wellness trends such as using Himalayan salt lamps and utilizing selenite and shungite for protecting and harmonizing you, your loved ones, and your environment.

In Part 5, to gain confidence in using healing crystals for self-growth and transformation, consider enrolling in a class. You will experience even more awareness of how crystals can be used. You'll want to share your knowledge with your friends and family.

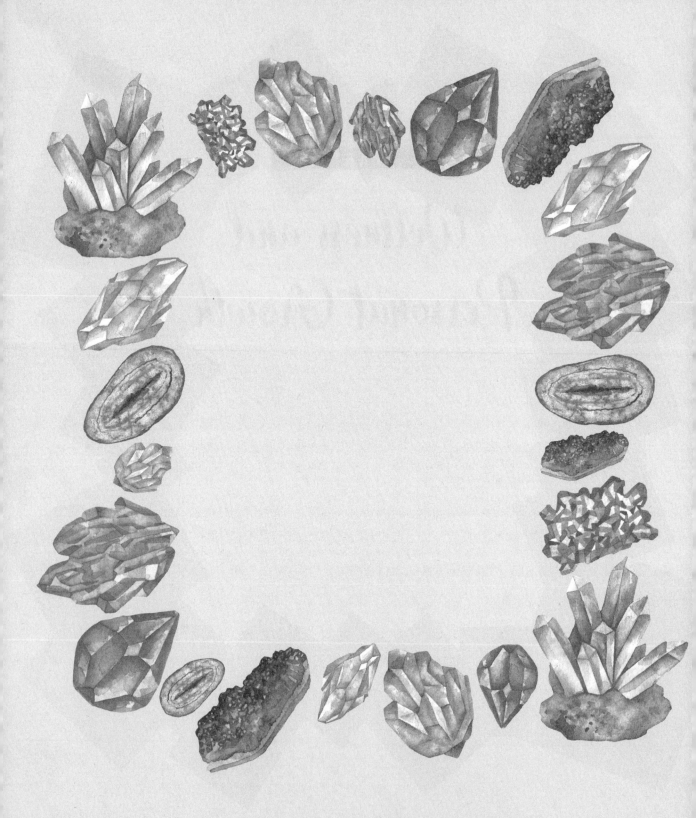

CHAPTER 20

Crystals for Wellness

Healing crystals are showing up in new products all the time as the science of crystals expands. Inventors are understanding more about the amazing properties of crystals and using them in new technology to improve our lifestyle. We now have new ways to use crystals for our health and wellness, even though ancient healing methods using crystals still exist.

We still need a connection with nature for healing to take place. We need the natural earth elements to help us heal through sacred geometry. There are many crystals that support wellness, and they are easy to obtain.

Learn How to ...
- ◆ Pickle your crystals with salt.
- ◆ Use a Himalayan salt lamp to harmonize and protect your space.
- ◆ Heal your body using Epsom salts.
- ◆ Find new products made from crystals.
- ◆ Follow crystal fashion trends.

Salt Crystals

You may be wondering why there's a section on salt crystals. Yes, salt is a healing crystal, and it has been used for thousands of years to flavor and preserve food, as medicine, and to draw out poisons. We take for granted what is in our salt shakers. There's a lot more to salt crystals to appreciate.

Kosher and Pickling Salt

There's an expression in cooking that all salt is the same. That is, all salt is sodium chloride. Table salt typically has iodine added. Why, you ask? Iodine is an essential element that helps prevent developmental problems, goiter, and other thyroid problems. The most common natural sources of iodine are seaweed, fish, dairy products, eggs, enriched grain products, and plant foods grown in iodine-rich soils. It's added to salt to prevent iodine deficiencies in those who live away from the coastlines and who consume foods that are low in iodine.

Table salt contains added iodine from potassium iodate, as well as stabilizers, anticaking agents, and granulated rock salt. However, Himalayan salt and sea salts have naturally occurring iodine in smaller amounts. Kosher salt and pickling salt do not contain iodine.

For crystal cleansing, some say it doesn't matter since the properties of sodium chloride are the same. However in my experience, there is a vibrational refinement with other minerals present in the salt and with different salt crystal shapes. Himalayan salt has trace minerals, such as calcium and magnesium, that not only provide electrolytes for hydration and balance, but the minerals also temper the crystals and add healing vibrations. As I mentioned in Chapter 8, those who are sensitive will know the difference. Many chefs know there is a difference too. Personally, I prefer sea salt or kosher salt over iodized salt. Crystals don't need iodine.

By the time we ingest salt, it's ground into small grains for our popcorn or our salt shakers. Did you know there are some lovely crystalline salt formations? Just like snowflakes, there's an abundance of geometric patterns found among different salt types. My favorite salt formations are those that are square or are pyramid shaped. I like the idea of tiny pyramids adding some energy to a salt water bath. Consider using salt flakes for powering up crystals while cleansing them of unwanted energy.

Himalayan Salt Crystals

Over the past few years, Himalayan salt crystal products have become widely available for wellness and healing, as well as for use in cooking both as a flavoring and as a preservative. Be sure your salt product is authentic and has been mined from the Kalabagh or Warcha salt mines near the Himalaya Mountains in Pakistan. The Khewra mine is the oldest but does not necessarily produce the best quality salt lamps.

Himalayan salt lamps come in many sizes and colors but are usually pink. The gentle pink glow of the Himalayan salt is attributed to the inclusion of minerals. They make attractive pieces for any room and create a mindfully relaxing space. Salt lamps have a carved-out cavity where a small low-wattage light bulb is placed to warm the salt. The salt lamp should be solid and not be crumbly from impurities. The lamp assembly should use UL-certified components and rest on a quality wooden or onyx base capable of carrying the lamp's weight stably. Salt naturally pulls water molecules from the air, and it is not unusual to see the salt lamp sweat. That is why a safety-approved lamp assembly is important. The lamp pulls water molecules from the air and literally purifies whatever air pollutants it can grab from the air. The water evaporates due to the heat of the lamp, and the unwanted particles stay in the crystal.

The release of negative air ions help rid the air of dust, smoke, and other pollutants that can cause respiratory problems. Some spas have salt rooms, sometimes called *salt caves*, that are lined with bricks of Himalayan salt. After 30 to 45 minutes of exposure in a salt room, you will feel like you do after a hike in the woods (also called *forest bathing*) where there are natural ions everywhere. The salt rooms provide increased meditative absorption in a negative ion space, as well as providing respiratory health benefits. There are handheld dry salt inhalers that have similar health benefits to salt rooms and provide relief from sinus issues, allergies, and chronic obstructive pulmonary disease (COPD).

Studies show that negative ions can increase serotonin in the brain and can contribute to stress reduction. A Columbia University study found a 58 percent improvement in seasonal affective disorder (SAD) sufferers when they were exposed to negative ion treatment. There are also sleep and rejuvenation benefits from locating a salt lamp in your bedroom. (Plus, it also doubles as a night light.) Himalayan salt lamps can neutralize harmful electromagnetic frequency (EMF) emissions from home electronic equipment and balance positive and negative ions, creating a calming environment. You might want to place your salt lamp near electronics or computer monitors. I have a small one that plugs into a USB port on my laptop.

Himalayan salt is the cleanest mineral known. The salt, known as *sodium chloride*, comes from the oldest sea salt formations on our planet that are 250 million years old! It contains 84 trace elements, such as magnesium, potassium, copper, and iron. Table salt is deficient in these minerals due to commercial processing such as bleaching. If you're soaking your crystals or yourself in a salt bath, it's best to use something nature provided. Your crystals will love to be cleansed in a Himalayan salt bath.

Remember that crystals can absorb and retain color as an energy vibration. Putting your crystals around the base of a salt lamp will keep them purified, and the soft glow of the lamp provides gentle, purifying, healing energy that blends in with the crystals' matrices. Place your hands on the lamp to warm your hands in winter or to ground your energies as needed. The salt lamp balances positive and negative ions; therefore, it helps reduce electromagnetic radiation. I have a round salt lamp that also functions for feng shui in the corner of a room. It not only reduces the EMFs from a nearby television, cables, and cable box, but it also functions to cleanse energy and circulate it away from the corner. It is also near to the bed for my dog—Tara, my Lhasa Apso—and I'm sure she benefits from the salt lamp as well.

There are many other forms of Himalayan salt:

- **Salt slabs**—Look for Himalayan salt blocks. Slabs can be heated and used for cooking or serving food. The salt enhances the flavors, and the heat keeps the food warm. Put your feet on warmed slabs for 15 minutes to detoxify and purge impurities from your body. Use a cold salt block and place your healing crystals on it overnight to remove unwanted energies. Remember, some crystals and jewelry may corrode or pit if they are in touch with salt over time.

- **Crushed salts**——To make dry bath salts, add aromatherapy oils and gem essences to a ½-cup of crushed salt in a lidded container and then shake to distribute the oils. Add the salts to a bath to enjoy their deeply penetrating qualities. You will feel so relaxed—what a perfect spa experience. Why not bottle your blended bath salts for a friend? Drop a crystal inside and add a customized label as a gift. Try geranium aromatherapy oil with a carnelian crystal or ylang aromatherapy oil with a garnet crystal for a special night in. What's your favorite combination?

- **Carved salt lamps**—Salt lamps come in many shapes—some oval ones are left in a rough natural state while others are carved and polished into pyramids, squares, and globes. You may have seen the "fire-bowl" salt lamps and wondered what they were all about. Who doesn't like to stare into the warm glowing embers of a fire pit? A lamp is placed under the salt bowl. Chunks of salt, usually in 1-2 inch cubes sit in the bowl and absorb the heat. They can be removed and used to treat a headache or be placed on areas of the body to soothe pain or at joints to improve mobility.

Healing and Detoxing with Epsom Salts

Magnesium sulfate, commonly known as *Epsom salts*, is a mineral compound used by the body to maintain a number of systems, including the cardiovascular system, the digestive system, and the skeletal system. When you're under stress, your magnesium level can become depleted, leaving you with symptoms including fatigue, muscular and cardiopulmonary issues, irregular sleep, and breathing problems. If you're not eating properly or avoiding taking a supplement, try a nice soak in Epsom salts. Add some crystals to rebalance your subtle system. Here are some other lovely ways to soak up this essential mineral salt:

♦ **Magnesium footbath**—Put ½ cup of Epsom salts into a bucket that you can place both feet into and add about 4 quarts of warm water. The water should at least cover the tops of your feet and your ankles. Soak your feet for 30 minutes up to twice a week. The magnesium is absorbed through your skin, relaxing your legs and body, and makes you feel comfy and relaxed. Feel free to add any of the following crystals to the bath:

  ♦ **To uplift:** use amber, clear quartz, amethyst, carnelian, citrine, aventurine, lepidolite, rhodochrosite, rose quartz, or sodalite.

  ♦ **To ground nervous tension and stress:** use dark colored crystals such as bloodstone, hematite, onyx, basalt, smoky quartz, jasper, or tiger eye.

♦ **Aromatherapy foot soak**—After filling a foot bathtub, add ¼ cup of Epsom salts, ¼ cup of Himalayan salt crystals, and a few drops of a favorite aromatherapy oil to the water. Add some tea tree oil to the bath water to help reduce any bacteria. As you add the salt crystals, let your toes wiggle and play with them. If you have a crystal ball about the size of a golf ball, tuck it under your foot and roll the sphere around under your arch to loosen tight tendons and relieve plantar fasciitis pain.

♦ **A full detox bath**—Add 2 cups (16 oz.) Epsom salts, 1 cup (8 oz.) baking soda, and 1 cup (8 oz.) sea salt to your bath water. Add a few drops of aromatherapy oil, such as sandalwood for mental relaxation, bergamot for stress reduction, or geranium for spiritual upliftment. Add some gem water or crystals to your bath to ground your stress. Soak for 20 to 30 minutes and then pat yourself dry or air dry to maximize the benefits.

♦ **Dry pillow**—I treated a lame horse named Ellie using an Epson salts pillow. Her foreleg was swollen just above the knee joint, and she was walking slowly. To create the dry pillow, I poured about a pound of dry Epsom salts into a doubled-up nylon pantyhose stocking and tied the ends. Then I wrapped the elongated pillow around her ankle and left it there for about 15 minutes. She seemed comfortable with the extra attention and stayed still. After unwrapping her leg, it was clearly visible that the swelling had lessened and was almost completely gone. You can make a pillow of Epsom salts for your personal use. Follow the instructions above and add a few crystals—such as hematite, tourmaline, and amazonite or jade and rose quartz—to help reduce pain and swelling. Lay the packet on tender joints.

Crystals Can Enhance Your Beauty Routine

The shelves at many stores are stockpiled with cosmetics and tools to aid you in upping your beauty routine. Did you know that crystals can be a part of that routine, too?

Cosmetics Infused with Crystals

How incredible to now have the most luscious beauty secrets available in cosmetics. Minerals have been part of cosmetics for years. I remember my grandmother's fluffy facial powder puff and the box of powder that clearly had ground pearl in it. There were even a few pearls set into the lid. How elegant and luxurious to grind up expensive jewels and put a mysterious glow on your skin. Imagine rubies, sapphires, tourmalines, diamonds, and amethyst infused into your skin. You would feel like a queen!

You can restore natural vitality to your skin using these crystals today. I often note after a crystal therapy session how a client's face looks relaxed with a radiant glow. Even sagging skin and wrinkles seem to lessen. Your energy is purified by the crystals and their marvelous sacred geometry provides youthful cellular rejuvenation.

Wouldn't you like to make an improvement to your facial and hand creams and toners? Adding crushed gemstones to creams has been used for centuries to beautify a woman's complexion. However, new methods use biotechnology to micronize the gemstones. Some cosmetic manufacturers have added micro-powdered jade, pearls, rubies, sapphires, quartz, amethyst, amber, and even diamonds or gold to creams. Shungite is known for its electro-magnetic protection and is added to acne creams. These microparticles cleanse and detoxify the skin, increase circulation, speed cellular healing and repair, tone and relax muscular substructures, improve your skin's complexion and texture, and leave a crystalline finish. Skin looks and feels energized. In other words, crystals will make you look beautiful!

I use a night cream that contains amethyst. As soon as I apply the cream, I can tell it is different than other facial products. My skin feels more hydrated, less stressed, and more relaxed. As a DIY project, use your crystals to fortify your creams. Here's how:

- ◆ Drop a carnelian into your toner or day cream for smooth revitalized skin.
- ◆ Add amethyst for tissue repairs and to impart a healthy glow.
- ◆ To calm the eruptions and inflammation of acne, add amber, carnelian, or snowflake obsidian.

◆ Add moonstone or snow quartz to night creams for relaxing myofascial and for cellular purification.

◆ For facial relaxation, add rose quartz to toners and wrinkle removers.

Wrinkle Rollers

As part of a self-care routine before bedtime, take 5 minutes to relax the tension from your face. There are crystal facial rollers made from rose quartz, jade, or other smooth crystals, or you can simply use a massage roller made from a crystal ball.

Massage and facial rollers help compress fat tissues, firm muscles, and reduce puffiness by increasing lymphatic drainage which flushes out toxins and reduces water retention. The crystal roller can be kept in the fridge and used cold to firm tissues, or it can be heated in warm water then used for opening pores and working with serums or oil products to increase their absorption. For lymphatic drainage, glide the facial roller down the sides of your neck in the direction of your heart. For a facial treatment, always roll upwards lightly to prevent sagging skin and pay special attention to those frown lines. Use the roller gently around your eyes as the tissues in that area are thin and only a light touch is needed. For the forehead, roll upward, paying special attention to the area between the brow. Remember that your third eye chakra is located in your forehead, so you may like to slow down when using a crystal rolling tool to prevent additional stress to that chakra.

Using a rounded massage tool is another way to massage and relax facial muscles. Roll lightly over oiled skin so you won't stretch the skin. I like to use the tip of the massage tool and gently press acupuncture points around the eyes to reduce wrinkles and to relieve sinus headaches. *Vogue* reports there is growing popularity of an ancient healing facial using a flat rose quartz or jade called a gua sha. This smooth tool is gently drawn across the skin following meridian lines to increase lymphatic drainage, tone the skin, and stimulate blood flow.

Diffusers

You can use your crystals both inside and outside of a diffuser. The same crystals you use for making gem water can be added to diffuser water. Place the water for the diffuser in a clear glass container with crystals for a few hours in sunlight before adding the gem water to the diffuser. The water will be saturated with your crystal's energy and fill the room with energizing droplets of crystalline mist. Who knew there were so many uses for a diffuser!

I put my crystals right inside the diffuser. The water chamber in your diffuser should be wide enough to set a small crystal into it. Remember, the crystal will displace some of the water, so add the water after you have placed the crystal. It's best to use the same types of crystals that were used to make gem water. Try tumbled stones such as rose quartz, amethyst, clear quartz, moonstone, amber, agates, or sodalite in your diffuser. As a tip, use distilled water so that your diffuser doesn't get lime deposits.

To fortify the water and the mist from the diffuser externally, place crystals all around the outside of the diffuser following a grid pattern. As the droplets of mist fall around the diffuser and onto these crystals, the water on the crystals will evaporate into the air and provide a subtle healing effect.

Chakra Oils

One of the nicest ways to treat yourself is to use essential oils with crystals. The resonance of the crystals amplifies the energy of the essential oil. Use the following table to find complementary scents to crystals that help activate the chakras. You can combine several scents. An aromatherapy diffuser works best to bring the scent into the room.

Select an oil and one of the complementary chakra crystals from the list to help amplify the healing effects of the oil. Place the oil on the crystal, rub it in, and set the crystal on the chakra for up to 10 minutes. A drop of rose oil on rose quartz will create a soothing loving vibration that will help open the heart chakra. However, if rose oil is dropped on lepidolite, the effects will be physically relaxing and relieve stress. Try different combinations for different healing effects.

Chakra Oils Chart

Chakra	Essential Oils	Gemstones
1—Root	Vetiver Sandalwood Cinnamon	Smoky quartz Obsidian Garnet
2—Sacral	Ylang-ylang Tangerine	Carnelian Citrine
3—Solar plexus	Peppermint Rosemary Clary sage Lemon	Malachite Yellow calcite Hematite Citrine
4—Heart	Rose Neroli Melissa Jasmine	Rose quartz Pink tourmaline Lepidolite Fluorite
5—Throat	Geranium Frankincense	Turquoise Blue calcite
6—Third Eye	Cedarwood Patchouli Amber	Lapis lazuli Blue topaz Celestite
7—Crown	Myrrh	Amethyst

Serene Selenite

I mentioned selenite in Chapter 13 in the form of crystal angels to help awareness in the dream state and to activate the pineal gland for deeper levels of consciousness and psychic awareness. Selenite assists in connecting with intuition and wisdom. There are now so many forms of this lovely crystal, it's worthwhile to mention it again. Selenite is becoming the crystal of the now age. Let's take a closer look and find some new uses for this crystal of liquid moonlight.

◆ **Towers**—Selenite tower formations are usually round, unpolished, and come in different heights. Each tower has a graduated tip to help channel and elevate the energy for cleansing. You will need four towers, one for each corner of a room, to add ongoing purification. Smaller ones can be added to crystal grids and layouts. Since selenite towers are round, their energy circulates and creates a shield. Add extras to a larger room to ensure complete coverage. They are great for feng shui to circulate energy.

◆ **Spirals**—Maybe these spirals remind you of a unicorn horn. Use one in the center of a grid to attract the mystical unicorn or use it as a wand with the elements to direct energy. The horn represents the feminine, the purity of heart, and is a symbol of bestowing magic and miracles.

◆ **Hearts**—This precious shape is perfect to give as a gift of love. Selenite hearts can be left next to a bedside to provide restful sleep. If they are held at the heart or in the palm of the hand, the selenite will settle your emotions and any negative thoughts. They are also like a breath of fresh air and will help alleviate tension about relationships.

◆ **Wands**—These longer flat shapes are about 7-inches long and about ½-inch thick and are used to scrub off unwanted energy. Rub the crystal like a scrub brush in your aura about 5 to 7 inches away from your body. Don't forget to remove any unwanted energy from under your feet and from the soles of your shoes. You can also use the wand in the aura cleansing exercise outlined in Chapter 10.

◆ **Lamps**—Just like Himalayan salt lamps, selenite lamps are carved with a small opening for a light bulb. They also come as thick candle holders for tea lights. The light and energy from these lamps are so gentle; they radiate purification and clear the environment of negative energy. I sometimes change the light bulb in my lamp to red, green, or blue to change the mood.

◆ **Charging plates**—Instead of charging jewelry crystals in sunlight or moonlight, lay them on a selenite plate overnight to accomplish the same task. Leaving them in the moonlight on the plate will add a huge energy bonus. Charging plates vary in size, with the most practicable one to hold your crystals and jewelry measuring about 8-by-4-inches wide and about a ½-inch thick. The charging plate can also double as a wand for a big aura cleanse.

♦ **Harmonizers**—Highly polished, smooth drums of selenite are about 4 inches long. They are made to hold, one in each hand, and create a nice energy blast to calm your emotions, such as before a yoga session, after a tough day at the office, to remove pain, or to relax before sleep.

Shungite

As mentioned previously, crystals seem to come out of the earth when they are needed. One of the most important crystals available on the market to benefit Millennials and Baby Boomers is shungite, the "stone of life." Shungite is a rich carbon-based material that was formed in sea beds long ago. It's a very pure material that is transformed through volcanic heat. Although this crystal has been around for a while, it's become popular with health fans specifically since it contains fullerenes, a type of long-lasting antioxidant. Just having shungite in your environment dampens electromagnetic radiation from electrical equipment. Some studies of natural fullerenes have shown that they stimulate tissue regeneration and possess anti-viral and anti-inflammatory properties. It comes in a raw black form used for healing purposes, and an elite or noble shungite that looks like hematite and is highly shiny. Either one is good to use.

Shungite relates to the first chakra. It is an outstanding grounding tool, especially as an anchor for those who do astral travel, are healing partners with Earth, or are involved in rearranging energy patterns where there has been a disturbance. Its prepared gem essence is helpful in Reiki sessions to help with transitions, insomnia, and as a revitalizer of energy. If you wear shungite, you will find it leaves some particles on your skin. They are harmless and can be washed off.

Shungite can cleanse water of bacteria. As a form of really dense carbon, shungite acts as a water purifier. Sold in small stone chips, these chips can be placed inside a small cotton bag and then added to a water container. Wash off any dust in a sieve under running water before placing the chips in the bag. For every gallon of water, use 40 grams (1.4 ounces) of shungite chips and let sit for at least 24 hours. The longer you leave the shungite in the water, the more active the water becomes.

Use shungite water to fill your pet's water bowl. You can also add it to your bath water to detoxify. As a powder, shungite can be mixed into a paste and left on the body to heal skin issues, arthritic conditions, injuries, bruises, and sprains.

As shungite is a soft material, like selenite, it can be made into many different shapes such as pyramids, and spheres. There are thin shungite discs that can be attached to cellphones, computers, or other electronics to reduce EMFs. The shungite shape that interests me the most is a cube, which seems menacing to electromagnetic energy and energy pollution from microwaves and WIFIs. It reminds me of a warrior's shield, and it can be used as a workhorse to ground and stabilize energy. The square shape is an emblem of the earth Platonic solid, the hexahedron, as mentioned in Chapter 2. This is one crystal that has many benefits that we could all use at this time.

Trendy Crystals by Design

Designer clothes that use crystals are not just pretty; they support the healing processes and visually send a signal that you have some awareness about healing crystals. However, it's just fashion unless you know what you have on your clothing and why it's there. If people ask, tell them what crystals you have and why you wear them.

Sadly, men's fashion doesn't incorporate much jewelry or gems. I would like to see men use crystals more. Perhaps they could be incorporated as part of a men's wellness spa experience or sewn into the inside of a garment somewhere to add some flash, some pizzazz, and some healing. Belt buckles are great places for men to use crystals—turquoise is a favorite on Western silver belts and bolo ties. There is a new trend in men's accessories—jeweled cufflinks. Look at historical pictures of royal men: jewels in turbans, brooches on sashes, and bejeweled capes. Now we're talking!

What are the latest crystal fashions? The crystals that seem to be getting around a lot are tourmaline, rose quartz, selenite, and topaz. Jasper-type colors of gold, amber, brown, and orange are also popular in the home and office. They are warm earth colors that create a noncompeting space. Such colors are great for winding down stressful energy and for connecting with nature, especially if you live in a sky house (i.e., an apartment or high-rise condo). During turbulent times, we look to the earth for stability and strength. During times of optimism, we look to the skies for ideas and growth. Check out fashion and color trends as a barometer on which crystals can be used to support our lifestyle and environment.

New Products with Tourmaline

As with other gemstones, powdered tourmaline is added to cosmetics and when pressed onto your skin, generates negative ions. (Without pressure, no negative ions are released.) Tourmaline has also been added to cosmetics to alleviate eczema. You see tourmaline used in sleep aids, air purifiers, ionizers, and other negative ion–generating products including pet mats. There are bedsheets made with tourmaline that when under pressure (when you're laying down), release negative ions. The use of tourmaline is not harmful, but it should never be ingested. There is still debate on the actual results of negative ion used in treating bronchial asthma, however. Look for more uses of gemstones in technology for health benefits.

CARVED IN STONE . . . .

Carnelian: I strengthen your spiritual core. I give you the resolve to move past old matters. I give you courage to use the gifts that were given to you. I give you the radiance of your inner beauty.

CHAPTER 21

Your Personal Path to Growth and Healing

By the time we reach adulthood, we're all but numbed to the mystery of life. The one bright spot in this is that when people feel their soul is empty, they often go looking for ways to fill it. As a seeker who has found crystals, you've surely discovered by now that they give something back. The very energy of crystals reconnects you to the earth, your spiritual home. Your energy has become revitalized and your subconscious awakened. Your healing abilities have become activated. Your spiritual development has become a natural truth to live by.

Now that you've started, your journey with crystals is endless and can continuously aid your self-transformation. Once you are comfortable working with crystal energy, don't be afraid to start looking at *yourself* as a healer and share your gift with others.

Learn How to ...

♦ Find further training in crystal healing.

♦ Explain to others about the healing benefits of crystals.

♦ Describe the signs of spiritual progress with crystal healing.

Commitment to Working with Crystals

When you make a commitment to working with crystals, they make a commitment to you, too! The beauty of working with crystals is that they are always there for you—anytime, anywhere, and under any circumstances. They will comfort your emotions when you feel raw and exposed, and they will open your eyes to what you are missing in life.

We all fall into ruts from time to time, and your crystals are like a rescue rope pulling you out. Think of it this way: if someone told you he could give you a pill that would help you meditate more deeply and be more at peace with yourself, would you take it? A lot of people would, and yet they think twice about working with a natural source of the same sort of relief. If someone handed you a crystal and said, "Here you go. Hold this sodalite crystal every night before bedtime and you will sleep better, and wear it during the day and you will feel calmer," wouldn't that be a better option than taking a pill?

It's really a shame that so many people end up with closed minds when it comes to exploring new areas of the mind and soul. After all, when we were children, exploring new things was not only encouraged, but was necessary and meaningful for development on physical, psychological, spiritual, and emotional levels. People have frowned on new age ideals. However, there isn't a "new age" because we have been blending new ideas into mainstream thinking forever. It really is the *now age*. So, why should we believe that limiting growth as adults is a positive step?

•

Crystal Comments

Here are some comments I've received from people new to crystals whose belief in them seems strong, if not a little humorous!

♦ I started working with rose quartz and kunzite and noticed their effects on my sleep. I have moonstone as well. This practice is a little bit scary for me because of its dramatic impact. However, I do realize the need for change.

♦ I have been working with crystals, and I have to say that I think that my bladder and kidney problems have resolved completely. I have also found that working with crystals for my foot problem brings amazing results.

♦ When programming crystals, I have read that one should be as specific as possible. Does this then mean I can state the amount of money I require and the date that I need it?

♦ My brother-in-law had Ross River virus (a type of flu common to the South Pacific) a while ago. I gave him petrified wood to put in a grid under his bed, and he was healed almost overnight. His friend got the same virus. He passed along the crystals to his friend, who had great success with them, too. So, now two skeptics are big believers, which is great.

♦ I like crystals because they are attractive, although I'm a skeptic as to their healing properties. However, I liked what you said. It makes sense.

♦ I currently own a blue lace agate bracelet, and I have been trying to connect with it to heal the goiter associated with my thyroid problem. Usually I only put the bracelet directly on my thyroid gland for a few minutes before I sleep. As I do so, I also talk to it to ask for healing.

♦ Crystals are truly amazing. Recently I came across snowflake obsidian chips in a shop. I reached for them without a thought. Almost immediately I felt their energy. When I finally released them from my hand, the crystal shop owner who then picked them up remarked that the obsidians were pretty warm.

You can see that people just like you reach out for crystals and that for many the experience is intuitive. None of these people had crystal healing training, yet each one found his or her way to a healing experience because of crystals.

Imagine the Possibilities!

Because crystals provide mental clarity, I'd really like to see our aging population take advantage of crystal therapy. Crystals such as tourmaline could specifically be used to offset Alzheimer's disease, dementia, and other geriatric diseases.

As previously mentioned, crystals are also helpful to increase awareness and consciousness. The development of psychic abilities is cumulative, meaning the abilities build slowly over time. Let's say you've been wearing crystals and your extrasensory perception has become razor sharp. If you remove the gemstones from daily wear, these powers won't disappear, but your awareness of them might diminish. Starting back again with crystals will reactivate your power, and you will continue to build on top of what you already started.

Due to stress, our emotions and thinking are sometimes in jeopardy. Using the various crystal-healing techniques discussed throughout this book can actually transform negative emotional states and help us to become happier people. Now that's a convincing crystal argument if I ever heard one!

Working with Crystals Every Day

If you have a crystal collection, don't let it sit there gathering dust—use it! And if you can't think of any good reason to pull those gemstones out, look back through this book. If you are not personally experiencing physical or emotional difficulties, perhaps someone you know could benefit from some healing.

If you don't already have a crystal collection, I hope by now you've read and learned enough about the healing power of crystals that you'll be inspired to go out and bring some home!

Go ahead and add to your collection as you find it necessary. But remember that a balanced crystal collection isn't just about having a range of different colored stones. It's about having a range of power, including the different-shaped crystals I talked about in Chapter 15 and 20. That way, you'll have some that gently release their energy and some that are more active with their power.

Ideally, when a new crystal comes into your life, you want to spend some time with it and learn about what it has to offer. The crystal, in turn, will help to attune you to a new higher frequency. Sometimes you have to let go of old energies to bring in the new. That's how crystal transformation happens!

Gaining Confidence as a Healer

In Chapter 17, I went over the guidelines for a crystal healing session. Don't forget what they say: practice makes perfect! How do you practice becoming a crystal healer? With a little help from your friends. Some of my students have volunteered to act as guinea pigs when I'm conducting a private healing class. In this way, we can learn from each other, both as a healer and as a client. But I also use new crystals on myself. If we do not know the effects a crystal has on our own bodies and minds, we can't recommend it to others.

Getting More Training in Crystal Healing

Feeling the subtle energy of crystals interacting with your own energy is not easy to do on your own unless you are already fairly sensitive, so attending a class is a great idea. Formal crystal training is available to anyone who wants to advance and perhaps become a healer. For example, a consortium called the Affiliation of Crystal Healing Organisations (ACHO) in England provides accreditation to crystal healing schools teaching a core crystal curriculum. (Some of the information provided in this book probably qualifies under such a program.) In countries where complementary therapies are formalized, certification from a holistic arts institution is often a requirement before treating clients.

If you are interested in learning more about crystals and you live in a remote area, you might have to travel to find a good class or instructor. However, there are also many online courses available, but you really can't learn about healing crystals unless you have a willing partner for hands-on experiences. Plus, it's difficult to get feedback from an online instructor because often there isn't one. Of course, the internet is a great resource to find an in-the-flesh instructor or school and to get a lot of information about individual crystals. Also remember that crystal devas will teach you what you need to know if you just ask. (And this requires no travel at all!)

Community colleges often provide courses in crystals, usually through health and wellness programs that offer other practices such as Reiki, reflexology, and aromatherapy.

Although some municipalities in North America require certification to acquire a special annual licensing for holistic practices, private crystal training courses are unregulated and are dependent on the instructor being knowledgeable about the topic. Many people who use crystals know quite a lot about them—but that won't necessarily make them good teachers. A good teacher not only knows about the crystals and how to use them but also is quite intuitive. Seek out an empath, a person with psychic abilities and emotional intelligence that allows him or her to remotely sense or feel what another person feels. As an empath, they can sense how a crystal is interacting with another person's energy and can guide that person in the healing experience.

Word of mouth is still the best way to find a great teacher. If you don't know anyone in the crystal community, ask holistic healers or the proprietors of metaphysical or gem shops if they can recommend someone.

Signs of Progress

Continual handling of crystals has its benefits, one of which is having a brighter complexion. Skin seems to clear up first, followed by increasing good luck, enjoying feelings of happiness, and noticing that other people want to be around you.

Not only will you develop greater sensitivity to the energy of crystals, but you'll also inherit some of their powers. You'll be full of energy and may even literally shock people, similar to when you rub your feet over a rug and then get an energy discharge when you touch metal. People will feel your expansion of energy. They might say that they feel your power. (Try to react modestly when this happens!)

You might find that if you meditate frequently with crystals, some interesting extrasensory perceptions develop, such as clairvoyance, precognition, or heightened sensory abilities like acute sense of smell or hearing. Your eyesight might become sharper, and you may be able to see and be more aware of things. Your intellect and memory will be clearer, especially if you remember to do your grounding exercises. You'll feel that you know things for which you have no prior knowledge or education. This is impressive, but not really surprising—this is a spiritual opening, after all! The natural gifts we are all born with will break through the barriers we place there. And yes, crystals can help in breaking through those barriers to a new level of awareness.

Compassion for All

Perhaps you picked up this book because you heard crystals can help with meditation and relaxation. But now you know that there is a huge component to using crystals for actual physical healing as well as emotional clearing and spiritual development.

Crystals in the form of silicon dioxide are everywhere—we even breathe in the dust of crystals! So doesn't that mean we are all living, moving crystals? Maybe it means we need crystals to help align ourselves with a bigger consciousness to find cures for what ails us. Those big crystals in the earth are holding us together. The closer we are to the universal vibration, the more aligned we are to our own oneness of being—our source energy.

You don't need to be shy about wearing or using crystals. Crystals are not associated with any religion or faith. They grow naturally in the earth and are already used in many industries, including pharmaceuticals, computer technology, and manufacturing. You are just using an aspect of their power for working on the subtle energies of your body—the human aura, the chakra system, the nadis, your internal organs and external body, your mind and emotions, and of course your own spirituality.

You are part of the twenty-first century with hope for emerging technologies that will provide a greater quality of life for all. You understand that science, medicine, and psychology are blending and a whole new sacred science is being born. Medicine will work alongside spirituality where the goal is compassion for all human life.

Please experiment with crystals because each one has a different purpose for each type of person. Let your intuition guide you to select the right one. Remember to periodically cleanse your crystals and to recharge them in the sun. May you enjoy the healing benefits of all crystals!

CARVED IN STONE . . . .

Why not have a crystal party where you get all your crystals together with like-minded friends and create a sacred space for meditation, music, chanting, drumming, and spiritual connection. Share your knowledge about crystal healing with each other, and celebrate your journey of self-transformation.

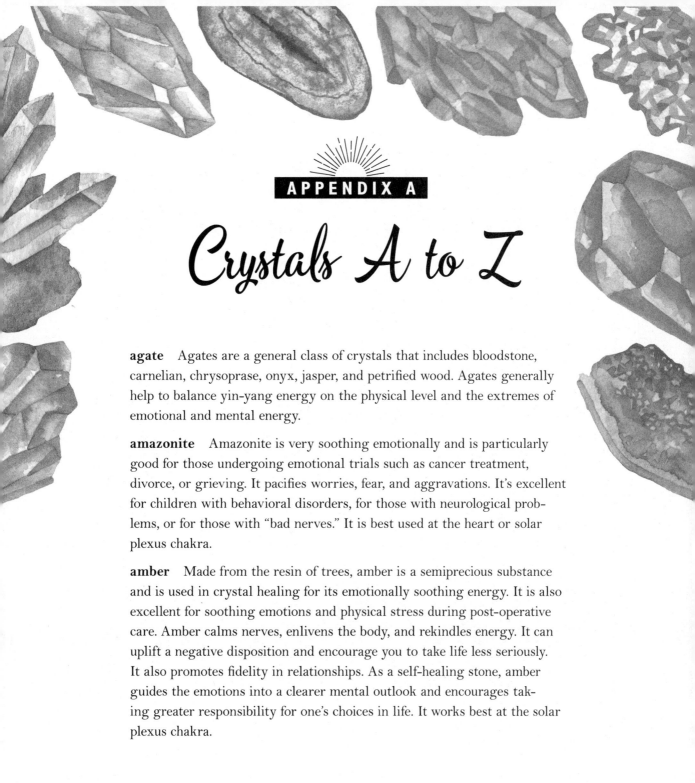

Crystals A to Z

agate   Agates are a general class of crystals that includes bloodstone, carnelian, chrysoprase, onyx, jasper, and petrified wood. Agates generally help to balance yin-yang energy on the physical level and the extremes of emotional and mental energy.

amazonite   Amazonite is very soothing emotionally and is particularly good for those undergoing emotional trials such as cancer treatment, divorce, or grieving. It pacifies worries, fear, and aggravations. It's excellent for children with behavioral disorders, for those with neurological problems, or for those with "bad nerves." It is best used at the heart or solar plexus chakra.

amber   Made from the resin of trees, amber is a semiprecious substance and is used in crystal healing for its emotionally soothing energy. It is also excellent for soothing emotions and physical stress during post-operative care. Amber calms nerves, enlivens the body, and rekindles energy. It can uplift a negative disposition and encourage you to take life less seriously. It also promotes fidelity in relationships. As a self-healing stone, amber guides the emotions into a clearer mental outlook and encourages taking greater responsibility for one's choices in life. It works best at the solar plexus chakra.

amethyst   One of the Master Healers, amethyst has the ability to transmute negativity and provide an improved outlook on life by promoting flexibility, cooperation, and peace. As a transformer, amethyst's job is to take lower dysfunctional vibrations and clear them by transmuting them to a higher vibrational level. Amethyst facilitates expansion of the third eye and expands psychic abilities by connecting intuitive receptors to the crown chakra. For physical healing, amethyst is used to regulate thyroid conditions and alleviate the pain of arthritis. It heals all things at all levels.

ametrine   Due to heat-treatment, one half of the stone is shaded amethyst and the other half is citrine—hence its name. Ametrine acts as a catalyst and speeds up intellectual recognition of spiritual ascension. This would be a good crystal for initiating a quickening.

angelite   This crystal holds light angelic energy and provides a shield of light around the wearer. Like celestite, it activates the subtle energies of the upper chakras providing communication paths and clarity for channeling and telepathy.

Apache tears   This crystal stimulates emotional spontaneity and the release of barriers that prevent you from experiencing deep emotions. This stone is excellent for transmuting one's own negativity under stressful situations. The Apache tear is a dark black stone of obsidian and, when held up to the light, appears transparent. However, it has been noted that as the grief one feels goes into the stone, it can turn it opaque. It is best used in the hands or solar plexus.

apatite   This apply-named crystal provides relief for overeaters by helping to normalize one's appetite. Apatite comes in a variety of chakra colors. It also helps to access the devas and opens up the upper chakras to seekers of truth.

apophyllite   This crystal is an awesome third eye and crown opener. Apophyllite facilitates astral travel and helps to initiate a person to new levels of intuition. This crystal acts as a bridge to cross time dimensions and provides access to spiritual dimensions. It is best used in the third eye or crown chakra.

aquamarine   This crystal is very protective emotionally and helps you remain centered through complex issues. Aquamarine strengthens one's resolve to feel that life has a purpose. It is excellent for dispelling negative emotions originating from one's weaknesses: fears, phobias, and anxiety. Aquamarine releases false expectations. This crystal helps in your attunement to be of service to others and diminishes the self-centeredness that often gets in the way of genuine spirituality. It works best at your truth center, the throat chakra.

aqua aura quartz   Clear quartz that has been treated with a fine coating of gold is sometimes known as fairy quartz or rainbow quartz. Other metals such as titanium may be used and marketed under different names. The energy relates to the crown chakra and higher realms for attunement and realization of spiritual quests.

aventurine   Aventurine purifies the emotional body and soothes nerves. Aventurine strengthens and restores the heart energy, providing a balance of male and female energies. This crystal is green and very loving, embracing, and protective of the heart. Many children who are shy, timid, or suppressing their leadership qualities need a crystal like aventurine. This stone helps the individual to become active and initiate action on her own accord. Asthmatic children seem attracted to this stone because it opens up the lungs and they experience a sense of relief.

azurite   Azurite provides an opening to a deeper level of consciousness and cleanses and prepares the mind to work on a higher spiritual level to provide deeper understanding and acceptance. It works with the throat chakra to purify the intent behind one's spiritual activities.

azurite-malachite   This blend of two types of crystals that grow together provides a powerful sense of getting to core matters by probing and penetrating past the masks we bear. The truth is exposed by unlocking the past. Use this crystal at the third eye or throat chakra.

barite   Barite, the "relationship crystal" is one of the crystals that can be used to stimulate friendship and loyalty. It can be used to soothe emotions and remove toxins from the body as part of addiction recovery programs.

black onyx   Used for psychic protection, it is so black that it shields the wearer from attack. It allows the wearer to be sensitive to negative energies but not be harmed by them. Onyx alleviates mental confusion and absorbs grief. It is best used in your pockets or at the root chakra for grounding.

bloodstone   Has masculine yin qualities and a tremendous ability to heal organs in the middle torso: liver, stomach, pancreas, gall bladder, large intestine, and heart. Bloodstone dispels discouragement and gives strength and endurance to withstand endless difficulties. This crystal reduces stress and anxiety. It revitalizes and encourages unselfishness in relationships. It is grounding to an emotional heart and provides a support tool to those in distress or who suffer from anxiety. It also provides grounding for going deeply into spirituality and mystical matters without getting lost. Bloodstone is a great anchor or safety net and can be used with other crystals to provide safe-keeping of subtle energies. Hold this crystal in your hand or place it at your solar plexus.

blue lace agate   Connects you with your spiritual gifts and provides nonjudgmental support and loving, unconditional energy. It alleviates spiritual tension and emotional intensity. This crystal is calming when used at the throat chakra. It helps you to speak your truth, channel your higher thoughts, and facilitate expression of spirituality. It is calming whenever a major opening has occurred in a chakra. Wear it as a necklace or place it at your throat chakra.

Botswana agate   Soothes repressed emotions and is excellent for smokers whose nerves are on edge when used at the throat chakra. It can move you beyond self-limits. Used at the third eye, it provides communication access to the devas of the animal and plant worlds.

calcite   Clears and optimizes the energy in chakras, by color. Calcite is a gentle cleanser of emotional upsets and helps you move forward after releasing emotional restrictions. Pink or white calcite provides an opening of the higher chakras where a direct channel is needed for communicating with your Highest Self. Use it in your hand during meditation, or place it at your throat, third eye, or crown chakra.

carnelian Effectively heals skin, acne, herpes, scars, and wrinkles and addresses issues of self-esteem. Carnelian eliminates feelings of inadequacy and low self-worth. It works with amethyst to transmute with extreme negative states such as envy, fear, rage, and sorrow. This stone is especially good for recovery after an emotional disappointment. It transmutes sadness in your heart into the initiative to do something positive about the problem. This crystal encourages enthusiasm and is good for giving vibrancy to one's sexuality. Carnelian restores trust to spiritually jaded people and keeps the focus on a higher level rather than physical or emotional levels. Wear this crystal at the heart chakra or hold it in your hand during meditation.

celestite Provides openness and expansion of one's consciousness, giving you the ability to articulate messages from the higher realms. It facilitates the opening of the throat, third eye, and crown chakras; helps develop and heighten telepathic abilities; and provides a pathway for consciousness to enter the higher realms. It lets you speak authentically about spiritual matters. Celestite is said to be good to help those who fear heights and those with digestive disorders. Celestite keeps your crown chakra active for receiving messages from friends and family and from subtle spirit energies who use the dream state to teach us.

charoite This ray of purple light dispels fear and connects the third eye to the mental plane to help loosen the need for worldly attachments and to prepare for the vibration of giving and receiving unconditional love. It provides for deeper intellectual, creative, and analytical abilities. It is best worn at the heart chakra.

chrysocolla Grounds emotional energy and eases extreme emotional mood swings. It provides emotional strength, balances expression and communication of emotions, and releases distress and guilt. It is best used at the solar plexus chakra. It is a very active crystal and can expel negative emotional states, sometimes rather dynamically, so use chrysocolla with a rose quartz or jade crystal to temper the effects.

chrysoprase This lovely green crystal is used to alleviate alcoholism and to provide ease to feelings of depression. It allows you to take one day at a time, build on successes through small changes, and be patient with inner transformation. It is best used at the throat and third eye chakras.

citrine   This crystal increases a positive emotional influence and dispels negativity on the mental and emotional levels. It counters nonproductive energy and frees energy for spontaneous expression. The golden rays of citrine provide a complex energy structure that energizes the crown and sacral chakras. Citrine transmutes the grosser material and physical vibrations into higher spiritual aspects and provides protection for the aura. Use it at the heart chakra or hold it in your hand during meditation.

clear quartz   One of the Master Healers and a Universal Healer, clear quartz generates energy, brings energy in, or can send energy to someone else. It unblocks and transmutes negative energy and dispels negative disposition. It works as a translator for communication with all other forms of energy. It balances positive and negative electrical charges and provides clear thinking about issues and creating thoughts into reality. Clear quartz provides balance and harmony to all areas of your life, including love, health, and spirituality. The rainbow quartz neutralizes, dissolves grief and other sadness, and restores feelings of joy.

copper   A natural mineral necessary for the formation of hemoglobin to keep bones and nerves healthy, it is used for the treatment of arthritis. Copper is a conductive material and is able to pass electrical pulses along its matrix without interference. To that end, it also dispels complacency and lethargy and stimulates self-dependence.

coral   Although technically coral is not a crystal, it is semiprecious and often used in crystal healing for its blood purification properties. The common colors are red and white. Red is for physical ailments, and white is for accessing truth and higher communications. Coral quiets the emotions and dispels feelings of despair and despondency. It encourages a passionate energy and stimulates and strengthens female reproductive organs through tissue regeneration. This stone relates well to the spleen meridian for blood circulation and to purification of the kidneys and bladder. Red coral is considered to be the blood of Mother Earth by Amerindians and is considered particularly precious by Tibetan women for menstruation, fertility, and blood disorders.

diamond   Promotes trust and fidelity in relationships. Diamonds brighten and enliven your aura by clearing out stale energy. Diamonds provide spiritual confidence and activate the crown chakra. The brilliance of light from the diamonds dispels brain fog and gives clarity to meditation.

dioptase   This brilliant emerald-green crystal provides attunement for the third eye. Dioptase can provide a wake-up call for those still so attached to worldly problems that entering into higher states of consciousness is hardly possible. This crystal teaches one to live through her heart and to be in the moment. It can be used for easing pain, hypertension, and other physical ailments.

emerald   An ancient love stone, emerald helps to soften arrogance and promote cooperation. Emerald dispels negative thoughts and helps you hold onto what is practical. It cools an angry heart and promotes divine love and peace. This crystal is excellent for preserving love that is maturing into a long-term relationship. Emerald is an emotional heart soother. This crystal provides peace at the heart chakra, especially about matters that trigger anxiety. Instead of falling into a deep emotional pit, emerald will help focus and guide your action to stay centered on your life's purpose.

fluorite   Considered to be a crystal of high mental stimulation and creativity, blue fluorite relates to the throat chakra. Purple fluorite unblocks energy and opens the upper chakras, whereas red, orange, and yellow fluorite opens the lower chakras. Rainbow fluorite provides the full spectrum of healing that fluorite has to offer. All colors of fluorite calm the emotional body and stimulate intellectual certainty. Purple fluorite helps to break up blockages at all levels. This crystal holds intense white light and activates the third eye and crown chakras.

garnet   Effective for problems related to the second chakra and for correcting various gynecological issues, PMS, and infertility. It is best known for revitalizing the physical and emotional body. Garnet increases the life force and one's passion for life and regeneration. Garnet provides grounding for chaotic emotions and allows the release of love from within oneself. It is best used in the lower chakras.

gold   One of the purest of minerals on the planet, gold is the master of all metals. It gives a sense of power and connection to great strength, along with a sense of absolute purity. Gold has the ability to link with the matrix of other crystals and is an activator of their electrical circuitry. Gold also fortifies the energy fields to be more resilient to pain. As a refiner of energies, it has a role to play in purifying and balancing energy fields and to bring peace within one's self. Use it at the third eye and crown chakras.

halite   Also known as rock salt, its colors vary due to impurities. It has the ability to purify the environment. It clears chakras of negative imbalances and stimulates psychic abilities. If used externally for water retention, it can draw out excess fluids. Himalayan salt lamps are made from halite.

hematite   The natural magnetic quality of hematite makes it a perfect crystal to use instead of commercial magnets. Hematite is also a blood purifier and relates well to anger and other toxins stored in the liver. Hematite gives emotional support to new love and helps to ground love energy so it doesn't fly away when challenged. It protects the heart from small love wounds. Its shiny surface reflects back negativity and helps reduce stress to the whole body.

Herkimer diamond   An attunement tool, it provides expansion of consciousness and clears the channels to access higher spiritual levels for communication. It can sharpen your memory of dreams and provide healing at the mental and spiritual planes. It is best used at the third eye chakra.

howlite   Dyed sky blue to look like turquoise, it is named turquosite as an inexpensive alternative. Howlite dispels negative attitudes such as over criticalness and selfishness. It is best used at the solar plexus and third eye chakras.

iolite   Provides an ability to open the third eye for clarity of visions and other intuitive work. It is a protector while entering higher states of consciousness and provides unconditional love. It promotes self-change. It is best used at the third eye chakra.

jade   Known as a crystal of fidelity, tranquility, and as the "sport stone," it promotes agility and swiftness. Some say jade is for good luck. It soothes the emotions and provides emotional detachment and restoration after various traumas such as minor surgery, divorce, funerals, or loss of a job. It promotes peace, family harmony, and tranquility. It provides a sense of self-worth, self-sufficiency, and capability in dealing with any situation. It is best worn in the upper chakras.

jasper   Makes it easier to use one's own power and to know that it cannot be taken away. It calms aggressive energy and facilitates safety and protection during recovery periods (for example, from stress, operations, and other life traumas). Red jasper provides lively fresh energy and reduces feelings of being victimized. Yellow jasper balances hormones and protects the wearer during travel. Green jasper restores energy and focus during recovery from burnout.

kunzite   This lovely pink crystal is used for the prevention of heart disorders, for pain in the heart, and for post-operative recovery after heart surgery. Kunzite opens the emotional heart to an inner dimension of divine love while dispelling negativity. This gemstone alleviates emotional stress and provides peace to behavioral disorders. It is best used at the heart and crown chakras.

kyanite   Clears mental illusions and helps you to see a situation for what it is. Kyanite helps align the chakra system.

labradorite   Helps to keep the aura clear and protects it from imbalances. It provides for access to other levels of consciousness. It is a crystal of leadership and is good for teachers to help others reach their potential. It's an excellent crystal for past-life recall, improving inner vision, and helping with the perseverance of the spiritual journey. Labradorite relates best to the upper chakras, especially the crown.

lapis lazuli   A dark blue stone known to promote a clear mind and to provide spiritual protection, it unblocks and releases emotions from the heart for self-acceptance. Lapis lazuli has a third eye and crown connection to intensify inner visions and deeper connection through the crown chakra. Attunes the mental states of awareness and promotes self-acceptance of one's spiritual gifts. For intuitive people, lapis intensifies psychic power. The deep blue color stimulates expansion of consciousness in a supportive way, promoting purification and clarity of spiritual insight. This stone is highly prized for its protective powers and stimulation of all psychic senses.

larimar   A pale blue stone that promotes expression of one's emotions and opens the upper chakras and in particular the throat chakra. A stone of opening communications from the heart and lets love energy radiate. Builds confidence and lets you move past self-restrictions.

lepidolite   Reduces stress responses such as stiff shoulders and tight solar plexus and alleviates despondency. It provides grounding for "fly-away" emotions by providing detachment from situations so clarity of purpose can be seen. It can be very grounding when you don't know what else to do. Lepidolite operates on and unifies the upper chakras: heart, throat, third eye, and crown.

malachite This deep forest-green stone clears the heart chakra of past experiences by unblocking and absorbing any negative energies. Malachite allows you to stay tolerant, loyal, and practical. It is a heavy releaser of negative emotions and is best used in conjunction with rose quartz to bring peace to emotions during deep releasing. It can aid in breaking down old patterns, whether emotional (stuck patterns of behavior) or physical (tumors, swollen joints, or muscular). The most important aspect of this crystal's healing ability, however, is for the preventive health of the physical heart and liver. If you are attracted to this crystal, chances are you have a family history of heart-related problems and probably need a heart check-up.

marble Marble has the ability to absorb and retain energy and is soothing physically and mentally. It is best used in your hand during meditation to absorb the quiet qualities of each session.

moldavite A meteorite that is green and produces spacey prophetic, visionary dreams, moldavite is also a huge instigator of change or quickening. It is a major transformer and tool of consciousness and interdimensional communication.

mookite This Australian dream crystal is a variety of jasper and is used to enhance dream time and to recall messages from the dream state. It is also said to be helpful in speeding the healing of wounds.

moonstone Provides unconditional love and acceptance, as well as a sense of peace at emotional transition points (puberty, marriage, births, deaths, and menopause). Moonstone provides a depth of perception and discernment. It can increase creativity, intuition, and self-expression. It has physical rejuvenating qualities for the skin and hair and offers protection for travelers. It is best worn at the heart or solar plexus chakra.

moss agate Soothes self-esteem and battered egos. It strengthens positive emotional traits and promotes communications with the plant devas. Because moss agate relates strongly to the earth's energy, it has a powerful influence on women's healing and nurturing. It is best used at the heart, solar plexus, and sacral chakras.

obsidian This volcanic material is an important crystal used for grounding energies. When used at the solar plexus, it acts as a door opener and dispels negative emotions by releasing old energy patterns. Obsidian transmutes energy blockages into white light. It should be used in the lower chakras.

opal   The rainbow colors of opal provide a brightening of the aura. Opal helps to brighten a negative attitude and dispel a dark mood. It promotes spontaneity and is a tonic to uplift moodiness. It also helps to discern the truth and bring hope and happiness to the wearer. Opal is best worn at the heart and upper chakras.

pearl   Although not a gemstone, pearl is a natural material found worldwide from oysters. It stimulates purity and eases the pain associated with female physical issues, such as childbirth. The wearer and the pearl's energy integrate, and the luster of the pearl is a reflection of the inner spiritual glow of the person.

peridot   Peridot is often used as a dream stone and as a gemstone for physical regeneration and long life. It clears chakras and is best used after Reiki, crystal healing, and chiropractic and acupuncture treatments to maintain subtle body alignment. Peridot restores inner balance that is overpowered by egotistic drive and self-destruction. It is best used at the heart and solar plexus chakras.

petrified wood   A composite form of agate and jasper, it is calming to jittery types. It is especially good for calming fears when held to the solar plexus. It can be used to access past lives and the Akashic Record. It works on both the mental and emotional levels.

pyrite   Especially good for maintaining the purity of one's purpose and helping keep outside influences away, pyrite is like a small mirror—negative energy is reflected away and a protective shield of energy is created in the aura. It also provides a feeling of physical empowerment, that life in the physical form is perfect, and that love is abundant. Pyrite is all about perfection and flawlessness. It is best used for meditation and for Feng Shui to align the bagua to universal purpose.

quartz   *See clear quartz.*

rainbow moonstone   A form of colorless labradorite that looks like a miniature aurora borealis. *See moonstone.*

rhodochrosite   This golden pink crystal with white banding provides renewal and a way to turn self-criticism, anger, and loathing into compassion, love, and self-acceptance. Rhodochrosite is a soothing emotional balancer for use after a period of intense emotional stress. It works well to dissolve and transmute feelings of guilt. It is best worn at the heart chakra.

rhodonite   This crystal is pink with black veins and provides excellent grounding for a heart chakra experiencing heartbreak. It can also stimulate the heart chakra and mental levels into a higher purpose for humanity. It relates to the root chakra but is best worn at the heart chakra so rhodonite's lessons can be absorbed at a more conscious level.

rock crystal   Rock crystal is composed of natural quartz crystal. *See clear quartz.*

rose quartz   A Master Healer and a heart chakra opener, rose quartz oozes compassion into all centers of the body. The wearer becomes aligned with a gracious and gentle energy where even tough emotional wounds can be soothed. It dispels negative emotional states, such as despondency and possessiveness, and promotes harmonious relationships. It also cools inflammations as well as emotional issues related to pain. It enhances one's ability to give and receive love by opening the heart chakra and stimulating greater flexibility in communications. It mellows out a reluctant heart and provides peace in relationships through harmony. Rose quartz is used for meditation, to still one's aggressive thoughts, and to provide mental tranquility. It is best used in the upper chakras but can be used elsewhere on the body as needed.

rooster tail quartz   A crystal that balances physical, emotional, and spiritual energies and provides encouragement to self-transformation.

ruby   Encourages and preserves romantic love and promotes the ideal relationship. This crystal brings focus to the heart and releases disoriented and trapped love energy. It protects the heart from unnecessary love-suffering and promotes the attainment of love objectives: health, happiness, wealth, and spiritual knowledge. It is best worn at the heart chakra.

rutilated quartz   This Master Cleanser, with its fine "angel hairs," will unlock and unblock stagnant energy. This crystal breaks up old energy patterns and promotes clarity on issues. Rutilated quartz helps move you past outdated thought patterns so you can embrace new values. It pulls apart complex emotional issues and unblocks chakras to allow negative energies to dissolve. Rutilated quartz can be used anywhere as needed to unblock energy.

sapphire   Very calming, it imparts patience and leadership abilities. It can amplify intuition and promotes emotional and mental maturity.

selenite This frozen white light is a bridge between the crown chakra and the most subtle of energies. Selenite offers support and a sense of purpose from your higher self. It allows you to reach beyond your emotional state to the higher psycho-spiritual centers such as altruism, compassion, and love. It can provide teachings on various subjects by contacting the crystal deva. It is best used at the crown chakra overnight to provide attunement and refinement for the higher chakras.

shugite Known as the stone of life, this carbon-based crystal is used for physical healing as well as for its metaphysical properties such as grounding and for its purification of water. It is a stone for spiritual transformation, aligning you to what is needed.

silica *See clear quartz.*

silver When silver is worn, energy is retained and circulates throughout the subtle body. Silver also provides a balance when used with other crystals. It activates the upper chakras.

smoky quartz A Master Healer, its job is to clear and transmute negative emotions. It draws out pain and releases negative emotions that can be causing physical pain. This crystal is excellent for grounding all kinds of negative energy such as mood swings, aggressive actions, ill temper, and generally nasty thoughts. Smoky quartz is an excellent crystal to use in times of stress and to rebuild emotional burnout by offering protection during the healing period. It reduces the fear of failure, unblocks self-limitations, and lets you risk trying some new experiences. It is best used at the lower chakras but can be used elsewhere on the body for grounding energy as needed.

sodalite Calming emotions and numbing mental chatter caused by emotional stress, sodalite helps alleviate insomnia caused by overactive mental chatter. It helps to dispel irrelevant thoughts, provides mental focus, and maintains logical reasoning with regard to emotional upsets. Sodalite promotes issues of trust and enhances companionship and the commonality of goals with others. It is best used in the upper chakras.

Stone of sanctuary A form of opaque white quartz crystal that promotes affiliation with divine love, peace, and provides for soothing and calmness to the emotions.

sunstone This stone increases personal power, chances of success, and boosts sexual energy. It lifts low feelings and increases positive thinking and hopefulness. It's a lucky stone and bringer of good fortune and wealth.

sugilite   Sugilite helps you become more sensitive to higher spiritual values and will support your alignment with them as you develop more conscious awareness. It's a crystal that's spiritually inspiring and takes you into a contemplative space. It can also help dispel headaches. It is best used in the upper chakras or held in your hand during meditation.

tanzanite   Considered to be the crystal for the new millennium. Its qualities include .opening your heart chakra to appreciate that your journey on the planet is a spiritual gift and remind you that you are guided by the wisdom of the heart. Tanzanite can be used at the third eye as an initiation to communicate with higher spiritual realms.

tiger eye   Provides mental and emotional discipline for people who are unable to appreciate self-responsibility. This stone is excellent for grounding psychic energy and providing security for opening up the psychic centers. It's useful as a grounder to put action to one's thoughts, especially if you are a dreamer or procrastinator. Tiger eye is about being practical. It is best used at the solar plexus or heart chakra.

topaz   A manifestation crystal that works well with the mental energies to create one's projections, golden topaz is known as a builder of faith and crown activator. It helps you recharge with golden light saturating your aura. Blue topaz opens and reconditions the third eye to see at a higher level. Use topaz in the upper chakras.

tourmaline   Tourmalines are very electrical and energetic. Green tourmaline is a major unblocker of emotional energy by keeping energy circuits open and energy flowing. Pink tourmaline activates and soothes the heart and provides feelings of intense beauty while preventing victimization. Tourmalines are initiators of access to higher levels of consciousness and are best worn in the upper chakras or used in meditation as part of a layout or held in your hand.

tumbled crystals   Stones that have been smoothed to a glossy finish using a physical process.

turquoise   A Master Healer, detoxifier, and protector of the physical body, including during travel, turquoise aligns all subtle bodies and works with the meridians to unblock and promote the flow of chi. Turquoise is best known as a stone of communications, working enthusiastically with the throat chakra. It's a stone that provides for the expression of creativity, not only vocally through speech and singing, but also through activity. It provides emotional detachment and focus on self-accomplishment without entanglement with others. It can be used anywhere on the body.

yang crystals   These include carnelian, diamond, fire opal, garnet, lapis lazuli, malachite, obsidian, rutilated quartz, smoky quartz, and sapphire.

yin crystals   These include agates, amber, amethyst, aquamarine, calcite, clear quartz, fluorite, jade, moonstone, and rose quartz.

zoistite   Used like malachite for the direct release of repressed emotions, it amplifies awareness about the issues. It connects the root and heart chakras for mutual release and integration of energies.

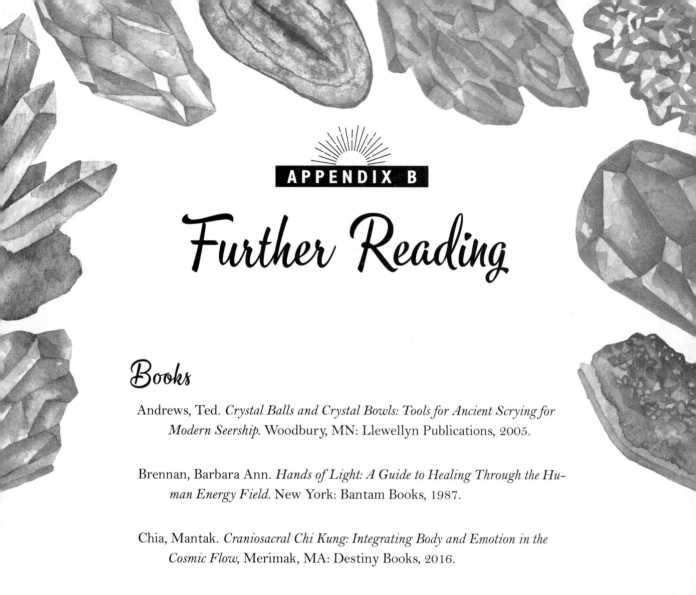

APPENDIX B

Further Reading

Books

Andrews, Ted. *Crystal Balls and Crystal Bowls: Tools for Ancient Scrying for Modern Seership*. Woodbury, MN: Llewellyn Publications, 2005.

Brennan, Barbara Ann. *Hands of Light: A Guide to Healing Through the Human Energy Field*. New York: Bantam Books, 1987.

Chia, Mantak. *Craniosacral Chi Kung: Integrating Body and Emotion in the Cosmic Flow*, Merimak, MA: Destiny Books, 2016.

Gardner, Joy. *Color and Crystals: A Journey Through the Chakras*. Freedom, CA: The Crossing Press, 1988.

The Group of 5. *Crystals and Stones: A Complete Guide To Their Healing Properties.* Berkeley, CA: North Atlantic Books, 2010.

Johari, Haroish. *Chakras: Energy Centers of Transformation.* Rochester, VT: Destiny Books, 2000.

———. *The Healing Power of Gemstones in Tantra, Ayuveda and Astrology.* Rochester, VT: Destiny Books, 1988.

Judith, Anodea. *Wheels of Life: A User's Guide to the Chakra System.* Woodbury, MN: Llewellyn Publications, 1999.

Lefevre, Clemence. *Himalayan Salt Crystal Lamps For Healing, Harmony, and Purification.* Rochester, VT: Healing Arts Press, 2009.

Mason, Henry M. *Crystal Grids: How to Combine and Focus Crystal Energies to Enhance Your Life.* Woodbury, MN: Llewellyn Publications, 2017.

Mason, Henry M. *The Seven Secrets of Crystal Talismans: How to Use Their Power for Attraction, Protection, and Transformation.* Woodbury, MN: Llewellyn Publications, 2008.

Melody. *Love Is in the Earth: A Kaleidoscope of Crystals.* Richland, WA: Earth-Love Publishing House, 1991.

———. *Love Is in the Earth: Laying-On-of-Stones: The Journey Continues.* Richland, WA: Earth-Love Publishing House, 1992.

Rafael, Katrina. *Crystal Enlightenment: The Transforming Properties of Crystals and Healing Stones, Vol. 1.* Santa Fe, NM: Aurora Press, 1985.

———. *Crystal Healing: Applying the Therapeutic Properties of Crystals and Stones, Vol. 2.* Santa Fe, NM: Aurora Press, 1987.

———. *The Crystalline Transmission: A Synthesis of Light, Vol. 3.* Santa Fe, NM: Aurora Press, 1990.

Ryan, Karen. *The Complete Idiots Guide to Crystals.* Indianapolis: Alpha Books, 2010.

———. *How to Use Your Pyramid.* Mississauga, ON, Canada: The Crystal Tiger, 1998.

———. *Spiritual Aromatherapy: The Subtle Effects of Essential Oils on the Human Spirit.* Mississauga, ON, Canada: The Crystal Tiger, 1997.

Sibley, Uma. *Crystal Ball Gazing: The Complete Guide to Choosing and Reading Your Crystal Ball.* New York: Fireside, 1998.

———. *The Complete Crystal Guidebook: A Practical Path to Self-Development, Empowerment, and Healing for the Beginner to the Advanced.* San Francisco: U-Read Publications, 1986.

———. *The Ultimate Crystal Guidebook: A Practical Path to Personal Power, Self-Development and Healing.* New York: Skyhorse Publishing, 2016.

Simmons, Robert, and Naisha Ahsian. *The Book of Stones, Who They Are and What They Teach.* East Montpellier, VT: Heaven & Earth Publishing, 2007.

Smith, Michael G. *Crystal Power.* St. Paul, MN, Llewllyn, 2007.

Tulku, Thondrup Rinpoche. *The Healing Power of Mind: Simple Meditation Exercises for Health, Well-Being, and Enlightenment.* Boston: Shambala Publications, Inc., 1996.

Webb-De Sisto, Marion. *Crystal Skulls: Emmissaries of Healng and Sacred Wisdom.* Bloomington, IN: Xlibris Corporation, 2002.

Wilde, Stuart. *Affirmations.* Taos, NM: White Dove International, 1987.

Internet Sources

Crystal Skulls, www.crystalskulls.com—An authoritative website and source for crystal skulls. Events listing for meeting up with the ancient skulls and their keepers.

Crystal Vaults, www.crystalvaults.com—This website was founded by Henry Mason and has an amazing amount of information about crystals and free guides. Join the blog and learn even more from others.

Healing Crystals, www.healingcrystals.com—A source of good information about crystals that will help educate you before purchasing.

Heaven and Earth, www.heavenandearthjewelry.com—Robert Simmons and Kathy Helen Warner, founders and owners of Heaven and Earth, provide a source for high-vibration crystals, new crystals, and authoritative books.

Hudson Institute of Mineralogy, Mindat.org—This website is the world's leading authority on minerals and their localities, deposits, and mines worldwide.

Judy Hall, www.judyhall.co.uk—Stay up to date on new crystal finds and their metaphysical meanings.

The Labyrinth Society, www.labyrinthsociety.org—Good source of articles on and images of labyrinths. Plans and instructions are included for making a Chartres labyrinth, in addition to being a great online shop for labyrinth tools and contacts for workshops worldwide.

Veritas, www.veriditas.org—The organization trains and supports labyrinth facilitators globally and organize pilgrimages to labyrinth sites.

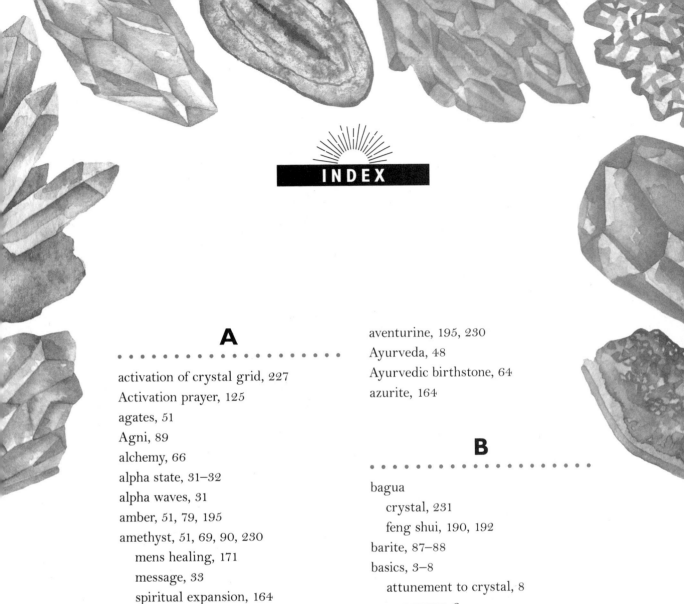

INDEX

A

activation of crystal grid, 227

Activation prayer, 125

agates, 51

Agni, 89

alchemy, 66

alpha state, 31–32

alpha waves, 31

amber, 51, 79, 195

amethyst, 51, 69, 90, 230

   mens healing, 171

   message, 33

   spiritual expansion, 164

angelite, 87–88, 90

apophyllite, 12, 164, 230

aquamarine, 51, 90

aromatherapy foot soak, 262

astral travel, 164

attunement

   definition, 93

   method, 93

aventurine, 195, 230

Ayurveda, 48

Ayurvedic birthstone, 64

azurite, 164

B

bagua

   crystal, 231

   feng shui, 190, 192

barite, 87–88

basics, 3–8

   attunement to crystal, 8

   awareness, 6

   currency, 5

   Google searches, 6

   growing popularity, 6

   healing, description of, 4

   healing properties, knowing about, 7

   new crystals, 7–8

properties, 4

renaming of crystals, 7

Rooster Tail quartz, 7

Stone of Sanctuary, 7

urban lifestyle, 6

U.S. Gold Rush, 7

varieties, 3

visual inspiration, 4

wellness, 5

word origins, 4

beauty routine enhancement, 263–264

cosmetics, 263

facial relaxation, 264

night cream, 263

wrinkle rollers, 264

being, levels of, 60

beta state, 31

beta waves, 31

bioenergetics circuit, 235

bloodstone, 164

blue lace agate, 164, 273

blue tiger eye, 195

brain-imaging technology, 30

brainwaves, types of

alpha waves, 31

beta waves, 31

delta waves, 31

theta waves, 31

Bravais lattice systems, 12–13

bullying, 176

buying crystals, 35

C

calcite, 51, 165, 230

message, 97

spiritual expansion, 165

carnelian, 51, 230

message, 270

spiritual expansion, 165

celestite, 12, 90, 230

dream enhancement, 195

message, 168

spiritual expansion, 165

Celtic sea salt, 88

chakras

activation, 82–84

alignment, 72, 94

attunement, 97

clearing, 119

color therapy and, 54

crown, 195, 238

crystal kit, 253

energies, rebalancing of, 7

heart, 66, 93, 103, 112

Middle Eastern traditions, 48

oils, 265–266

sacral, 266

sensitivity to crystal energy, 118

solar plexus, 81

stubborn, 94

third eye, 238, 266

throat, 120

charoite, 165

chronic obstructive pulmonary disease
(COPD), 260

citrine, 92, 165, 230

clear mind, 29

clear quartz, 51, 69, 165

clearing techniques, 117–127

    aura clearing with partner, 122–125

    chakra alignment and balance, 121–122

    chakra congestion, 119

    Crystal Therapy System, 119–121

    crystal wand, 125–127

        activation, 125

        exercises, 126

        focus, 126

    intense release of energy, 121

    vortexes of energy, 118

    wand wonderment, 125

clinical settings, spiritual healing in, 27

color therapy, chakras and, 54

colored gemstones, demand for, 7

comets, 239

communication, stone of, 113

conductivity, 186–187

    copper, 186

    gold, 186

    metal, 186–187

    platinum, 186

    silver, 186

    titanium, 186

constitutional crystal, 99, 103

copper, 10, 67, 186

copper carbonate, 245

corpora arenacea, 167

cosmetics, 263

    naturally sourced, 19

    regulation of, 19

crafts, 243–254

    crystal water uses, 246

    gem essences, 247–249

        amethyst, 248

        application, 248–249

        carnelian, 248

        creation, 247–248

        dose, 248

        hematite, 248

        rose quartz, 248

        tiger eye, 249

        turquoise, 249

    gem water, 244–246

        benefits, 245

        creation, 244, 246

        steeping, 245

    money tree, 252

    moon juice, 246

    power packs, 249–251

        combinations, 250

        sleep packs, 250–251

        uses, 249–250

crown chakra, 195, 238, 266

crown chakra crystals, 97

crystal bagua, 231

    bagua chart, 231

    dream board, 231

crystal energy, 22

crystal grids, 95, 224–230

    creation, 224–228

        activation, 227

        choosing crystals, 225

        design, 225–226

        dismantling, 228

intent, 224

maintenance, 228

meditation, 228

programming of focus crystal, 225

spot selection, 225

crystal layout vs., 224

emotional balance, 230

Flower of Life grid, 228–230

Metatron's Cube, 230

symbol activation, 230

health and wellness, 230

mental alertness and mindfulness, 230

psychic development, 230

wealth and abundance, 230

Crystal Grids, 225

crystal healers, 64

definition, 64

shift in energy dynamics, 64

crystal party, 277

crystal singing bowls, 242

crystal skulls, 236–241

cleansing and recharging, 239

comets, 239

communication with, 241

components, 238–239

healing with, 237

maintaining and working with, 240

meditation, 241

Mitchell-Hedges crystal skull, 237

selection of, 237–238

types, 240–241

welcoming, activating, and naming, 239

crystal water uses, 246

crystalline matrix, basic blocks of, 25

crystalline structures, 12–13

crystals

attunement, 8

Bravais lattice systems, 12–13

connection to the divine, 84

constitutional, 99, 103

crown chakra, 97

crystalline structure, 254

developing sensitivity to, 77

double-terminated, 105

dow, 108

ethical mining of, 20

first, 23

focus (grids), 225

love, 69

meditation, basic, 79

meteorite, 7

multipurpose, 183–196

daily uses, 184–185

dream enhancement, 195–196

feng shui, 190–194

jewelry, 185–189

prosperity, 190

physical attributes, 66

power of, 221

preparations, 85, 97

quartz, definition of, 4

record keeper, 165

renaming of, 7

sleeper, 91

stem cells, 25

teacher, 109

transcendent nature, 66

transmitter, 225

value of, 38

vibrations of, 68

water, living consciousness in, 25

yang, 51

yin, 51

currency, 5

D

Dalai Lama, 144

Dead Sea salt, 88

delta waves, 31

design of crystal grid, 225

detox bath (Epsom salts), 262

diamond, 51, 77

message, 8

spiritual expansion, 165

diffusers, 265

dioptase, 165

dismantling of crystal grid, 228

divine energy, cosmic receptacle of, 24

double-terminated quartz, 230

dow crystal, 108

dream enhancement, 195–196

amber, 195

aventurine, 195

blue tiger eye, 195

celestite, 195

Herkimer diamond, 195

jade, 195

labradorite, 195

moldavite, 195

mookaite, 196

moonstone, 196

multipurpose crystals, 195

Druids, ancient, 64

E

earth energy, 90

electroencephalograph (EEG), 31

electromagnetic fields (EMFs), 185, 215

electromagnetic frequency (EMF) emissions, 260

emerald, 7

message, 155

spiritual expansion, 165

emotional balance, 230

emotional properties (pyramids), 42

emotional relaxation, 81–82

emotions, unwanted, 28

empath, 276

ending relationships, 155

energy

crystal, 22

divine, cosmic receptacle of, 24

earth, 90

feminine, 89

harmonizing, 77

healing, 23

intense release of, 121

medicine, 247

movement between cells, 24

piezoelectric, 66

shifting of, 47

signatures, salt, 88

subtle, 14, 72, 80

life force, 48

Tibetan medicine, 48

traditional Chinese medicine, 49

training yourself to feel, 77

unwanted, 121

vortexes of, 118

wave, 14

yang, 51

yin, 51, 90

Epsom salts, 261–262

aromatherapy foot soak, 262

dry pillow, 262

full detox bath, 262

magnesium footbath, 262

essential oils, 217

expansion crystals, 163–164, 166

F

facial relaxation, 264

families, 169, 181

fears, teen healing and, 175

feng shui, 6, 190–194

bagua, 190–192

harmonizing segments, 192–194

maintain bagua, 194

toning down, 194

finger labyrinths, 236

fire opal, 51

fishtail formation, 160

five master healers, 140

Flower of Life grid, 228–230

merkaba, 230

Metatron's Cube, 230

sacred geometry, 230

symbol activation, 230

fluoride, 167

fluorite, 51, 90, 230

focus crystal (grids), 225

forest bathing, 260

frankincense oil, 214

G

Gaia

concept of, 22

as cosmic receptacle of divine energy, 24

garnet, 51, 60, 67, 230

gem essences, 247–249

amethyst, 248

application, 248–249

carnelian, 248

creation, 247–248

dose, 248

hematite, 248

rose quartz, 248

tiger eye, 249

turquoise, 249

gem water, 244–246

benefits, 245

creation, 244, 246

steeping, 245

gemstones

Ayurvedic, 73

colored, demand for, 7

crushed, 65

jyotish, 73

lab-grown, 40

lunar, 188

natural electromagnetic radiation of, 72

solar, 188

Geostone, 7
gold, 186, 230
Gold Rush (U.S.), 7
golden topaz, 165
Google searches, 6
Great Pyramid of Giza, 32
grids (crystal), 95, 224–230
  creation, 224–228
    activation, 227
    choosing crystals, 225
    design, 225–226
    dismantling, 228
    intent, 224
    maintenance, 228
    meditation, 228
    programming of focus crystal, 225
    spot selection, 225
  crystal layout vs., 224
  emotional balance, 230
  Flower of Life grid, 228–230
    Metatron's Cube, 230
    symbol activation, 230
  health and wellness, 230
  mental alertness and mindfulness, 230
  psychic development, 230
  wealth and abundance, 230
grounding stone, 178

H

halite, 67, 88
Hawaiian red clay sea salt, 88

healer
  crystal, 64
    definition, 64
    shift in energy dynamics, 64
  master, 140
  universal, 69
healing, 63, 74
  circles, 33
  community, 39
  crystal healer, 64
    definition, 64
    shift in energy dynamics, 64
  crystal skulls, 237
  description of, 4
  energy, 23
  faith, 63
  Hindu method of, 72
  intent, 32
  labyrinth, 232–236
    benefits, 234
    cathedrals, 233
    center point, 233
    Chartres design, 235
  mindfulness, 232
  physical, 131, 142
    balance, 132–133
    permission, 142
  properties, 7
  psychospiritual, 66
  spirit, 63
  spiritual, 157, 168
  spontaneous, 67
  water, 25–26

heart chakra, 66, 93, 103, 266

hematite, 66, 250

Herkimer diamond, 195, 230

Himalayan salt, 259–261

   crushed salts, 261

   salt lamps, 261

   salt slabs, 261

Hindu method of healing, 72

hospitals, spiritual healing in, 27

howlite, 87

Hudson Institute of Mineralogy, 40

jewelry, 185–189

   bracelets, 188

   earrings, 189

   metal conductivity, 186–187

   pendants, 189

   pouches, 189

   rings, 187–188

   wearing, 185–186

Jewelry TV, 7

Judaic-Kabbalah symbol, 229

jyotish gemstone, 73

I

igneous rock, 11

intention

   mindfulness, 76

   programming crystal water through, 244

   sixth sense, 78

intimidation, teen healing and, 176

intuition, 68, 184

iolite, 165

J

jade, 7, 51

   dream enhancement, 195

   mens healing, 171

jasmine, 79

jasper, 181, 230

K

kosher salt, 258–259

kunzite, 66, 90, 250, 273

kyanite, 122, 166, 230

   grid maintenance, 228

   message, 127, 210

L

lab-grown gemstones, 40

labradorite, 249

   dream enhancement, 195

   mens healing, 171

   spiritual expansion, 166

labyrinths, 232–236

   cathedrals, 233

   center point, 233

   Chartres design, 235

crystal healing with, 235–236

healing benefits, 234

unicursal design, 233

lapis lazuli, 51, 96, 230, 245

mens healing, 171

message, 74

lattice, 12–14

axis, 13

Bravais systems, 12–13

helix, 13

resting, 14

layouts, 199, 210

leadership stone, 177

lepidolite, 230

power packs, 251

spiritual expansion, 166

light radiation, 89

love crystal, 69

love stone, 139

Lululemon Lab, 6

lunar gemstones, 188

luxury wellness, 5

M

magnesium footbath, 262

magnesium sulfate (Epsom salts), 261

malachite, 19, 51, 230, 245

marble, 11, 88

Mason, Henry M., 225

master transformer, 69

mature relationships, 155

mazes

center point, 233

multicursal design, 233

meditation

altered states of consciousness from, benefits of, 32

clear mind, 29

with crystal grid, 228

crystal skulls, 241

enhancement, 79

essential oils and, 79

group, 30

guided, 29

pyramid structure, 32

mens healing

amethyst, 171

jade, 171

lapis lazuli, 171

mental relaxation, 81–82

merkaba, 230

message

amethyst, 33

calcite, 97

carnelian, 270

celestite, 168

diamond, 8

emerald, 155

garnet, 60

jasper, 181

kyanite, 127, 210

lapis lazuli, 74

for Seeker, 242

sodalite, 196

turquoise, 116

metamorphic rock, 11

metaphysics, 67

   alpha state, 31–32

   beta state, 31

   brainwaves, types of, 31

   Gaia, concept of, 22

   healing energy, 23

   healing water, 25–26

   meditation, 29

      altered states of consciousness from, benefits of, 32

      clear mind, 29

      pyramid structure, 32

   mindfulness

      crystals and, 28

      definition of, 28

      exercise, 28

      practice of, 28

   psychoenergetics, 33

   stem cells, 25

   unwanted emotions, control of, 28

meteorite crystal, 7

mindfulness

   awakening and, 76

   crystals and, 28

   definition of, 28

   exercise, 28

   grid, 230

   healing, 232

   practice of, 28

minerals

   barite, 10

   formation, 10

   gypsum, 10

   halite, 10

   importance for body function, 10

   magnetite, 10

Minotaur at Knossos, 233

Mitchell-Hedges crystal skull, 237

moldavite, 7, 40, 249

   dream enhancement, 195

   spiritual expansion, 166

money tree, 252

mookaite, 196, 249

moon juice, 246

moonstone, 51

   dream enhancement, 196

   power packs, 251

Moroccan amethyst, 7

multicursal design (maze), 233

multipurpose crystals, 183–196

   daily uses, 184–185

      electromagnetic equipment, 185

      intuition, 184

      students, 184

   dream enhancement, 195–196

   feng shui, 190–194

      bagua, 190–192

      harmonizing segments, 192–194

      maintain bagua, 194

      toning down, 194

   jewelry, 185–189

      bracelets, 188

      earrings, 189

      metal conductivity, 186–187

      pendants, 189

      pouches, 189

rings, 187–188
  wearing, 185–186
  prosperity, 190
museum quality specimens, 39
music, healing and, 216

N–O

nadis, 78
Native American groups, healing lodges
  of, 64
natural scents, 79
naturally sourced cosmetics, 19
neuroscience studies, 30
new relationships, 154
night cream, 263
Nördlinger Reis meteor, 40

obsidian, 51, 173, 273
opal, 13
out-of-body experience, 164

P

partnering together, 155
patchouli, 79
pearls, 87
petrified wood, 273
pharmaceutical industries, crystals used
  in, 65
physical healing, 131–133, 142
physical relaxation, 80–81

pickling salt, 258–259
piezoelectricity, 15
pineal activation, 166, 168
platinum conductivity, 186
Platonic solids, 23, 200
power of crystals, 221
power packs, 249–251
  combinations, 250
  hematite, 250
  kunzite, 250
  lepidolite, 251
  moonstone, 251
  sleep packs, 250–251
  sodalite, 251
  uses, 249–250
prayer chimes, 213
preparations (crystals), 85, 97
prescription healing kit, 253
protection stone, 178
psychic balancing stone, 178
psychospiritual healing, 66
purchasing crystals, 35
purple fluorite, 166
pyramids, 42–43
  crystal types, 42
  emotional properties, 42
  mental properties, 42
  physical properties, 42
  programming, 43
  spiritual properties, 42
  uses, 43
pyrite, 230

Q

Qi Qong, 49

quartz

clear, 12, 51, 67

crystals, definition of, 4

double-terminated, 230

electricity applied to, 19

Rooster Tail, 7

rose, 51, 69, 90, 112, 230, 273

rutilated, 51

smoky, 51, 113

Stone of Sanctuary, 7

R

record keeper crystal, 165

red coral, 174

Reiki session, 60

relationships, healing, 154–155

challenges and struggles, 154

ending relationships, 155

mature relationships, 155

new relationships, 154

partnering together, 155

relaxation, 80–82

importance of, 80

mental and emotional, 81–82

technique guidelines, 80–81

rhodonite, 230

Rooster Tail quartz, 7

root chakra, 266

rose quartz, 51, 69, 90, 230, 273

ruby, 230

rutilated quartz, 51

rutile, 12

S

sacral chakra, 266

sacred geometry (Star of David), 207

salt bath, alternative to, 88

salt crystals, 258–262

Epsom salts, 261–262

aromatherapy foot soak, 262

dry pillow, 262

full detox bath, 262

magnesium footbath, 262

Himalayan salt, 259–261

crushed salts, 261

salt lamps, 261

salt slabs, 261

kosher salt, 258–259

pickling salt, 258–259

table salt, 258

salt water bath, 87

sandalwood, 79

sapphire, 7, 51

Scientific Center of Clinical and

Experimental Medicine, 24

scrying, 44

sea salt, 87

seasonal affective disorder (SAD), 260

sedimentary rock, 11

Seed of Life, 229

Seeker, message for, 242

selenite, 230, 266–268
   charging plates, 267
   harmonizers, 268
   hearts, 267
   lamps, 267
   spirals, 267
   tower formations, 267
   wands, 267
self-esteem crystal, 177
sensitivities, 75–84
   chakras activation, 82–83
   clarity of mind, 78
   meditation enhancement, 79
   nadis, 78
   sixth sense, 78
   spiritual stimulation, 83
   wonderment, 77
Shaolin monks, 70
shungite, 268–269
   cleansing of water, 268
   first chakra, 268
   popularity, 268
   properties, 269
silver, 186
singing bowls (crystal), 242
sixth sense, 78
skulls (crystal), 236–241
   cleansing and recharging, 239
   communication with, 241
   components, 238–239
   healing with, 237
   maintaining and working with, 240
   meditation, 241
   selection of, 237–238

   types, 240–241
   welcoming, activating, and naming, 239
sleeper crystal, 91
smoky quartz, 51, 90
sodalite, 230
   message, 196
   power packs, 251
sodium chloride, 260
solar gemstones, 188
solar plexus chakra, 81, 266
spiritual expansion, 164–166
   amethyst, 164
   apophyllite, 164
   azurite, 164
   bloodstone, 164
   blue lace agate, 164
   calcite, 165
   carnelian, 165
   celestite, 165
   charoite, 165
   citrine, 165
   clear quartz, 165
   diamond, 165
   dioptase, 165
   emerald, 165
   golden topaz, 165
   iolite, 165
   kyanite, 166
   labradorite, 166
   lepidolite, 166
   moldavite, 166
   purple fluorite, 166
spiritual healing, 157, 168
spiritual stimulation, 83

spontaneous healing, 67
Star of David, 206–207
   in Hinduism, 206
   in Judaism, 206
   sacred geometry, 207
   Shakti triangle, 206
   Shiva triangle, 206
star tetrahedron, 230
stem cells, 25
stones. *See also* gemstones
   Ayurvedic birthstone, 64
   bloodstone, 164
   of communication, 113
   grounding, 178
   leadership, 177
   love, 139
   moonstone, 51, 196
   protection, 178
   psychic balancing, 178
   Stone of Sanctuary, 7
   sunstone, 230
   woman's, 174
subtle energy, 14, 48, 72, 80
sunstone, 230

T

table salt, 88, 258
Tai Chi, 49
teacher (crystal), 109
theta waves, 31
third eye chakra, 238, 266
third eye crystals, 97
throat chakra, 120, 266

Tibetan Buddhism, 65
Tibetan chimes, 213
Tibetan medicine, 48, 65
tiger eye, 230, 245
tigle seeds, 49
ting cha (chimes), 88
titanium conductivity, 186
tools. *See* transformational tools, 223–242
topaz, 12, 230
tourmaline, 96–97, 230, 274
transformational tools, 223–242
   crystal bagua, 231
   crystal grids, 224–230
      creation, 224–228
      crystal layout vs., 224
      emotional balance, 230
      Flower of Life grid, 228–230
      health and wellness, 230
      mental alertness and mindfulness, 230
      psychic development, 230
      wealth and abundance, 230
   crystal singing bowls, 242
   crystal skulls, 236–241
      cleansing and recharging, 239
      communication with, 241
      components, 238–239
      healing with, 237
      maintaining and working with, 240
      meditation, 241
      selection of, 237–238
      types, 240–241
      welcoming, activating, and naming, 239
   labyrinth, 232–236

benefits, 234

cathedrals, 233

center point, 233

Chartres, 235

crystal healing with, 235–236

finger, 236

maze, 233

mindfulness healing, 232

transmitter crystals, 225

Tree of Life, 229

trendy crystals, 269

turquoise, 14, 66, 230

message, 116

as stone of communication, 113

U

unicursal design (labyrinth), 233

universal healer, 69

unsettled feelings, teen healing and, 175

unwanted emotions, control of, 28

urban lifestyle, 6

U.S. Department of Health and Human Services, 5

U.S. Gold Rush, 7

V

value of crystals, 38

Vedic fire god, 89

vesuvianite, 12

vibrations of healing crystals, 68

vortexes of energy, 118

W

wand, 125–126

activation, 125

exercises, 126

focus, 126

water

gem, 244–246

benefits, 245

creation, 244, 246

steeping, 245

healing, 25–26

uses, 246

water crystals, living consciousness in, 25

wellness, 5, 257–270

beauty routine enhancement, 263–264

cosmetics, 263

facial relaxation, 264

night cream, 263

wrinkle rollers, 264

chakra oils, 265–266

diffusers, 265

dimensions of, 5

luxury, 5

salt crystals, 258–262

Epsom salts, 261–262

Himalayan salt, 259–261

kosher salt, 258–259

pickling salt, 258–259

table salt, 258

selenite, 266–268

charging plates, 267

harmonizers, 268

hearts, 267

lamps, 267

spirals, 267

tower formations, 267

wands, 267

shungite, 268–269

cleansing of water, 268

first chakra, 268

popularity, 268

properties, 269

tourmaline, new products with, 270

trendy crystals, 269

Western medical community, 8

woman's stone, 174

womens healing

obsidian, 173

red coral, 174

wrinkle rollers, 264

X–Y–Z

yang, 51

yin, 51, 90

yoga, 48

YouTube, 6, 167